THACKERAY

AND THE FORM OF FICTION

THACKERAY

AND THE
FORM OF FICTION

BY JOHN LOOFBOUROW

PRINCETON, NEW JERSEY

1964 · PRINCETON UNIVERSITY PRESS

Publication of this book has been aided by
the Ford Foundation program to support publication,
through university presses,
of works in the humanities and social sciences

Printed in the United States of America
by Princeton University Press, Princeton, New Jersey

PREFACE

HE significance of Thackeray's literary achievement has tantalized perceptive critics over the years. One of the first—Walter Pater—posed a provocative judgment in *Appreciations*: "Different classes of persons, at different times, make of course very various demands upon literature," he wrote, "but all disinterested lovers of books will always look to it, as to all other fine art, for a refuge, a sort of cloistral refuge, from a certain vulgarity in the actual world. A perfect poem like *Lycidas*, a perfect fiction like *Esmond*, the perfect handling of a theory like Newman's *Idea of a University*, has for them something of the uses of a religious 'retreat.' "

The passage is part of Pater's essay on "Style" and the context is peculiarly appropriate to Thackeray. Style is a vital element in Thackeray's fiction—it is an instrument upon which he develops an almost entirely new range of effects. Subtleties of language have been less associated with mid-Victorian writers than with more recent novelists, and this fact has tended to obscure the full meaning of Thackeray's narrative method. But, like the novels of Henry James, Thackeray's fiction depends as much upon its expressive as upon its dramatic elements; and to appreciate the quality of his novels, their language must be explored as carefully as the stylistic effects of the later writer.

Thackeray's work must be read like witty poetry—a poetry expressed in delicate conceits and sustained allusions rather than in the traditional narrative rhetoric of his own time. Nevertheless, style in Thackeray is seldom pure sound effect. Readers who crave the subtle harmonies of words can find endless delight in his novels; but Thackeray's harmonies are as significant as they are delightful, and his

v

most sonorous sequences are never without the counter-point of suggestive meanings. This book is an attempt to explore the expressive elements of Thackeray's style, to indicate their significance, and to show how they fuse in his major novels to create both form and content.

CONTENTS

Preface   v

I. New Relationships in Style, Form,
and Content   3

II. Parody of "Fashionable" Fiction
(1837-1848): *Vanity Fair*   14

III. Parody of Chivalric Romance
(1845-1849): *Vanity Fair*   33

IV. Neoclassical Conventions:
Vanity Fair, Pendennis, The Newcomes   51

V. Form, Style, and Content in
Vanity Fair   73

VI. Allegorical-Biographical-Historical
Epic: *Henry Esmond*   92

VII. *Esmond* as Epic   118

VIII. Style and Form in *Esmond*   167

IX. Style and Content in *Esmond*   188

Index   231

THACKERAY

AND THE FORM OF FICTION

CHAPTER I

NEW RELATIONSHIPS IN STYLE, FORM, AND CONTENT

THE modern novel is very different from the novels of the eighteenth century. Defoe, Fielding, Smollett suggest a clear, uncluttered stage, upon which characters and their actions stand out in bold relief. Relationships are of minor interest, and thoughts and emotions are insignificant; it is as though actors and adventures had an absolute, objective existence, independent of contingencies and even of the novelists' art. E. M. Forster, Virginia Woolf, Henry James write in a different artistic world, where the first impression is often of the expressive medium itself—of the suggestive presentation of relationships and the play of metaphors evoking emotions that eventually coalesce into persons and events. Eighteenth-century novels are discussed in terms of plot, characters, style; contemporary novels in terms of expression, themes, emotions. The difference is not definitive but it is real, and novelists of the nineteenth century are often grouped with one or the other of these kinds of fiction—Trollope, Scott, Jane Austen with the eighteenth-century convention; George Eliot, Meredith with the modern mode. Thackeray is an ambiguous figure; he is frequently associated with a sentimental Victorian image that is gradually losing its clarity, or he is paired with Trollope among the later exponents of the eighteenth-century tradition.

New creative means, however, are needed for new artistic effects; and while the techniques of contemporary fiction have frequently been analyzed, the prior developments have not been carefully defined. The changes that transformed the eighteenth-century convention into the modern

3

novel were, of course, diffuse and various; many years of experimentation separate Fielding's work from E. M. Forster's. But halfway through the nineteenth century there was a shorter period of intense activity—similar to the slight but irreversible diversion, by a genetic mutation, of a continuous process of evolution—and Thackeray's writing is a major factor in this crucial development.

Despite the tendency to associate Thackeray with a familiar tradition, his important novels represent a new kind of writing. The significance of his work has been obscured by its apparently conventional elements; whereas many of Thackeray's conventions were used for unprecedented artistic purposes, for instance, when he adopts the mannerisms of popular fiction to represent the compulsive emotional drives that animate his characters. In developing such creative methods, Thackeray fundamentally altered the accepted relationships between words and content, style and form. Subject and expression are unified in his novels as they had not been before; and in this achievement, his use of language is the critical element.

Thackeray's prose is an innovation in English fiction—a major element in the transition from the novels of Fielding or even the Brontës to the novels of Henry James and E. M. Forster. Thackeray was the first English novelist to create a narrative medium in which form and content are derived from the expressive patterns of the language itself. For example, he can produce an emotional climax by means of allusive verbal effects where there is literally no "plot" climax in the narrative action. Earlier English novelists set forth a preconceived incident in language designed primarily for communication. In Thackeray, intense, suggestive images give to literal event a further dimension, or even discredit appearance and create a divergent imaginative reality of their own. The difference becomes apparent when novelists of the eighteenth century are juxtaposed with writers like Proust and Joyce. In Richardson and Fielding, style is an instrument for dramatic effect, tragic or comic; it tells and embellishes the story. In their novels, the incident precedes its expression—language may ornament or intensify, but it never creates event; it is common to all writers, adapted but not fundamentally modified. Such prose is to the novel's content as clothing to a body. The expressive relationship is very different in later fiction. In Proust and Joyce, style is as integral to content as texture is to the cloth itself; very often, style is the story—the words are themselves the dramatic event.

The new relationship between matter and language is a continuous theme in Thackeray's artistic development. His first literary pieces were parodic or derivative. From successive interactions of parody and imitation, he gradually developed a suggestive, allusive prose that included in its own resources the elements of form and content; and, even so early as *Vanity Fair*, his language has the complex participation in narrative event that we have come to expect in the modern novel. No earlier novelist attained such verbal richness, and later novelists, from George Eliot to Vladimir Nabokov, are indebted to Thackeray's experimentation. This is not to say that such writers imitated Thackeray's style, or even that they knew his work. George Eliot certainly learned from Thackeray,[1] and it would be possible to schematize a kind of indirect transmission—for example, Proust was indebted to Eliot, Nabokov learned from Proust. But it is more rewarding, and probably more realistic, to conceive of Thackeray's novels as a new form which has become characteristic of the species without relating individual writers by demonstrable "influence" to the original variant.

The most important source of narrative content in Thackeray's prose is the satirical allusion to typical literary conventions. Even when these conventions are modified by

Thackeray's personal manner, they retain their suggestive force and summon up meaningful, familiar images. But the significance of the allusions must be recognized before their effect can be appreciated. Such literary images—sentimental idealisms, chivalric codes, neoclassical mannerisms —may mirror states of mind or represent emotional events; they may be satiric fantasies or poetic insights; and their purpose must be understood in the narrative context. This recognition is helpful in reading *Vanity Fair*, where Thackeray first integrates and purposefully controls his allusive sequences; it is essential for *Henry Esmond*, where the expressive patterns are subtler and more significant.

The narrative conventions which are so rich a source of allusion for Thackeray are more than literary curiosities. They are still alive in the popular literature of today. The sentimentalities of "fashionable fiction" fill the pages of current magazines, only superficially altered. "Criminal romance" is Hollywood's stock in trade, and the "chivalric convention" is vigorous in the Western movie. The neoclassical pastoral recurs in modern tropical idylls and social Arcadias, and mock-epic is still the satirist's weapon for attacking heroic pretense. The expressive artifices that are parodied in Thackeray's fiction are familiar forms expressing persistent human delusions; a brief acquaintance with the appropriate patterns and rhetoric makes Thackeray's satire as relevant now as it was in his own time.

In analyzing *Vanity Fair*, it is important to discriminate basic prose "textures"—sentiment, romance, pastoral, mock-epic. A word like "textures" is needed to indicate the quality of these modes; for Thackeray's allusive conventions are not discrete "styles" but aspects of an expressive unity. They are as inseparable from his sustained narrative medium as the nap of velvet from its substance. To recognize the significance of these conventions, it is helpful to explore their historical development; and Thackeray's early imitations and parodies merit discussion since his treatment of allusive materials is most quickly understood in the simpler context of this early work. After such historical and stylistic analysis, it will be far easier to appreciate the integration of traditional modes in a complex narrative, and *Vanity Fair* can be approached as an entity.

In *Henry Esmond*, *Vanity Fair's* expressive experiment is given new artistic value. Verbal patterns in *Vanity Fair* seem to create effective form *ex nihilo* and its literal "plot" is a vestigial convention. In *Esmond*, both literal and imaginative form are effective, the one a counterpoint to the other. The verbal textures of Thackeray's previous work interact in *Esmond* with literal elements of historical event and objective plot structure. And *Esmond's* biographical-historical modes are used in a new way. They are part of a serious attempt to write a novel that will fulfill the epic function—epic not in an impressionistic but in a definable sense, and in a way not attempted by earlier writers.

The epic structure had been applied to eighteenth-century fiction in *Tom Jones*; but Fielding's innovation, though it helped to raise the novel's prestige, was systematic rather than organic. *Tom Jones* and *Amelia* demonstrated that comic prose narrative could accommodate the traditional voyage pattern and its questing hero, but Fielding sought in the epic mode no equivalent for contemporary reality; in style and content his novels were an extension of the mock-epic convention. Epic form was not an indispensable medium for what he had to say (the voyage metaphor, for instance, has no inherent relevance to Tom Jones's experience). Writers like Proust and Joyce, on the other hand, have sought a different organization for the "epic novel." In these novelists, the questing hero represents the essential characteristics of his culture and seeks for answers to its fundamental problems; his epic experiences are a microcosm of national history. Classical epic

7

events—in *Ulysses,* the epic form itself—become imaginative symbols of the hero's emotional experience.

When Thackeray wrote *Henry Esmond,* he was experimenting with such an enlargement of the novel's scope. *Esmond's* epic purpose is indicated not by literal parallels with Homer and Virgil but by a sequence of classical allusions characterizing the hero's role and initiating climaxes that mirror heroic events in creative metaphor. As in *Ulysses* and *Remembrance of Things Past,* echoes of familiar literary conventions in *Esmond* simulate the hero's personal assimilation of the artistic traditions of his culture. Esmond's experience is characteristically subjective and is typically conveyed by the textures of the prose itself; the novel's irreducible elements of historical event and temporal structure combine with its expressive textures as objective fact is correlated with subjective experience.

To respond fully to *Henry Esmond,* a preliminary effort is required as it is with *Vanity Fair.* Biography and history —*Esmond's* ostensible modes—must be considered during their development in the eighteenth and early nineteenth centuries. A scrutiny of the traditions of this recent past will show how these conventions acquired epic possibilities for Thackeray's predecessors, and how this potential came, in time, to be associated with the novel; the process will help to clarify Thackeray's inherited concepts of the function of the novel and of the significance of epic. *Esmond's* most important classical allusions must be identified; and, at the same time, prose textures analyzed in *Vanity Fair* will be recognized in their new context.

Most of Thackeray's major literary modes are present in *Vanity Fair.* First, there is "fashionable" fiction—partly because it became popular at nearly the same time that Thackeray began writing, and partly because this impressionistic medium is fundamental to Thackeray's prose, acting as a common denominator between his novels and the fiction of his time. As recent as the romantics, it is the recurrent butt of Thackeray's early parodies; transmuted and assimilated, it is a major theme in *Vanity Fair*. Next, there is chivalric romance—epitomized by Scott, but with a background in the eighteenth century that must be considered for its relevance to Thackeray's treatment of the genre. Romance runs through *Vanity Fair* like a counterpoint to the "fashionable" manner and is essential to the coloring of character and the creation of structure. Finally, one finds the eighteenth-century genres of pastoral and mock-epic, reflecting Thackeray's affinity for neoclassical satire; in *Vanity Fair*, although polished and pointed beyond the scope of his early parodies, they are static interludes, but in his later novels they are creatively assimilated. After fashionable, chivalric, pastoral, and mock-epic modes have been considered in *Vanity Fair* for their allusive content, their place in the context of Thackeray's narrative prose, their interaction to create form and content, *Henry Esmond* may be read continuously, its textures, allusions, and cumulative patterns identified as they develop, and its complex relation of form to content considered. In addition, critical analysis may suggest how Thackeray reconceived the process of creating fiction, and found for the English novel a new and fertile field that has become the province of writers like Meredith, James, and Forster.

ii

By the middle of the nineteenth century, when Thackeray began to publish, English fiction had adopted a variety of conventions. Richardson, practicing the familiar letter-narrative, had created the novel of sentiment. Fielding had produced his comic epic in prose, partly derived from Cervantes but taking its structural framework from classical models. Chivalric romance had been introduced in Walpole's *Castle of Otranto*. The novel of manners,

9

most closely related to drama, had been practiced by Sterne, Burney, Edgeworth, and perfected by Jane Austen. Later writers produced novels in which such conventions multiplied and divided. The sentimental mode degenerated into the "fashionable" manner of Catherine Gore and Bulwer Lytton. Among its variants were a semi-Byronic melodrama and a facile version of the novel of manners. Fielding's mock-epic was reflected in adventure fiction from *Roderick Random* to *Pickwick Papers*. Romance resulted in two conventions: through the gothicism of writers like Radcliffe and Lewis, it influenced Dickensian symbolism in such novels as *Bleak House* and *Great Expectations*; as chivalric tradition, it shaped historical novels from Scott to Cooper and led to the mock-romance of Meredith's *Egoist*.

Thackeray's first ten years as a professional writer (roughly 1836-1846) were spent in journalistic experimentation with these literary conventions. His most direct method was overt parody. *The Professor* (1837), for example, mimics the sentimental and criminal conventions of "fashionable" fiction. In *The Second Funeral of Napoleon* (1841) sustained satire on neoclassical decorum foreshadows Thackeray's subsequent assimilation of the mock-epic convention. *A Legend of the Rhine* (1845) combines chivalric burlesque with parody of the sentimental and gothic modes; *Rebecca and Rowena* (1849), a comic sequel to Scott's *Ivanhoe*, is closely related to Thackeray's treatment of Amelia and Rebecca in *Vanity Fair*. These early pieces dance back and forth between parody and imitation, sometimes jerkily, sometimes with considerable grace; but it is already clear that literary conventions are more than verbal patterns for Thackeray. They represent significant human viewpoints, often popular fantasies whose morbid aspects Thackeray attacks by satirizing the expressive textures associated with them. Thackeray's militant concept of the satirist is suggested by

10

a passage in his lectures on the English humorists: "I think of the works of young Pope as I do of the actions of young Bonaparte or young Nelson. In . . . the presence of the great occasion, the great soul flashes out, and conquers transcendent."² Like Pope, Thackeray was a fighter with words.

Thackeray's first novels were *Catherine* (1836) and *Barry Lyndon* (1844). *Barry Lyndon* is an imitation of Fielding's *Jonathan Wild*; it offered little scope for originality, but it gave Thackeray practice in controlling dramatic narrative and permitted him to experiment *in extenso* with eighteenth-century satirical conventions. *Catherine*, however, is unmistakably part of Thackeray's artistic development. In this earlier novel, textures of "fashionable" prose—the sentimental convention and its variant, the romance of crime—are elaborately exploited, and pastoral is ironically introduced in the climactic scenes. Although *Catherine's* expressive textures often fail to integrate with the narrative, they are forced to work together, and if their conjunction is sometimes constrained, it is always fruitful.

The expressive elements with which Thackeray experimented in these early pieces are epitomized in his illustration for the title page of *Vanity Fair*. On a tawdry stage, the author dressed as clown leans against a box of costumes from which he has taken a plumed helmet and a wooden sword; he holds up a cracked mirror to the disenchanted face that looks out from the performer's panoply; in the Arcadian distance rise the turrets of a castle. The traditional stage properties are emblems of Thackeray's literary heritage: chivalry, sentiment, pastoral, mock-epic—the professional costumes of his artistic persona.

Vanity Fair (1847-1848), Thackeray's first major novel, is the immediate result of his satiric apprenticeship, and it is very possibly his greatest work. It is not his subtlest, not his finest artistically, not his most profound; but it continues

11

to soar, like an imperfect and successful balloon, delighting observers who are not concerned with more specialized phases of performance and purpose. Here, for the first time, the varied materials of the early burlesques are woven together in an extended, progressive pattern. Sentimental parody provides the substance of Amelia's point of view and of her love for George; romance furnishes satirical metaphors for Rawdon and for the relation between George and Dobbin. Pastoral and classical myth suggest Becky's motives and comment on her devious intrigues.

But Thackeray's development does not end with *Vanity Fair*. His expressive resources are further extended in each of his later novels as well as in *Henry Esmond*. In *Pendennis* (1848-1850), the pastoral tradition—an isolated metaphor in *Vanity Fair*—becomes a sustained and integral theme. In *The Newcomes* (1853-1855), mock-epic—equally restricted in *Vanity Fair*—is combined with serious classical allusion to form a fundamental, organic narrative mode; and, in this novel, a new expressive resource appears: the fairy tale motif that had acquired its now-familiar romantic quality in the nineteenth century and was a source of significant allusion for Henry James.

The most important aspect of *Vanity Fair*, however, is not the simple presence of expressive conventions, but their synthesis in a continuous fiction. Isolated modes had often been parodied; and parody, as Jane Austen used it, had been an independent creative medium. But before Thackeray, most novelists followed some one controlling mode—romance with Scott, manners with Austen, burlesque with Fielding. In *Vanity Fair*, for the first time, multiple expressive traditions are assimilated in a sustained narrative, familiar conventions are integrated into a single, more intricate entity.

The major modes of *Vanity Fair*—textures of "fashionable" fiction and chivalric romance—are elements of organic form rather than ornamental elaborations. Satirical echoes of "fashionable" convention begin and conclude the novel, control its shape, and are diffused through the narrative; sentimental and melodramatic variants differentiate the pseudo-heroines, Amelia and Rebecca. Romance motifs create a contrasting sequence that inscribes sharp tangents of dramatic structure upon the diffused, continuous ground of the "fashionable" mode. The two conventions are both opposed and complementary; together they determine the effective form of *Vanity Fair*. Such elements must be analyzed in order to be fully appreciated, and in the course of this analysis the narrative unity may be temporarily obscured; but the purpose of the process is the eventual resynthesis of the novel's artistic elements, and when this has been accomplished, it should be possible to see *Vanity Fair* as a whole without sacrificing the richness of its cumulative patterns.

CHAPTER II

PARODY OF "FASHIONABLE" FICTION
(1837–1848): *VANITY FAIR*

THACKERAY'S prose began with parody and in this respect his work is in the sustained tradition of the novel: "To convince us of his essential veracity, the novelist must always be disclaiming the fictitious and breaking through the encrustations of the literary. . . . It is no coincidence that, from Rabelais to Jane Austen, so many realists have begun as parodists."[1] Unlike earlier novelists, however, Thackeray neither dissolved his parodic themes in an objective narrative medium nor precipitated them in a single satiric manner. Allusive conventions—verbal echoes of familiar literary traditions—originating in his parodies and imitations, coexist and find their consummation in the subtle suggestive textures of novels like *Vanity Fair*. Among these parodic conventions the first and perhaps the most fundamental is that of "fashionable" fiction.

"Fashionable" fiction was the product of certain writers of the Regency and later, sometimes called "silver-fork" novelists. The genre owed most to the "sentimental novel" of Richardson and his imitators, but its prose also reflected the rhythms of Sterne and the romantic rhetoric of Byron and Carlyle. The fashionable mode was more than an object of satire for Thackeray; its flexible rhythms, its affinity for digression, allusion, and metaphor, made it an ideal medium for the synthesis of diverse conventions that characterizes his mature prose. It is curious that the fashionable mode should provide the basis for Thackeray's personal idiom while remaining an object for parody. As a rhythmic medium, it is a neutral presence in his later prose;

14

but when fashionable textures are clearly recognizable, the mode is serving a satirical function.

In parodying the fashionable and other modes, Thackeray shares the satirist's traditional purpose of discrediting accepted illusion. Illusion is involved in most human experiences and may be attacked in various ways, dramatic or analytic; but Thackeray was mainly concerned with exposing the delusions expressed in artistic conventions themselves—the sequence of idealized poses or poeticized fantasies, the literary modes associated with social or psychological artifice. Thus, in an early critical review, he condemns the "fashionable" genre that makes artistic capital out of economic inequality: "Has any sentimental writer organized any feasible scheme for bettering the poor? . . . At the conclusion of these tales . . . there somehow arrives a misty reconciliation between the poor and the rich; a prophecy is uttered of better times for the one, and better manners in the other; presages are made of happy life, happy marriage and children, happy beef and pudding for all time to come; as they do at the end of a drama when the curtain falls, and the blue fire blazes behind the scenes."[2]

Parody was Thackeray's primary means of "disclaiming the fictitious and breaking through the encrustations of the literary." Ultimately, as literary conventions were assimilated into his narrative medium, allusive satire transcended stylized travesty and came to represent significant states of mind, like Spenserian allegory. *Vanity Fair's* essential drama, for example, depends on the interaction of expressive modes that mirror emotional realities—the heroines' experience is projected through a sequence of fashionable textures, and the sentimental and melodramatic variants of "fashionable" fiction that characterize Amelia and Rebecca control the novel's dual dramatic pattern. And Thackeray's early parodies of "fashionable"

15

fiction prepare the patterns of *Vanity Fair*: in these preliminary pieces, the satire is straightforward and its dramatic purpose is indicated explicitly by the author.

Some of Thackeray's sharpest initial attacks on the
fashionable mode were directed against the fiction of
Catherine Gore. Mrs. Gore's novels, exploiting hackneyed
idealizations, represented the purely sentimental aspect of
"fashionable" fiction. Her work was not without merit:
Thackeray's parody is always most effective when aimed at
writers for whom he has a certain admiration, even envy.
In developing the tradition of Richardson and Sterne, Mrs.
Gore and the "silver-fork" novelists contributed to a new
understanding of romantic love; but this insight was vi-
tiated by a cult of saccharine insincerity. The sentimental
mode, refined and diffused, satirizes Amelia in *Vanity Fair*;
it is parodied, however, as early as *The Professor* (1837).
The Professor is a crude burlesque in the eighteenth-
century manner. Its heroine, Adeliza Grampus, is a fish-
monger's daughter whose sensibilities have been morbidly
excited by a course of sentimental fiction (like Miss
Lennox's Female Quixote). "Slim as the Monument on
Fish Street Hill," she falls in love with a scoundrel.
" 'Dandolo!' would she repeat to her confidante, Miss Binx;
'the name was beautiful and glorious in the olden days;
five hundred years since, a myriad of voices shouted it in
Venice, when one who bore it came forward to wed the
sea—the doge's bride!' "[3] When Adeliza gives her heart to
Dandolo, the author exclaims: "Love! Love! how ingenious
thou art! thou canst make a ladder of a silken thread, or a
weapon of a straw; thou peerest like sunlight into a dungeon; thou scalest, like forlorn hope, a castle wall; the keep
is taken!—the foeman has fled!—the banner of love floats
triumphantly over the corpses of the slain!"[4] This apostrophe is not unlike the passages in Thackeray's major
novels describing emotions that are partly genuine. In his

later manner, the imagistic, freely associative quality of fashionable rhetoric permits the hidden motivations of his characters to emerge in suggestive, thematic metaphor. In *The Professor*, however, Thackeray precludes a naive acceptance of conventional sentimentality in a footnote to the text: "We cannot explain this last passage; but it is so beautiful that the reader will pardon the omission of sense, which the author certainly could have put in if he liked."[4] What is explicit here is implied in the later novels. The satiric note is never absent from Thackeray's lyric harmonies, and this early annotation should be remembered whenever he appears to be "sentimentalizing" in his later work.

A few years after *The Professor*, Thackeray was writing a prose that combined satiric deflation with lyric insight in a creative medium that admitted no explanatory annotation. In a characteristic passage which offers a useful paradigm for the treatment of fashionable textures in *Vanity Fair*, evocative rhetoric transcends parody to render the realities of love:

"No mistake can be greater than that of fancying such great emotions of love are only felt by virtuous or exalted men: depend upon it, Love, like Death, plays havoc among the *pauperum tabernas*, and sports with rich and poor, wicked and virtuous alike. I have often fancied, for instance, on seeing the haggard pale young old-clothesman, who wakes the echoes of our street with his nasal cry of 'Clo'!'—I have often, I said, fancied that, besides the load of exuvial coats and breeches under which he staggers, there is another weight on him—an *atrior cura* at his tail— and while his unshorn lips and nose together are performing that mocking, boisterous, Jack-indifferent cry of 'Clo', clo'!' who knows what woeful utterances are crying from the heart within?"[5]

The controlled development of this passage is based on the juxtaposition of elevated classical phrases with realistic images—*"pauperum tabernas"* with "old-clothesman," *"atrior cura"* with "at his tail"—and poetic amplification as in "haggard pale young old" contrasted with satirical diminution in "exuvial coats and breeches." This is one of Thackeray's typical methods: the integration of the lyric rhythms and images of fashionable fiction with the harsher rhetoric of neoclassical satire and contemporary realism. Through such expressive interaction he is able to introduce a phrase that retains the emotional intensity of the fashionable mode but transmutes its insincere idealism into a valid insight—"who knows what woeful utterances are crying from the heart within?" Separated from its context, this sounds like a Victorian truism; its quality is altered by the insistence that love sports not only with "rich and poor" but with "wicked and virtuous alike." Wordsworth and Dickens had proclaimed the power of love among the poor, but they did not like to suggest that love might be experienced by a reprobate without modifying his moral character—where his personality remained vicious, the amorous impulse must be no more than animal lust. Lord Byron and Bulwer Lytton, despite their artistic insincerities, were the Victorian pioneers in this area of ethical ambiguity, where an increasing interest in subjective experience adumbrated the explorations of modern psychology.

Bulwer Lytton's romance of crime was a variant on the fashionable mode. Bulwer could produce vivid emotional insights as well as Mrs. Gore; but his analyses of the criminal impulse, like her investigations into romantic love, were debased by spurious idealisms and a facile "poetic" style. In the diary for 1832 Thackeray remarked, "Read Eugene Aram but was much disappointed (as usual) It is a very forced & absurd taste to elevate a murderer for

18

money into a hero—The sentiments are very eloquent clap-trap."[6] This eloquent clap-trap was both more dangerous and more impressive than the finery of Mrs. Gore; it recommended an ethic that seemed to Thackeray perverse and it commanded an admiration as fervent as the passion for Byron. Bulwer Lytton quoted the great philosophers and embellished his prose with classical allusions (a device at which Thackeray became a master—but with a different purpose); his morbid fictions seemed to offer profound and visionary insights. Here again, Thackeray attacked a writer for whom he had a certain admiration. "Bulwer has a high reputation for talent," he commented in his diary, "& yet I always find myself competing with him—This I suppose must be vanity—If it is truth why am I idle?"[6] He was not idle for long. In *Catherine*, an uneven but interesting novelette, Thackeray combined the sentimental parody of Mrs. Gore with a sterner satire on the lofty perversions of Bulwer. *Catherine's* love-burlesque anticipates the satirical-sentimental rendering of Amelia, George, and Dobbin in *Vanity Fair* as its travesty of criminal romance anticipates the ironic-melodramatic treatment of Becky, Rawdon, and Steyne.

Published in 1839-1840, *Catherine* was an acknowledged parody on Bulwer Lytton's *Eugene Aram* and *Ernest Maltravers*. Thackeray's purpose is explained at once: the novel, "in accordance with the present fashionable style," will deal with characters taken from the Newgate Calendar, "agreeably low, delightfully disgusting, and at the same time eminently pleasing and pathetic."[7] If fashion demands that fiction concern itself with crime, the public must be confronted with the real thing; criminals are apt to be cowardly, vulgar, ignorant: "They don't quote Plato, like Eugene Aram . . . or prate eternally about *tò kalòn*, like that precious canting Maltravers . . . or die whitewashed saints, like poor 'Biss Dadsy' in 'Oliver Twist.' "[8]

At the beginning of the novel, Catherine, a handsome, illiterate barmaid of muscular sensuality, is seduced by Count Maximilian de Galgenstein, a German adventurer with a commission in the English army. When the Count leaves her, Catherine marries John Hayes, a timid, miserly man from her own village. In his portrait of Hayes, Thackeray commences a serious reading of love. Hayes pursues Catherine "with a desperate greedy eagerness and desire of possession, which makes passions for women often so fierce and unreasonable among very cold and selfish men."[9] But Thackeray does not quarantine this unpleasant emotion by dismissing it as lust or otherwise distinguishing it from true love. The "agony of poor mean-spirited John Hayes" is as sincere as if he were a sympathetic protagonist; the characterization is an instance of Thackeray's insistent insight into human ambiguity. After many years of marriage, Catherine meets the Count again, and their revivified desire is described in language that modulates through the saccharine harmonies of Mrs. Gore to the reedy resonance of Bulwer Lytton:

"Or suppose, again, I had said, in a style still more popular:—The Count advanced towards the maiden. They both were mute for a while; and only the beating of her heart interrupted that thrilling and passionate silence. . . . The tears that rolled down the cheek of each were bubbles from the choked and moss-grown wells of youth; the sigh that heaved each bosom had some lurking odours in it— memories of the fragrance of boyhood, echoes of the hymns of the young heart! Thus is it ever—for these blessed recollections the soul always has a place; and while crime perishes, and sorrow is forgotten, the beautiful alone is eternal."[10]

There is a difference between this suggestive parody and *The Professor's* simple burlesque. Here, expressive modulation represents a typical psychological sequence; the language mirrors the mind's movement from insipid delusion to vicious artifice. Sentimental poses—"The Count advanced towards the maiden. They both were mute"— open the scene; Mrs. Gore's rhythms echo in the "thrilling and passionate silence"; but it is Bulwer Lytton's rhetoric that is reflected in "the beautiful . . . eternal." And, at the climax of the passage, ambiguous metaphor weaves into the lush Lyttonian tapestry the symbols of its corruption. The lovers' "tears" are "bubbles," their "cheeks" are "choked and moss-grown," their "sigh" has "lurking odours in it," and these images convey unlovely emblems of a pseudo-poetic passion—a stagnant well, and, with a coarseness that pungently materializes these aging libertines, the rancid smell of their amorous breath.

Catherine's dénouement is a travesty of fashionable melodrama where Thackeray's insistence on the violence of real crime exposes the psychological impulse responsible for the popularity of criminal romance. The etherealized brutality of Bulwer Lytton's novels had accustomed the public to a satisfaction it would not own by name. Thackeray insists on the unpalatable reality. On an impulse, Catherine murders her husband. Immediately thereafter, she and the Count meet in a scene of romantic reunion:

"At this moment the moon, which had been hidden behind Westminister Abbey, rose above the vast black mass of that edifice, and poured a flood of silver light upon the little church of St. Margaret's. . . .

"Catherine . . . had been standing against a post, not a tree—the moon was shining full on it now; and on the summit, strangely distinct, and smiling ghastly, was a livid human head.

"The wretched woman fled. . . . [The Count] was taken

up a hopeless idiot, and so lived for years and years; clanking the chain, and moaning under the lash."[11]

This melodramatic retribution (the livid head is that of the murdered Hayes) is a further parody designed to satirize the sensational conclusions in which Bulwer Lytton distributed poetic justice. Thackeray follows the facile images and arbitrary contrasts of this spurious climax with a contemporary account of the body's discovery (for his narrative is based on fact): " 'Yesterday morning, early, a man's head, that by the freshness of it seemed to have been newly cut off from the body, having its own hair on, was found by the river's side. . . . The head was much hacked and mangled in the cutting off.' . . . We very much doubt if Milton himself could make a description of an execution half so horrible as the simple lines in the *Daily Post* of a hundred and ten years since, that now lies before us . . . as bright and clean as on the day of publication."[12]

This insertion of a lump of unassimilated journalism is a crude device; it represents an early phase in Thackeray's integration of "realism" with allusive parody. The story progresses by jerks and starts—now Thackeray fills pages with parody, again he resumes his narration and half forgets its satirical purpose. The climax of *Catherine* is a pastiche of imitation and quotation, recalling the kind of wit perfected by Swift in "The Tale of a Tub": it ceases to be a novel and becomes an essay skillfully woven of random fragments.

During the next ten years Thackeray learned a great deal; *Barry Lyndon*, his imitation of Fielding, gave him practice in sustained narrative, and voluminous satirical journalism enabled him to develop his parodic verbal textures and integrate them into expository prose. These advances contributed considerably to his success in *Vanity Fair*, but they are refinements rather than departures. The work already discussed fairly represents Thackeray's early treatment of fashionable convention and it should be possible now to identify its expressive textures in *Vanity Fair* and to see how they participate in a full-scale narrative. *Vanity Fair* (1847-1848) is Thackeray's first major synthesis of literary conventions; variants on the fashionable mode—idealized crime and sentimental love—are major themes. From the trial and error of his earlier narrative experiments, Thackeray has learned to fuse the elements of his allusive parody into an effective expressive medium, to imply his satirical contrasts with a casual phrase, to advance his characters in real experience while reading events in terms of conventional poses. In *Vanity Fair*, the fashionable mode yields not only satirical insights but psychological content and dramatic form. Of the variants of "fashionable" fiction, since the sentimentalism of Mrs. Gore is more diffuse and continuous in the novel, it will be simplest to begin with the comparatively concentrated textures of Bulwer Lytton's melodramatic manner.

Thackeray's parody of the criminal romance finds its magnificent justification in his treatment of Becky Sharp. Despite her brilliant career, Becky is, like Catherine, a child of poverty and disorder: "Miss Sharp's father was an artist. . . . He was a clever man; a pleasant companion; a careless student; with a great propensity for running into debt, and a partiality for the tavern. . . . As it was with the utmost difficulty that he could keep himself, and as he owed money for a mile round Soho, where he lived, he thought to better his circumstances by marrying a young woman of the French nation, who was by profession an opera-girl."[13] Becky, like Catherine, is disappointed in her early expectations of a brilliant match, and her marriage with Rawdon Crawley, whose love is as earnest as that of "mean-spirited John Hayes," is a compromise with respectability. The earlier novel's parody of the conventional love affair between peasant girl and nobleman is extended in Becky's intrigue with the Marquis of Steyne, and in the portrait of Steyne, aristocracy is more keenly satirized than in the previous version. Thackeray saves *Vanity Fair's* most effective caricature of the Marquis for the end of the novel; it is a lethal list of titles that echoes the satirist's chant from Fielding to Joyce and Nabokov:

"Everybody knows the melancholy end of . . . the Most Honourable George Gustavus, Marquis of Steyne, Earl of Gaunt and of Gaunt Castle, in the Peerage of Ireland, Viscount Hellborough, Baron Pitchley and Grillsby, a Knight of the Most Noble Order of the Garter, of the Golden Fleece of Spain, of the Russian Order of Saint Nicholas of the First Class, of the Turkish Order of the Crescent, First Lord of the Powder Closet and Groom of the Back Stairs, Colonel of the Gaunt or Regent's Own Regiment of Militia, a Trustee of the British Museum, an Elder Brother of the Trinity House, a Governor of the White Friars, and D.C.L."[14]

With the beginning of the sequence, "Hellborough, Pitchley and Grillsby," Mephistopheles threatens to explode like the farcical devil of a morality play. Steyne's House of Gaunt has already betrayed a "mysterious taint of the blood"; his son, once a "dandy diplomatist," is now under confinement, "dragging about a child's toy, or nursing the keeper's baby's doll."[15] The satirical series of titles recalls the dubious significance of the Marquis' own personal and family names, with their emblematic reference to his hereditary qualifications: Gaunt—grim—attenuated; taint—stigma—Steyne.

The climactic scene between Becky and Steyne, like the final sequences between Catherine and the Count, divests the actors of their conventional literary disguises; but in

Vanity Fair there is no dissociation between narrative and interpretation. Thackeray is not forced to suspend action while he develops significance or to sacrifice continuity to parody. The word now moves with the event; parody is implicit in the textures of dramatic exposition. Nevertheless, Thackeray has learned a great deal from *Catherine*. His preliminary rendering of crime's "grand scene" is extended ironically in *Vanity Fair*; phrases that were intrusive asides in the uneven parody of the early novel are now controlled by the integration of expressive textures— thus, an epithet from *Catherine's* parodic climax becomes the passing discord "wretched woman" that anticipates the dissolution of Becky's Byronic glamor.

Vanity Fair's "grand scene" is a gloss on social success. Becky is indebted to the lechery of the Marquis of Steyne; she is about to satisfy the debt. Unannounced, her husband, Rawdon, enters:

"Steyne was hanging over the sofa on which Becky sate. The wretched woman was in a brilliant full toilette, her arms and all her fingers sparkling with bracelets and rings; and the brilliants on her breast which Steyne had given her. . . . Becky started up with a faint scream as she caught sight of Rawdon's white face. At the next instant she tried a smile, a horrid smile, as if to welcome her husband: and Steyne rose up, grinding his teeth, pale, and with fury in his looks. . . .

"There was that in Rawdon's face which caused Becky to fling herself before him. 'I am innocent, Rawdon,' she said; 'before God, I am innocent.' She clung hold of his coat, of his hands; her own were all covered with serpents, and rings, and baubles. . . .

" 'Come here,' he said.—She came up at once.

" 'Take off those things.'—She began, trembling, pulling the jewels from her arms, and the rings from her shaking fingers, and held them all in a heap, quivering and looking up at him. 'Throw them down,' he said, and she dropped them. He tore the diamond ornament out of her breast, and flung it at Lord Steyne. It cut him on his bald forehead. Steyne wore the scar to his dying day."[16]

In the discredited context of criminal romance, a farcical Satan and a melodramatic Eve have played the primordial scene for laughs. The Fallen Becky—"wretched woman" . . . "brilliants on her breast which Steyne had given her" . . . " 'I am innocent' " . . . "all covered with serpents, and rings, and baubles." Steyne, the Tempter—"hanging over the sofa" . . . "grinding his teeth" . . . "fury in his looks." The "bald forehead" of this second-rate serpent is bruised by the clumsy Adam, Rawdon—"Steyne wore the scar to his dying day." In the parodic context, this biblical sequence is a moral nightmare; its dramatic integration is a mature achievement, but the precision of its satiric effects is the result of Thackeray's early parody of criminal fiction.

Textures of criminal romance in *Vanity Fair* have two functions. One, which will presently be considered, is formal; the melodramatic mode is one of the major elements in the effective artistic pattern of *Vanity Fair*. The other, like parody in *Catherine*, fulfills the satirist's traditional purpose—to discredit literary artifice and to achieve a diminishing perspective on Becky's factitious brilliance. One of the ironies of literature is that Becky's heroic adventures have been taken as seriously as though she were Bulwer Lytton's own; it is the same response that once made Satan the hero of *Paradise Lost*. But Becky is not a Byronic heroine. Her protector, Steyne, is caricatured like Catherine's Count, and Becky nurses no romantic dream of glory. In the third-class Continental boarding houses, "Becky liked the life. She was at home with everybody in the place, pedlars, punters, tumblers, students and all."[17] For Becky, vaulting ambition is a shopgirl's fantasy of financial heaven: "I think I could be a good woman if I had five thousand a year. I could dawdle about in the nursery, and count the apricots on the wall."[18] Her affectations are the shopgirl's own: "The humble calling of her female parent Miss Sharp never alluded to."[19] Like Catherine, she has "the dismal precocity of poverty";[20] on the Continent, she was "a boarding-house queen: and ruled in select *pensions*. She never refused the champagne, or the bouquets, or the drives into the country, or the private boxes."[21] Becky Sharp is no contradiction in this "novel without a hero."

The further, formal, function of the rhetoric of crime in *Vanity Fair* offers an instance of Thackeray's developing integration of style and structure. The criminal romance convention projects an artistic pattern in the Becky-Rawdon-Steyne narrative that is not dependent on the literal plot—an image of amorous melodrama that belies Becky's commonplace nature and satirizes her poetic pretensions. This sequence has a quality of its own, and after its climax in the grand denunciation scene, Amelia dominates the novel. Textures of criminal romance unify the Becky-narrative, defining it as an entity within the larger context. At the same time, sentimental textures, because of their literary kinship to the conventions of criminal romance—a relationship already exploited in *Catherine*—are a means of correlating Amelia's role with Becky's. The fundamental reciprocity of sentimental and criminal conventions within the fashionable mode integrates the Amelia-Becky narratives within the total conception, and this expressive integration results in a dramatic unity that has sometimes seemed a critical paradox because of the novel's disparate literal "plots."

Vanity Fair's version of the sentimental convention—

"fashionable" fiction's alternate mode—provides an inclusive expressive context that begins and ends the novel. Sentimental textures are persistently associated with Amelia; and their satirical significance discredits a critical misinterpretation that corresponds to the Byronic glamorization of Becky—the frequent, contemptuous appraisal of Amelia as an idealized heroine. It was hardly Thackeray's intention to fabricate a conventionalized ingénue. He wrote to his mother, who had objected that Amelia was selfish, "My object is not to make a perfect character or anything like it. . . . Dobbin & poor Briggs are the only 2 people with real humility as yet. Amelia's is to come."[22] No doubt, Thackeray's echoes of Mrs. Gore have been taken too seriously; it is the satirical content of this allusive sentimentality that indicates Amelia's artistic significance.

Vanity Fair's opening sequences—Becky's flirtation with Jos Sedley and Amelia's romance with George Osborne—are woven from fashionable staples:

"The argument stands thus—Osborne, in love with Amelia, has asked an old friend to dinner and to Vauxhall —Jos Sedley is in love with Rebecca. Will he marry her? That is the great subject now in hand.

"We might have treated this subject in the genteel, or in the romantic, or in the facetious manner. . . . Suppose we had shown how Lord Joseph Sedley fell in love, and the Marquis of Osborne became attached to Lady Amelia, with the full consent of the Duke, her noble father. . . . But my readers must hope for no such romance."[23]

As long as Amelia is an inexperienced girl, the sentimental echoes have—like certain passages in *The Professor* —the genuine freshness and pathos of youth. The proper fruition of these naive emotions is suggested in a passage that anticipates Amelia's healthy development: "She had, too, in the course of this few days' constant intercourse, warmed into a most tender friendship for Rebecca. . . . For the affection of young ladies is of as rapid growth as Jack's bean-stalk, and reaches up to the sky in a night. It is no blame to them that after marriage this *Sehnsucht nach der Liebe* subsides. It is what sentimentalists, who deal in *very* big words, call a yearning after the Ideal, and simply means that women are commonly not satisfied until they have husbands and children on whom they may centre affections, which are spent elsewhere, as it were, in small change."[24]

But Amelia's idealisms do not fructify in reality. Her worship of George Osborne is morbid; its abnormality is emphasized by an allusion to Titania's degradation: "Perhaps some beloved female subscriber has arrayed an ass in the splendour and glory of her imagination; admired his dulness as manly simplicity; worshipped his selfishness as manly superiority; treated his stupidity as majestic gravity, and used him as the brilliant fairy Titania did a certain weaver at Athens. I think I have seen such comedies of errors going on in the world. But this is certain, that Amelia believed her lover to be one of the most gallant and brilliant men in the empire: and it is possible Lieutenant Osborne thought so too."[25]

Here are Mrs. Gore's sentimentalities turned sour. It is Amelia's pathos that she cannot outgrow this attitude and continues to worship her dream-hero after he dies so that she is unable to reciprocate Dobbin's devotion. And Dobbin, too, is confused by the conventional idealizations, beginning with his schoolboy admiration for George: "He believed Osborne to be the possessor of every perfection, to be the handsomest, the bravest, the most active, the cleverest, the most generous of created boys."[26] He respects Amelia's fantasy-romance from residual loyalty to naive ideals, and continues to humor her illusions long after he has learned to impose sterner values on himself.

The sentimental enchantment is broken by a crisis in Dobbin's life; parodic literary textures dissolve as a function of psychic readjustment, and stylistic modulation mirrors Dobbin's disillusionment. Exasperated by Amelia's indifference, he at last confronts her with reality: "I know what your heart is capable of: it can cling faithfully to a recollection, and cherish a fancy. . . . I knew all along that the prize I had set my life on was not worth the winning; that I was a fool, with fond fancies, too, bartering away my all of truth and ardour against your little feeble remnant of love. I will bargain no more. . . . I have watched your struggle. Let it end. We are both weary of it."[27]

When, a few pages later, Dobbin returns to Amelia, the narrative texture returns to sentimental parody, and the effect is startling. Every saccharine phrase rings with irony. The insipid artifice which has deluded Dobbin is pointedly parodied; and Thackeray's key phrase—"the last page of the third volume"—assures us drily that this is satire on artistic as well as human affectations. The truth bites through in his climactic characterization of Amelia— "tender little parasite": "The vessel is in port. He has got the prize he has been trying for all his life. The bird has come in at last. There it is with its head on his shoulder, billing and cooing close up to his heart, with soft outstretched fluttering wings. This is what he has asked for every day and hour for eighteen years. This is what he pined after. Here it is—the summit, the end—the last page of the third volume. Good-bye, Colonel.—God bless you, honest William!—Farewell, dear Amelia.—Grow green again, tender little parasite, round the rugged old oak to which you cling!"[28]

From Amelia's chirping in Miss Pinkerton's school, with Becky as realistic chorus, to her final billing and cooing and fluttering of impotent wings—a travesty of divine love —in this valueless reunion with Dobbin, the novel projects a typical psychological development from innocent indulgence to compulsive involvement in deluded idealism. The sentimental disguise has become a shirt of Nessus, clinging about harsh emotions that struggle for expression. In *Vanity Fair*, emotional growth is also aesthetic development, and, as immature responses are discarded, the charm of facile literary modes is dispelled.

Parodic textures of criminal romance contour the Becky-Rawdon-Steyne action in *Vanity Fair*, textures of sentimental satire shape the Amelia-George-Dobbin sequence; their artistic relationship unifies the two narratives. The fashionable modes, as in the best passages of *Catherine*, are so subtly blended that no juncture is apparent. But the parodist's negations are not Thackeray's only purpose; there is a coda to this satiric sonata. Amelia and Dobbin marry; their wilful evasions of reality have robbed them of a full relationship, but their meagre fruition is better than glamorous sterility. We meet them again on the last page of *Vanity Fair*. They have a child, of whom Dobbin "is fonder than of anything in the world":

" 'Fonder than he is of me,' Emmy thinks, with a sigh. But he never said a word to Amelia that was not kind and gentle; or thought of a want of hers that he did not try to gratify.

"Ah! *Vanitas Vanitatum!* which of us is happy in this world? Which of us has his desire? or, having it, is satisfied?—Come, children, let us shut up the box and the puppets, for our play is played out."[29]

Critics have been generally puzzled to excuse Thackeray's dismissal of his characters. But perhaps it is now possible to see why, in shutting up these "puppets," Thackeray does not give his people away. Some of them were puppets indeed and capable of no development. They crumple into rags, like the Satanic caricature of the Mar-

31

quis of Steyne—"The richly dressed figure of the Wicked Nobleman . . . which Old Nick will fetch away at the end of this singular performance."[30] Others, whose vigorous reality is revealed to the reader but not to their fellow actors, assume conventional masks and frustrate the realistic satisfaction of their natural impulses. In the world of the novel they continue mechanically to play their fraudulent parts; like Becky, who appears as a puppet in Thackeray's last illustration, a pious widow at a charity bazaar above the caption "Virtue Rewarded; A Booth in Vanity Fair." But the rarest characters are those with a capacity for genuine emotional response. They were puppets only so long as they acted an illusion, pulled by the strings of the fashionable mode. In foregoing their fantasy-happiness and ceasing to demand imagined satisfactions, Amelia and Dobbin become human beings, and walk away from us at the end of the novel, leaving their outgrown miniatures behind them.

CHAPTER III

PARODY OF CHIVALRIC ROMANCE

(1845–1849): *VANITY FAIR*

$\mathcal{C}$ HIVALRIC romance motifs are of equal importance with fashionable textures in *Vanity Fair*; together, they form the novel's extended expressive modes. Fashionable textures—the parodied rhetoric of sentimental love and romantic crime—diffuse through the narrative as an ambience of shifting perspectives and ambivalent values. Romance motifs—satirized elements of familiar chivalric convention—form intersecting asymmetrical patterns. In the fashionable mode, the effect is of variation and modulation; in the chivalric mode, of persistent relationships and qualities. The incongruities of romance clichés are caricatured in delusive love-idealisms, destructive chivalric codes, hero-heroine-clown-squire-villain patterns, disoriented motifs of purity, humility, courage, adoration. And Thackeray's treatment of romance was not without sequel. In the later English novel, this ironic reorganization of chivalric materials is a recurrent technique. Meredith's *Egoist* is triumphantly in the tradition of chivalric parody; Joyce's *Ulysses* is pointed with satirical romance allusions more obvious but not less functional than Thackeray's, as in the passage at the hospital where "young Stephen and sir Leopold" meet in the company of "right witty scholars."

An important aspect of romance in *Vanity Fair* is determined by Thackeray's eighteenth-century heritage. For though the romance convention in England is very old, the medieval tradition was obscured between Chaucer and Dryden and was not an effective part of the Victorian inheritance. If Thackeray sometimes alludes to earlier, more robust romance conventions, they do not significantly modify the quality of his semi-satiric interpretation of chivalry.

Eighteenth-century romance—a combination of medieval mystique and gothic fantasy—was the defiant creation of progressive poets and nostalgic scholars in a neoclassical world; by mid-century it was an established concept. In 1762 Richard Hurd recalled "the magic of the old Romances," and lamented the loss of that "world of fine fabling." His elegy was coincident with a turning point in the development of English fiction. Like the poets, the later eighteenth-century novelists were ready to turn from the reasonable study of mankind to more freely imaginative explorations—and in 1765 *The Castle of Otranto* was published. It was a romantic challenge to contemporary "realistic" practice; and the changing interpretation of the relationship between romances and novels that continued through the century is part of Thackeray's literary heritage.

The eighteenth century had begun by rejecting romance and demanding realism in the novel. The theory, though not the practice, is clearly exemplified by Congreve, whose preface to *Incognita* (1692) proclaimed a revolt against the French historical romances of the seventeenth century:

"Romances are generally composed of the Constant Loves and invincible Courages of . . . Mortals of the first Rank . . . where lofty Language, miraculous Contingencies and impossible Performances, elevate and surprize the Reader into a giddy Delight. . . . Novels are of a more familiar Nature; Come near us, and represent to us Intrigues in practice . . . not such as are wholly unusual or unpresidented, [but] such which not being so distant from our Belief bring also the pleasure nearer us."[1]

During the half-century following the publication of *Incognita*, novelists were continually exploring new techniques for conveying the impression of reality; and at the

34

same time they began to formulate for the novel a "realistic" aesthetic. Their achievement is epitomized in Smollett's definition of 1753: "A novel is a large diffused picture, comprehending the characters of life, disposed in different groups, and exhibited in various attitudes, for the purposes of an uniform plan, and general occurrence, to which every individual figure is subservient."[2] Although Smollett may have been engaged in special pleading, his emphasis on the "characters of life" agrees with the practice of other mid-century novelists. But this condition of aesthetic certitude was ephemeral. Hurd's nostalgia for the lost fableland of the Middle Ages was symptomatic; and in a few more years Horace Walpole, the champion of a newly romantic novel, prefaced his second edition of *The Castle of Otranto* with a declaration that reads like an answer to Congreve:

"[*Otranto*] was an attempt to blend the two kinds of romance, the ancient and the modern. In the former, all was imagination and improbability: in the latter, nature is always intended to be, and sometimes has been, copied with success. Invention has not been wanting; but the great resources of fancy have been dammed up, by a strict adherence to common life. But if, in the latter species, Nature has cramped imagination, she did but take her revenge, having been totally excluded from old romances."[3]

This critical ambivalence was Thackeray's point of departure. Thackeray had a special affinity for the historical novel of Scott and Dumas, and, as *Henry Esmond* suggests, an intense interest in history itself—a medium which had acquired great intellectual and artistic prestige in the nineteenth century. But since, after Scott, the historical novel was ineluctably in the romance tradition, its significance was complicated for Thackeray, who was initially a satirical realist, by the inherited dispute over the claims

35

of "nature" and "romance" in the novel—an argument
pursued by nineteenth-century novelists from Jane Austen,
who satirized the gothic variant of eighteenth-century
romance, to Henry James, who insisted that the novelist
should "regard himself as an historian and his narrative
as a history."[4]

Thackeray began by defending the "naturalistic" aesthetic: he maintained that "the Art of Novels *is* to represent Nature: to convey as strongly as possible the sentiment
of reality—in a tragedy or a poem or a lofty drama you
aim at producing different emotions; the figures moving,
and their words sounding, heroically."[5] It is not surprising
that he found Hugo's *Notre-Dame de Paris* "a work of
genius, though it is not perhaps a fine novel."[6] But his
attitude toward the idealizations of romance altered and
his irony became more complex as his work matured.

It is possible, without being unduly schematic, to indicate successive stages in Thackeray's assimilation of romance in the years before *Vanity Fair*, as long as one remembers that his earlier attitudes are not replaced, but
only modified, by later ones. In 1832, for example, the
discussion of "romanticism" in his diary is skeptical: "The
poets and dramatists of the old time had to combat agst the
coldness of custom, & yet circumscribed in metre time and
subject they occasionally produced true poetry. . . . In the
time of Voltaire the heroes of poetry and drama were fine
gentlemen, in the days of Victor Hugo they bluster about
in velvets and moustachios and gold chains, partly as in old
times creating & partly following the prevailing fashion."[7]

In 1840 the tone of a passage from *The Paris Sketch
Book* is affectionate: "Jacques Louis David is dead. He
died about a year after his bodily demise in 1825. The
romanticism killed him. Walter Scott, from his Castle of
Abbotsford, sent out a troop . . . who . . . did challenge,
combat, and overcome the heroes and demigods of Greece

and Rome. *Notre Dame à la rescousse!* Sir Brian de Bois Guilbert has borne Hector of Troy clean out of his saddle."[8]

In 1847 Thackeray suggests his reconciliation of romance with social satire in a figurative phrase from *The Book of Snobs*: "And I arm myself with the sword and spear, and taking leave of my family, go forth to do battle with that hideous ogre and giant, that brutal despot in Snob Castle, who holds so many gentle hearts in torture and thrall."[9] In *The Book of Snobs* Thackeray analyzed the pettiness and commercialism of the Victorian social code. As he had attacked facile idealisms with the argument of reality, so he attacked the materialism which society calls "realistic" with the idealism of romance. This concurrent discrimination and assimilation is exemplified in two of Thackeray's shorter narratives—*A Legend of the Rhine*, based on Dumas, and *Rebecca and Rowena*, a parody of *Ivanhoe*. Both are directly related to his treatment of romance in *Vanity Fair*.

A Legend of the Rhine, written in 1845, two years before *The Book of Snobs*, is a burlesque adaptation of a forgotten tale by the older Dumas called "Othon l'archer."[10] The *Legend*, Saintsbury remarked, "is a fantastic parody of serious modern followings of ancient romance. But there is nothing in it in the least offensive or even antagonistic to Romance itself."[11]

Thackeray's *Legend* opens with a contemplative prelude which has no equivalent in Dumas: "They are passed away:—those old knights and ladies: their golden hair first changed to silver, and then the silver dropped off . . . their elegant legs, so slim and active in the dance, became swollen and gouty . . . the roses left their cheeks, and then their cheeks disappeared, and left their skulls, and then their skulls powdered into dust, and all sign of them was gone. And as it was with them, so shall it be with us."[12]

Ubi sunt? To satirize the pretty-fantasy structures of the modern romance-novel, Thackeray has recalled a convention of medieval poetry, the *memento mori*; and the courtly nineteenth-century chivalric image—"slim and active in the dance"—yields to the medieval dance of death— "They are passed away." The insistence upon the physical fact of mortality is prelude to a grimly slapstick stretto on a theme excised from the published version of an earlier manuscript—"I wonder is there any single good feeling that war inspires, and are not the very best of the qualities elicited by it, coarse brutal savage of a low order of intelligence?"[13] Here, a realism reminiscent of true medieval romances strips away the heroic disguise from knightly combat: "His mouth foaming—his face almost green—his eyes full of blood—his brains spattered over his forehead, and several of his teeth knocked out . . . Sir Gottfried fell heavily from the saddle of his piebald charger; the frightened animal . . . plunged out his hind legs, trampling for one moment upon the feet of the prostrate Gottfried, thereby causing him to shriek with agony."[14] The *Legend's* princely protagonist is a denizen of that Dresden world where the "humblest of romance heroes, Signor Clown, when he wants anything in the Pantomime, straightway finds it to his hand,"[15] and the love sequences are postured in the sentimental radiance of the fashionable novel: "Once more their eyes met—their hearts thrilled. They had never spoken, but they knew they loved each other for ever."[16] Thackeray does not let us forget the incongruities in these idealizations: the handsome hero, for example, is a knightly narcissist, furious at having to sacrifice his "golden curls—fair curls that his mother had so often played with!"[17] And the *Legend* has also the dark antiheroine of romance, the "Lady of Windeck": "Her form was of faultless beauty; her face pale as the marble of the fairy statue." This chivalric enchantress is given to dubious puns—serving magic dinner to a bewitched victim, she offers him "a devilled turkey wing. 'I adore the devil,' said he. 'So do I,' said the pale lady." Questioned about the source of this voluptuous meal, she adds "The kitchen is *below.*"[18] The lady's sorry conceits are sufficient satire on the eighteenth-century convention of the gothic temptress. *Rebecca and Rowena* (1849) is a further parodic development. In this satirical continuation of Scott's novel, Thackeray insinuates the reality of contemporary Victorianism beneath the masks of chivalric romance. "Is it necessary to describe them? No: that has already been done in the novel of 'Ivanhoe,' "[19] his *Legend* comments; for the Scott novel was the prototype of later chivalric fiction, remaining throughout the nineteenth century a pattern for parodists and imitators. *Ivanhoe* exploited all the conventional romance motifs—the blond heroine and her dark anti-type, the courageous hero, the humble squire, the knightly combat ethic, the mystique of chivalric love. Thackeray's *Rebecca and Rowena*—"A Romance Upon Romance"—satirizes the stylized Victorian versions of these ideal roles. In this double-edged parody, realistic descriptions of modern social motivation seem to validate, by contrast, the idealized conventions of chivalry—a metamorphosis that recalls *The Book of Snobs.* At the same time, romance conventions are discredited when Thackeray's fictional characters invoke them in conformity to a self-righteous social code.

If *A Legend of the Rhine* burlesqued the realistic violence disguised by chivalric conventions of masculine combat, *Rebecca and Rowena* satirizes the "civilized" brutality beneath the mask of feminine etiquette. Thus, Thackeray deftly caricatures the irreproachable Victorian lady in his portrait of Scott's insipid heroine, Rowena: "Those who have marked her conduct during her maidenhood, her distinguished politeness, her spotless modesty of demeanour, her unalterable coolness under all circumstances, and her lofty and gentlewomanlike bearing, must be sure that . . . Rowena the wife would be a pattern of correctness for all the matrons of England."[20] This gentle gelid language is a prelude to Rowena's first narrated action, when, as punishment for making an anti-clerical joke, she orders Wamba the Jester to be whipped:

" 'I got you out of Front-de-Boeuf's castle,' said poor Wamba piteously, appealing to Sir Wilfrid of Ivanhoe, 'and canst thou not save me from the lash?'
" 'Yes, from Front-de-Boeuf's castle, *where you were locked up with the Jewess in the tower!*' said Rowena, haughtily replying to the timid appeal of her husband. 'Gurth, give him four dozen!' "[21]

The thin, insistent treble of the italicized phrase is all that is needed to define the lady's emotions. A deeper layer is exposed in the tissue of this sentimental Rowena when, after the supposed death of Ivanhoe, she contracts "a second matrimonial engagement": "That Athelstane was the man, I suppose no reader familiar with life, and novels which are a rescript of life, and are all strictly natural and edifying, can for a moment doubt. . . . Did women never . . . fall in love with donkeys, before the time of the amours of Bottom and Titania? . . . Yes, Rowena cared a hundred times more about tipsy Athelstane than ever she had done for gentle Ivanhoe."[22]

In *Vanity Fair*, Amelia worships George Osborne "as the brilliant fairy Titania did a certain weaver at Athens." Here, in the parodic context of this "Romance Upon Romance," the connotations of the Titania metaphor are reinforced. Shakespeare's fable identified the animal impulse at the heart of man's imagined fairylands, magical or chivalric; Thackeray's allusion is a reminder that fantasy is equally frequent and reality equally disparate in the most civilized society. In the quoted passage, the modish "amours" deftly shifts the scene from the forest of Arden to the fashionable nineteenth-century drawing room.

Rebecca and Rowena, extending and refining the insights of *A Legend of the Rhine*, makes, in its formal development, a decisive departure from Thackeray's earlier chivalric burlesques. The *Legend* does not alter conventional romance patterns: the heroine and the hero are blond, the villain dark, the hero warlike, the conventional code of knightly combat shapes the action; the story parallels the conventions it mocks rather than developing divergent structures. *Rebecca and Rowena*, on the other hand, purposefully inverts the formal romance relationships and creates a nascent pattern of its own. Here, dark Rebecca is the heroine, blond Rowena a character part. Ivanhoe is a mutation of the romance hero, pacific and introverted instead of aggressive and conformist; King Richard is a buffoon, the clown a social crusader. This inversion of chivalric axioms repatterns the subsequent action. The crusade is a scene of inefficient butchery rather than of chivalrous virtue. Ivanhoe's ultimate marriage (to Rebecca) is a union of melancholy and anonymity, rather than the fairy-tale consummation of conventional romance.

Thackeray's adaptation of the chivalric tradition in *Vanity Fair* depends on a similar repatterning of motifs; and the novel may be read in this respect as a deviant *Ivanhoe*. But romance mutation is considerably more complex in Thackeray's major novels than in the parodies; uniting the burlesque of the *Legend* with the satirical inversion of *Rebecca and Rowena*, it is more than a simple combination of the two. At a given point, Thackeray may parody romance convention; again, he may invert it; but more often, his treatment is neither a burlesque nor an inversion, but a kind of subtle distortion, an unfamiliar mating between ideal and real that produces idiosyncratic variants.

Vanity Fair's chivalric themes are premised in the title page drawing, with its stage helmet, its wooden sword, and its cluster of medieval turrets. And it is not difficult to analyze the novel in terms of allegorized romance: Amelia and Becky figure as bewitched heroine and delusive enchantress (sentimentality and selfishness); George and Rawdon as false knights (vanity and brutality); Dobbin as disguised prince, identified at last as the true knight (humility). But these are abstractions, deprived of their active participation in *Vanity Fair's* eccentric equilibrium. The novel's romance continuity, with its significant distortions, must be sampled in dynamic contexts.

The travesty of the beautiful prince of romance persists in *Vanity Fair* as the portrait of a Regency dandy. George Osborne is a chivalric hero for the clownish William Dobbin, who bears him "such an affection, as we read in the charming fairy-book, uncouth Orson had for splendid young Valentine his conqueror."[23] This idealization is immediately disordered by the generic narcissism that was typified in the *Legend* by the hero's distress at losing his golden curls: Osborne, remarking that Dobbin " 'is not an Adonis, certainly,' . . . looked towards the glass himself with much *naïveté*; and in so doing, caught Miss Sharp's eye fixed keenly upon him, at which he blushed a little, and Rebecca thought in her heart, '*Ah, mon beau Monsieur*! I think I have *your* gauge.' "[24]

The *Legend's* brutal image of knightly valor recurs in *Vanity Fair* in the shape of Rawdon Crawley, Officer in Her Majesty's Dragoons, a "large young dandy,"[25] who "had already . . . fought three bloody duels, in which he gave ample proofs of his contempt for death."[26] This champion competes with his father for Becky's favor, and their amorous rivalry hints of the jungle—"if he came down the corridor ever so quietly, his father's door was sure to open, and the hyaena face of the old gentleman to glare out."²⁷ It is consonant with *Vanity Fair's* subtler re-orientation of romance patterns that, in the climactic scene of Becky's exposure, when the Marquis of Steyne is humiliated, Rawdon should appear "strong, brave, and victorious"²⁸ by contrast with the fashionable villain. George Osborne, on the other hand, the hero of a fairy-tale, a fantasy creation dependent on the sentimental connivance of Dobbin and Amelia, evaporates in a gallant passage whose only pathos is his wife's: "then George came marching at the head of his company. He looked up, and smiled at Amelia, and passed on; and even the sound of the music died away."²⁹

William Dobbin, the enharmonic clown, is an anti-romantic dissonance in this context: "a very tall ungainly gentleman . . . in the hideous military frogged coat and cocked-hat of those times."³⁰ The uniform which is "handsome" in the romance figurations of George and Rawdon becomes "hideous" in Dobbin's eccentric image; and this incongruity finds its gloss in a cadenza on the chivalric war-motif that was travestied in the *Legend* and satirized in *Rebecca and Rowena*: "Time out of mind strength and courage have been the theme of bards and romances . . . I wonder is it because men are cowards in heart that they . . . place military valour so far beyond every other quality?"³¹

The "heroines" of *Vanity Fair* refract further chivalric obliquities—Rebecca and Rowena in prismatic distortion. Rebecca Sharp is deviously related to *Ivanhoe's* Rebecca of York, but the exotic reference is rather satiric than sentimental. Physically, however, Becky is a morbid mutation of the blond romance heroine: "small and slight in person; pale, sandy-haired, and with eyes habitually cast down." She assumes all the masks of romantic evil prefigured in the *Legend's* dark lady: as false purity, Rebecca is "dressed in white, with bare shoulders as white as snow—

the picture of youth, unprotected innocence"; as the merciless "belle dame" she is Delilah, Cleopatra, the "Dame Blanche"; as a Lamia she "writhes and twists about like a snake," her hands are "all covered with serpents," she forces "a horrid smile"; as an enchantress her "bright green eyes streamed out, and shot into the night," and she appears at roulette with "shining eyes and mask"; in Satanic metamorphosis she is "a spider" whose laborious web is torn by a housemaid's broom. But these are only aspects of a sustained ambivalence—she is both a "good-natured soul," and "an artful little minx"; it may be "only a question of money" that makes "the difference between her and an honest woman."[32]

Amelia, the abortive romance heroine, has the dark hair of her anti-type; she is "poor little Emmy," with "a rosy, round, happy face"; Osborne seems to her "a fairy prince" stooping to "a humble Cinderella." Her treatment of Dobbin—"how cold, how kind, how hopeless, how selfish"—recalls the satirical Rowena rather than Scott's ethereal heroine; the sentimental folly of her "blind devotion" subordinates Dobbin's sincerity to Osborne's stereotyped chivalric image—"She had her picture of George for a consolation." It is the fetish of a fantasy-knight to which she has clung in an ecstasy of adolescent idealism: "All her husband's faults and foibles she had buried in the grave with him: she only remembered the lover, who had married her at all sacrifices; the noble husband so brave and beautiful, in whose arms she had hung on the morning when he had gone away to fight, and die gloriously for his king. From heaven the hero must be smiling down."[33]

This deft disordering of stylized romance relationships and qualities is not mere ingenuity. It is a much more significant reading of the romance-illusion than the direct parody of the burlesques. *Vanity Fair* does not wholly discredit romantic idealisms; but reality is not the reverse of romance, any more than it is its fulfillment. Chivalry is vindicated, but in deviant ways, as when the "amazing champion," Dobbin, son of "a grocer in the City," attacks "Cuff, the unquestioned king of the school," to protect the little "prince," George Osborne, from punishment: "Perhaps Dobbin's foolish soul revolted against that exercise of tyranny; or perhaps he had a hankering feeling of revenge in his mind, and longed to measure himself against that splendid bully and tyrant, who had all the glory, pride, pomp, circumstance, banners flying, drums beating, guards saluting, in the place."[34]

Romance intensities are verified in unexpected contexts —Amelia's love for George changes in the violence of Waterloo from girlish devotion to real passion, as genuine as the shock of her image while she watches him prepare for battle: "She came out and stood, leaning at the wall, holding this sash against her bosom, from which the heavy net of crimson dropped like a large stain of blood."[35] Chivalric motifs of love and combat appear in aspects of modern convention; as anthropologists read in myth the primitive impulses of violence and desire, emotional realities are discovered here in the idealisms of romance.

So, *Vanity Fair* reinterprets in contemporary terms the traditions of chivalric romance. Poetic formulas remain, their content is converted; basic relationships persist, realistic contexts alter their terms. But the patterns are still present. Behind *Ivanhoe* are the images of fables as distant as the *Faerie Queene*, for Ivanhoe was itself, in some respects, a reinterpretation of Spenser. In the *Faerie Queene* England's champion serves celestial Una, is seduced by dark Duessa, discovers her iniquity after saving her from a pretended rape, and returns, enlightened, to the golden heroine. In *Ivanhoe*, an English champion gives his romance allegiance to fair Rowena, rescues beautiful, dark-

haired Rebecca from rape by Front de Boeuf, and is finally
united with the virtuous Rowena. Scott's modification of
traditional types is a nineteenth-century chivalric idealization: in Rowena, Una's stern piety is sugared and diluted;
Scott's hero is a lustless Redcross; and the Spenserian
Duessa is generically altered in *Ivanhoe's* chaste Rebecca,
whose unconventional purity is a new poetic insight.

Vanity Fair's satirical context transforms all ideal conventions, but Thackeray's mythic evocations recall both
Scott and Spenser. Ivanhoe is split in two—George and
Dobbin are both "British lions," but George is a chivalric
truism, and Dobbin, questing for Amelia, is at once grail-
servant and clownish Caliban.[36] Amelia shares Una's capacity for love, but Amelia is also Rowena's sentimental
effigy and worships the worthless champion. George, like
Ivanhoe, admires Rebecca, but Rebecca chooses Rawdon,
the Victorian Front de Boeuf. Rebecca is a throwback from
Scott's idealized type to the traditional Duessa-image, yet
it is she who amiably unites a battered Rowena to an
Ivanhoe for whom the chivalric trophy has lost its value—
to a Dobbin who has discovered that Amelia is "not worth
the winning."[37]

Romance in *Vanity Fair* has a wide satiric range extending from sustained attacks on the chivalric glorification of
war that culminates in Waterloo to the exposure of the
morbid love-idealisms that mislead the deluded actors.
But the novel's romance motifs also define the actors'
persistent, fundamental emotional impulses of which these
false idealisms are the conventional distortions. Thus, although Amelia is obstinately deluded by her romantic
image of George, she has, as Thackeray points out in one
of his letters, the basic capacity for "LOVE—by w^h. she
shall be saved."[38]

And romance is further qualified in *Vanity Fair* by an
aspect of human mutability, the relativistic analysis of

psychological motivation. Thackeray's concept of character is not simple. A letter to his mother introduces the argument of salvation in *Vanity Fair* with the premise that Amelia is selfish; and the novel's persistent irony is a demonstration of this psychic ambiguity. The tender Amelia is "soft and foolish"; her precarious survival depends on a "feeble remnant of love."[39] Throughout the novel, the imaginative certitudes of romance are tested by an imagery of dubious motivation; psychological relativity modifies the symbolisms of emotional permanence—and the textures of "fashionable" fiction provide the medium for this exchange.

In *Vanity Fair*, psychological ambiguity is associated with fashionable textures, as emotional survival is with romance. The modes are mutually indispensable; romance tradition is a permanent reference point for fashionable parody, fashionable textures are a refracting medium for romance. In chivalric imagery, Osborne is a "Don Giovanni," a "Don Juan" torturing his amorous victim; in fashionable parody he is "swaggering and melancholy, languid and fierce. He looked like a man who had passions"; "Cupid," Becky calls him.[40] Rawdon in romance is a brutal Front de Boeuf—victor of "three bloody duels," a "celebrated 'blood' "; in comic perspective he is a "young dandy," "a famous buck," a "love-stricken dragoon."[41] Romance opposes the heroines in an eccentric duality of light and dark, sinister and pure: "poor gentle" Amelia is filled with "blind beautiful devotions," "Love had been her faith"; Rebecca is successively a "queer little wild vixen," a "dauntless worldling," a "bad angel," an "accomplished little devil," "unsurpassable in lies."[42] In the fashionable context, the two are sometimes almost identical—Amelia is "a figure in a book of fashions . . . a high-waisted gown with an impossible doll's face simpering over it"; Rebecca, "a vivified figure out of the *Magasin des*

Modes—blandly smiling in the most beautiful new clothes."[43]

In the romance context, the characters of *Vanity Fair* are consistent types; in fashionable perspective they are mixed, ambiguous creatures. As a chivalric hero, George Osborne is a gallant narcissist; in fashionable mutation, he is contradictory—ambitious, tender, remorseful. In romance, Rebecca is invariably malign and devious; in the fashionable context, she is good-natured and fond of her husband. Fashionable textures are a medium for multiple viewpoints, the values changing with the perspective— Osborne's father's ideals are justified by his social environment and are perhaps an excuse for George; a starving alderman would be as dishonest as penniless Rebecca. In the romance mode, values persist; beneath the chivalric cult of combat, brutality and destruction are ineluctable— "The war-chroniclers who write brilliant stories of fight and triumph scarcely tell us of these . . . you don't hear widows' cries or mothers' sobs . . . in the great Chorus of Victory."[44]

If fashionable textures are a diffuse, atmospheric medium, romance motifs are elements of compositional color. The formal contrast between Amelia and Rebecca—like a triangular opposition—is the most frequently cited instance of "narrative line" in *Vanity Fair*; but this opposition depends rather on the sequence of significant metaphors than on a "linear" organization of plot-events. There is much less realistic contrast between the two plot progressions than the concept of "opposing fortunes" suggests; literal experience does not consistently diverge through the narrative, nor do the plots differ greatly in objective outcome.

In *Vanity Fair*, it is the allusive sequences that project the geometric narrative patterns to which the reader responds. Romance motifs are the real means, for example,

of contrasting the heroines' experience—an instance of
this creation of dramatic design is the progressive opposition of heart-imagery that accompanies the heroines' emotional development. Amelia's "generous heart" becomes
successively an "imprisoned and tortured . . . little heart,"
a "bleeding disappointed heart"; Rebecca, the "practi-
tioner in Vanity Fair," pierces this image and Amelia is
"powerless in the hands of her remorseless little enemy"—
"Women only know how to wound so. There is a poison
on the tips of their little shafts."[45] Rebecca's heart-images
are negations—"I didn't break my heart about him"; "trill-
ing songs with a lightsome heart"; her maternal indifference is conclusive: "Mother is the name for God in the lips
and hearts of little children; and here was one who was
worshipping a stone!" Rebecca's apex is the serio-comic
"crime fiction" climax—on the dubious denials of her
"corrupt heart," a romance epitaph closes the scene: "all
her selfishness and her wiles, all her wit and genius had
come to this bankruptcy."[46] Amelia's most intense moment
is an emotional nadir, the separation from her son—"The
combat . . . lasted for many weeks in poor Amelia's heart";
her "tender heart" is not calmed until Amelia "owns that
it is she . . . who is guilty," "she herself, by her own selfishness and imprudent love."[47] If Amelia's heart-imagery
recalls the chivalric grail-metaphor while Rebecca's heart
turns to stone and corrupts like the wicked heart of
romance, there is parody as well as pathos in the romantic
rhetoric; but unlike fashionable metaphor, it persistently
emphasizes the fundamental emotional oppositions that
create the effect of formal design in Vanity Fair.

Vanity Fair's romance sequences, however, are not at
any point independent of fashionable textures; they are
different aspects of a narrative integration. The novel is a
synthesis, not a pastiche, of traditions. Its chivalric vistas
extend to the Faerie Queene and pass through the medium

of *Ivanhoe*, and Scott's rhetoric was borrowed by Bulwer Lytton whose novels Thackeray parodied in the fashionable mode. Thackeray's romance motifs inhere in the fashionable textures of his prose; *A Legend of the Rhine* is a parody on sentimental novels as well as a satire on chivalry. In *Rebecca and Rowena* and *Vanity Fair* his reorientation of traditional romance patterns is always in the context of the fashionable mode—the ironic, shifting context of multiple perspectives. In *Vanity Fair*, Becky's "grand scene," a parody of fashionable melodrama, is studded with fragments of romantic motif. The Waterloo sequence is a climax of romance intensities, but its continuous, dramatic textures are in the fashionable mode. Fashionable textures in *Vanity Fair* reflect a humanity diffuse and mutable as fish in the sea—sunned, shadowed, paired for the moment, as the water is bright or black, hot or cold. Romance motifs group individuals and mark the species, like the patterns of scale and color that identify primary characteristics. In formal terms, the novel's fashionable mode is a continuous, modulating context; its chivalric mode is the medium of sustained, thematic progressions.

CHAPTER IV

NEOCLASSICAL CONVENTIONS:

VANITY FAIR, PENDENNIS, THE NEWCOMES

"THEY say he is like Fielding: they talk of his wit, humour, comic powers. He resembles Fielding as an eagle does a vulture," Charlotte Brontë wrote of *Vanity Fair*. "His wit [bears] the same relation to his serious genius, that the mere lambent sheet-lightning playing under the edge of the summer-cloud, does to the electric death-spark hid in its womb."[1] Thackeray's "wit," finding new and unexpected formulations for romanticism, was an alien quality in the nineteenth-century novel. Miss Brontë deprecates the comparison with Fielding, but what she calls "the Greek fire of [Thackeray's] sarcasm" was his legacy from the eighteenth century. The literary resources of neoclassical objectivity—pastoral to parody poetic artifice, mock-epic to satirize heroic exaltation—were, for Thackeray, valid perspectives on nineteenth-century reality.

In the mid-nineteenth century, romanticism faltered at social fact, and pure rationalism could not interpret the intuitive aspects of experience. In 1870, Cardinal Newman expressed his sense of the ambivalence of perception and reality: "this universal living scene of things is after all as little a logical world as it is a poetical; and, as it cannot without violence be exalted into poetical perfection, neither can it be attenuated into a logical formula."[2] It was this awareness of the relativity of reality that Thackeray recognized in *Pendennis* (Ch. LXI)—"I see truth in that man, as I do in his brother, whose logic drives him to quite a different conclusion," the hero remarks of the two Newmans. During the years when *Vanity Fair* was being

51

published, there were signs that the romantic experiment would not succeed, but a retreat to neoclassical certitudes was no longer possible. New combinations of perception and expression were needed to express contemporary experience, as in the Renaissance, whose literature has been called "the register of a violent effort to catch up with the expanding conditions of life. With its realization that certain themes are still untreated goes the feeling that certain techniques are becoming outmoded. . . . A transitional sense of disproportion makes itself felt . . . mock-epic, which magnifies vulgarity, applying the grand manner to commonplace matters; and travesty, which minimizes greatness, reclothing noble figures in base attire."[3] So Thackeray, expressing a new sense of the multiplicity of reality, experiments with literary hybrids: chivalry mates with mock-epic, pastoral is paired with romance, sentiment is crossed with satire. If the adaptation of romance in Thackeray's novels was an unconventional development, his assimilation of pastoral and mock-epic represents an equally unexpected phenomenon—the unforeseen specialization and the improbable vigor of Augustan modes in a Victorian habitat.

Since neoclassical conventions were initially antagonistic to Thackeray's other narrative modes, it took him longer to weave them into the continuous fabric of his prose. In *Vanity Fair,* the neoclassical genres are not integral narrative textures; pastoral and mock-epic are pastiches, like the patches of fashionable parody in earlier novels. These unfused passages are easy to recognize; there are concentrated sequences in *Vanity Fair,* one of pastoral, one of mock-epic, and these compressed examples of Thackeray's basic methods make good subjects for analysis. But the use of neoclassical modes as part of sustained narrative must be explored in Thackeray's later novels—*Pendennis, The Newcomes.*

PASTORAL

Thackeray most often practiced pastoral in the Augustan manner—the mode was popular with the romantics, but Thackeray borrowed their effects only for secondary resonance. His Arcadian harmony was essentially neoclassical—and the neoclassical mode was never quite serious; it premised an impossibility and parodied itself. If Thackeray found in pastoral an image of improbable innocence, it was a result of eighteenth-century usage; and to appreciate the charm and irony that characterize the mode in *Vanity Fair* it is helpful to consider the development of the Augustan convention.

Eighteenth-century pastoral was purely Arcadian. The Renaissance had produced magnificent Christian hybrids, but Augustans admitted only the image of innocence that was envisioned in Sannazaro's *Arcadia*—"one of the great dreams of humanity."[4] Simplicity was the essence of this Augustan pastoral—not the simplicity of undisciplined nature, but a formal, though spontaneous, decorum; a pattern, like neoclassical nature, of original grace. So Dryden, describing Theocritus, remarks that "A simplicity shines through all he writes: he shows his art and learning, by disguising both," and Pope accepts Dryden's analysis of what is "becoming of a pastoral,"[5] which has, he says, "the general moral of innocence and simplicity."[6]

But innocence and simplicity, artfully imitated, turned into insipid artifice; it was this quality that discredited the pastoral Thackeray knew. Early in the eighteenth century the mode became suspect; the porcelain muse began to titter her lines and Augustans, unable to alter the decorum they had established, agreed that pastoral was unfit for serious company—Steele ridicules the religious connotation in *The Guardian*: "Damon, or sometimes the god Pan, is dead. This immediately causes . . . [the shepherd] to make complaints . . . his friend interrupts him, and tells him that Damon lives, and shows him a track of light in the skies to confirm it; then invites him to chestnuts and cheese."[7] The pastorals of Pope's early years primly conform to Augustan precept and warble that "The Groves of *Eden*, vanish'd now so long, Live in Description, and look green in Song."[8] But the reflections of the original Garden that shimmer through his youthful Arcadia are eventually replaced by a caricature of the pastoral paradise: "The suff'ring eye inverted Nature sees, Trees cut to Statues, Statues thick as trees"; and in the *Moral Essays*, Pope's pastoral lovers, like Steyne and Rebecca in *Vanity Fair*, hardly pretend to believe in their idyllic roles:

> Arcadia's Countess, here, in ermin'd pride,
> Is there, Pastora by a fountain side.
> Here Fannia, leering on her own good man,
> Is there, a naked Leda with a swan.[9]

The pastoral disenchantment continued throughout the century. Dr. Johnson remarked that pastoral was "not to be considered the effusion of real passion."[10] The "great dream of humanity" had become a sentimental joke. So, in Carlyle's translation, the pastoral imagery in *Wilhelm Meister* is an emblem of adolescent nostalgia: "The stuffed bunches of wool denominated lambs, the waterfalls of tin, the paper roses, and the one-sided huts of straw, awoke in him fair poetic visions of an old pastoral world."[11]

Through Carlyle and Johnson as well as the Augustans, Thackeray inherited the whimsical neoclassical convention, with a range that extended from silver-toned mockery to discordant satire. Of Gay's pastorals, he wrote: "They are to poetry what charming little Dresden china figures are to sculpture . . . and die of despair or rapture, with the most pathetic little grins and ogles."[12] In *Catherine*, romantic pastoral parodies "fashionable" fiction's purple passages; in *Pendennis*, Arcadian motifs represent the willful sentimentality of the factitious lovers. Thackeray used pastoral for compassion or ridicule but almost never to idealize his characters; and his expressive, if not his narrative, technique is fully developed in *Vanity Fair*. One of *Vanity Fair's* extended scenes is predicated upon the pastoral metaphor. In this Arcadian sequence, Rebecca flirts with the Marquis of Steyne, while her husband, Rawdon, unconscious of deception, plays high stakes with Lord Southdown. Pastoral imagery is smuggled in disguised as a "sheep-dog"—"I mean a *moral* shepherd's dog," Rebecca explains, "A dog to keep the wolves off me . . . A companion."

" 'Dear little innocent lamb, you want one,' said the Marquis; and his jaw thrust out, he began to grin hideously, his little eyes leering towards Rebecca.

"The great Lord of Steyne was standing by the fire sipping coffee. The fire crackled and blazed pleasantly. There was a score of candles sparkling round the mantelpiece, in all sorts of quaint sconces, of gilt and bronze and porcelain. They lighted up Rebecca's figure to admiration, as she sate on a sofa covered with a pattern of gaudy flowers. She was in a pink dress, that looked as fresh as a rose; her dazzling white arms and shoulders were half covered with a thin hazy scarf through which they sparkled; her hair hung in curls round her neck; one of her little feet peeped out from the fresh crisp folds of the silk: the prettiest little foot in the prettiest little sandal in the finest silk stocking in the world."

Here, a charming Dresden figure is set forth in a rhetoric whose pastoral decorum is barely disordered by the realistic images of crackling fire, coffee, and the ersatz blossoms on the town-nymph's meadow—"a sofa covered with a pattern of gaudy flowers." The tinkling pleasantry is more seriously disturbed by the aggressive wit of Arcadia's own Silenus as Steyne begins to crack jokes, grinning "hideously, his little eyes leering":

"'And so the Shepherd is not enough,' said he, 'to defend his lambkin?'

"'The Shepherd is too fond of playing at cards and going to his clubs,' answered Becky, laughing.

"'Gad, what a debauched Corydon!' said my Lord— 'what a mouth for a pipe!'

"'I take your three to two,' here said Rawdon at the cardtable.

"'Hark at Meliboeus,' snarled the noble Marquis; 'he's pastorally occupied too: he's shearing a Southdown: What an innocent mutton, heh? Damme, what a snowy fleece!'"

The Marquis' innuendoes are unmistakably indecorous. His jibe "what a mouth for a pipe" runs pastoral riot from derisive suggestions of shepherd's flute and lamb's bleat to a jeer at Rawdon's barracks-room smoking habits. When Steyne identifies Rawdon with the dubious Virgilian lover, Corydon, he impugns the virility of this military "Meliboeus" ("'How is Mrs. Crawley's husband?' Lord Steyne used to say to him. . . . He was Colonel Crawley no longer. He was Mrs. Crawley's husband.") The aristocratic Silenus' wit is insufferable, and the Shepherdess takes his latest conceit as an invitation to riposte. Sharpening the Marquis' quip about Southdown's "snowy fleece," she turns it into a pastoral pun that pierces the Marquis' Jason-image (knight of the order—seducer of his hostess—hero of the golden fleece) and quivers in Steyne himself: "Rebecca's eyes shot out gleams of scornful humour. 'My Lord,' she said, 'you are a knight of the Order.' He had the collar round his neck, indeed—a gift of the restored Princes of Spain." With Becky's allusion to the nobleman's Golden Fleece, the imputation of foul play ("shearing a

Southdown") is diverted from Rawdon, and the aristocrat's sneer at the gambling fraternity is returned with interest, for Rebecca's "knight of the Order" refers as well to the Marquis' former membership in that fraternity:

"Lord Steyne in early life had been notorious for his daring and success at play. He had sat up two days and two nights with Mr. Fox at hazard. He had won money of the most august personages of the realm: he had won his marquisate, it was said, at the gaming table; but he did not like an allusion to those bygone *fredaines*. Rebecca saw the scowl gathering over his heavy brow.

"She rose up from her sofa, and went and took his coffee cup out of his hand with a little curtsey. 'Yes,' she said, 'I must get a watchdog. But he won't bark at *you*.' "[13]

Thackeray's phrasing is as sure as Rebecca's in this silken transition from Arcadian artifice to narrative present; reality emerges in commonplace details—"sofa," "coffee cup," "watchdog"—that relate the pastoral coda to the imagery of the exposition. The scene's relevance to *Vanity Fair* as a whole is apparent: given a knowledge of the characters it stands for itself, an integral, appropriate allegory.

And yet, it is this quality of independence that marks the passage as immature. The scene is a beautiful embroidery, but it does not assist event; nothing is suggested that was not already premised, and pastoral imagery is not developed during the rest of the novel. The sequence remains pastiche like the parody in *Catherine*, but the expressive method is established, and Thackeray is ready now to integrate this mode into his narrative medium.

As *Pendennis* followed *Vanity Fair*, pastoral fused with dramatic continuity. In *Pendennis*, Arcadian motifs characterize the hero's flirtation with a questionable heroine in graceful parody of artistic and social pretense. There are no profound insights here, nor are they intended; the sequence is a succession of witty water colors, like Thackeray's drawings for the satirical ballet scenes in *Flore et Zephyr*. But, in contrast to the isolated tableau in *Vanity Fair*, the pastoral sequence in *Pendennis* moves freely through dramatic event, pastoral motifs creating as well as ornamenting the action; the metaphor is no longer confined to a brilliant cadenza but participates in the flow of narrative prose.

Early in *Pendennis*, allusive imagery discloses a mock-Arcadia of rural English brooks and gardens, the desultory hero, Pendennis, in the role of pastoral swain to Blanche, "the pretty little fish which played round his fly."[14] A coy prelude leads to a conventional pas-de-deux: "Under a piece of moss and a stone, he used to put little poems, or letters equally poetical, which were addressed to a certain Undine, or Naiad who frequented the stream, and which, once or twice, were replaced by a receipt . . . written in a delicate hand, in French or English, and on pink scented paper . . . whilst the tree was reflected into the stream, and the Brawl went rolling by."[15] As in *Vanity Fair*, Thackeray follows the neoclassical practice of satirizing pastoral artifice by introducing commonplace details—"letters equally poetical," "a receipt," "scented paper." But the romantic modulation of subsequent phrases—"the tree was reflected into the stream, and the Brawl went rolling by"—suggests an ironic reference to the Biblical Garden which the Arcadian idyll reflects, and the hint is reinforced a few pages later, when the first phase of this flirtation ends, by a semi-satiric recollection of the "Tree of Life which, from the beginning, has tempted all mankind."[16]

The hero's initial dalliance is inconclusive; other events supersede the artificial love affair and pastoral motifs fade away. The scene shifts to London: Blanche re-enters in a fashionable drawing-room; and Arcadian imagery reap-

pears, altered by the urban context to a decorator's
fantasy, like the pastoral setting in *Vanity Fair*—"the
carpets were so magnificently fluffy that your foot made
no more noise on them than your shadow: on their white
ground bloomed roses and tulips as big as warming-pans:
about the room were . . . chairs so attenuated that it was a
wonder any but a sylph could sit upon them . . . there
were Dresden shepherds and shepherdesses . . . light-blue
poodles and ducks and cocks and hens in porcelain; there
were nymphs by Boucher, and shepherdesses by Greuze,
very chaste indeed."[17] The sylph's attenuated chairs prepare this spurious Arcadian setting for the pseudo-heroine,
who has now become a "sylphide."[18] The quality of the
pastoral artifice is measured by the shopkeeper's unctuous
phrase "very chaste indeed."

After this central sequence, the pastoral continuity is
again diffused into narrative event; but the caricature of
civilized Arcadia has prepared for a recapitulation of
pastoral themes near the end of the novel. When the
ostensible lovers meet again in the country, their eulogy
of rural pleasures precedes an inadvertent confession of
pretense:

" 'And do you really like the country?' he asked her, as
they walked together.
" 'I should like never to see that odious city again . . .
one's good thoughts grow up in these sweet woods and
calm solitudes, like those flowers which won't bloom in
London, you know. The gardener comes and changes our
balconies once a week.' "[19]

The Arcadian settings, like the idyllic "thoughts" of the
pastoral couple, are synthetic—"The gardener comes and
changes our balconies once a week." Pursuit of artifice has
led to anti-paradise; a rhetorical coda satirizes the decorous
affectation: "What took place? O ringdoves and roses, O

dews and wild-flowers, O waving greenwoods and balmy airs of summer! Here were two battered London rakes, taking themselves in for a moment, and fancying that they were in love with each other, like Phyllis and Corydon."[20] Corydon, the epithet of Rawdon's displacement in *Vanity Fair*, identifies the present Arcadian hero, and in this epicene role the actor concludes his flirtation. *Pendennis's* pastoral episode is a divertissement, but its allegory is part of the novel's continuous action. From idyllic illusion and the acceptance of artifice to sterility in the ineffectual garden, the Arcadian metaphor has been assimilated into *Pendennis's* expressive textures, and pastoral convention has shared in the novel's continuity, creating, rather than interrupting, dramatic event.

MOCK-EPIC

Mock-epic in *Vanity Fair*, like pastoral, is a stylistic digression; but if pastoral is a charming arabesque, mock-epic is an intense, purposeful parable. In pastoral costume, Rebecca is only a decorative version of her usual self. In mock-epic, she is a less familiar personification. The novel's mock-epic metaphor, which has complex symbolic connotations, is also irreproachable shorthand for Becky's sexual behavior after her break with Rawdon:

"I defy any one to say that our Becky, who has certainly some vices, has not been presented to the public in a perfectly genteel and inoffensive manner. In describing this siren, singing and smiling, coaxing and cajoling, the author, with modest pride, asks his readers all round, has he once forgotten the laws of politeness, and showed the monster's hideous tail above water? No! Those who like may peep down under waves that are pretty transparent, and see it writhing and twirling, diabolically hideous and slimy, flapping amongst bones, or curling round corpses; but above the water-line, I ask, has not everything been proper, agreeable, and decorous, and has any the most squeamish immoralist in Vanity Fair a right to cry fie? When, however, the siren disappears and dives below, down among the dead men, the water of course grows turbid over her, and it is labour lost to look into it ever so curiously. They look pretty enough when they sit upon a rock, twanging their harps and combing their hair, and sing, and beckon to you to come and hold the looking-glass; but when they sink into their native element, depend on it those mermaids are about no good, and we had best not examine the fiendish marine cannibals, revelling and feasting on their wretched pickled victims."[21]

This flaunting decorum is not a prudish expedient—quite the reverse. Charlotte Brontë pointed out that Thackeray's "hint is more vivid than other men's elaborate explanations, and never is his satire [so keen as when] he modestly recommends to the approbation of the public his own exemplary discretion."[22] *Vanity Fair's* mock-epic rhetoric is gilded to attract attention, and its traditional allusions are whimsically mixed. Homer's sirens—bodiless melodies that paralyzed their victims—were not carnivorous water creatures. Perhaps the present mermaids acquired their tails and harps in Thackeray's favorite classical source, "Lempriere's delightful Dictionary": "Some authors suppose that they were monsters who had the form of a woman above the waiste. . . . The sirens are often represented holding, one a lyre, a second a flute, and the third singing." In *Odyssey* XII, Circe describes the Homeric sirens; but in Book X, she has sent Odysseus to Hades, and the full context of Homer's Circe-sequence, coalescing with the *Odyssey's* siren-image, suggests elements in the composition of Thackeray's mermaids. The sirens in *Vanity Fair* are amphibious creatures who "dive below" into "turbid water," and this imagery recalls, not Circe's description, but the "vast waters, strange currents" that Odysseus must fathom on his underworld journey; the present sirens' sojourn "among dead men" reflects an image from Agamemnon's speech in Hades: "all around, men slaughtered like white-tusked swine." The swine-image, however, also recalls Circe's domain; and *Vanity Fair*'s mermaids, "feasting on their victims," reflect as well the scene of Odysseus' return to the island where his men are "imprisoned in airless dens like swine." So, Circe herself becomes part of Thackeray's picture; in this setting, she presently gives the Homeric description of the sirens: "melodious hypnotists—for those whom the sirens on the moist grass pierce with song no wife and children wait." Unfathomed waters and carnage in Homeric Hades are the "turbid" "native element" of Thackeray's mermaids; and Circe's predatory aspect fuses with the sirens' lethal image in *Vanity Fair*'s "marine cannibals." Thackeray's "agreeable and decorous" style ("twanging" harps, "about no good," "fiendish cannibals," "pickled victims") is neoclassical—a mock-epic diminution of rhetorical decorum by means of incongruous epithets.

And there is another aspect to *Vanity Fair*'s mock-epic evocation, one of mythic suggestion. The classical metaphor's mocking hints of sexual promiscuity not only convey realistic aspects of Becky's experience but suggest a dimension of primordial sensuality, a reptilian concupiscence "writhing and twirling," "flapping amongst bones or curling round corpses"—an amoral Becky, a prehuman form, only "diabolical" and "fiendish" in its "coaxing," "cajoling," feminine impersonation when it becomes a "monster's hideous tail"—a fish out of water.

In Thackeray's later novels, *Vanity Fair*'s mock-epic experiment developed, like pastoral, into a sustained narrative mode; in *Henry Esmond,* the heroic metaphor is fundamental. The significance of epic in *Esmond* will call for analysis later on; here, however, the less intense but fully integrated use of epic in *The Newcomes* will exemplify Thackeray's mature method. But before discussing *The Newcomes*, it will be necessary to look at the literary background of the heroic techniques with which Thackeray was familiar; their history is longer than that of Thackeray's other modes, and his use of them is complex.

Renaissance burlesque had a fine tradition—Chaucer, Shakespeare, and Cervantes parodied pastoral and chivalry —but the mock-epic mode is a more recent phenomenon. True mock-epic is comic amplification; preserving the stylistic decorum of heroic convention, it elevates base materials while it satirizes their insufficiency. Conversely, travesty and burlesque discredit their models. Dr. Johnson makes the point in his Life of Butler: "Burlesque consists in a disproportion between the style and the sentiments, or between the adventitious sentiments and the fundamental subject. It, therefore, like all bodies compounded of heterogeneous parts, contains in it a principle of corruption. . . . We admire it awhile as a strange thing; but, when it is no longer strange, we perceive its deformity."[23] In Thackeray, burlesque, which accompanies mock-epic, needs no annotation; its techniques have remained the same from Petronius to Evelyn Waugh. But his mock-epic method is a legacy from the neoclassical satirists who were the first to discriminate among the different kinds of heroic imitation.

If Boileau is not indisputably mock-epic's creator, he is probably the first to discuss it critically; and he is very conscious of innovation. In the preface to *Le Lutrin* he announces his achievement: "C'est un burlesque nouveau, dont je me suis avisé en notre langue: car, au lieu que dans l'autre burlesque, Didon et Énée parloient comme des harengères et des crocheteurs, dans celui-ci une horlogère

et un horloger parlent comme Didon et Énée."[24] This first
critical recognition of mock-epic makes a special point of
the factor of amplification. Dryden pursues the argument
in his "Discourse Concerning Satire": "[Boileau] writes
. . . ['Le Lutrin'] in the French heroic verse, and calls it an
heroic poem; his subject is trivial, but his verse is noble. I
doubt not but he had Virgil in his eye, for we find many
admirable imitations of him, and some parodies. . . . This,
I think, my Lord, to be the most beautiful, and most noble
kind of satire. Here is the majesty of the heroic, finely
mixed with the venom of the other; and raising the delight
which otherwise would be flat and vulgar, by the sublimity
of the expression."[25] Dryden's distinction between "imitations" and "parodies" is important; in true mock-epic, the
mode is imitation not caricature—incongruity is confined
to the content of the chosen subject.

It was Johnson who most convincingly argued that
"noble verse" and dramatic conventions suitable to "an
heroic poem" could be adapted to elevate a "trivial subject." The idea is expressed in his discussion of *The Rape
of the Lock*: "Pope brought into view a new race of
beings, with powers and passions proportionate to their
operation. The sylphs and gnomes act, at the toilet and the
tea-table, what more terrifick and powerful phantoms
perform on the stormy ocean, or the field of battle. . . . New
things are made familiar, and familiar things are made
new. . . . The subject of the poem is an event below the
common incidents of common life . . . yet the whole detail
of a female day is here brought before us invested with so
much art of decoration, that, though nothing is disguised,
every thing is striking."[26] Unlike burlesque, mock-epic
reveals the triviality of its subject only in the contrast
between elevated manner and undignified matter. The
derogatory rhetoric of burlesque is never appropriate in
mock-epic, where the nobility of the heroic language

should sustain the epic decorum, while implicit contrast both satirizes the inadequacy of the content and suggests the presence of the ideal in the commonplace. The opening lines of Pope's *Dunciad*, for instance, like many mock-epic passages in Thackeray, are rhetorically unexceptionable. They are comic rather than heroic epic by a process of induction alone—"The mighty mother, and her son, who brings The Smithfield muses to the ear of kings." "Smithfield" is not inherently satiric, although its incidental absurdity is a useful cue to readers; only the cunning precision of the epithets ("mighty" with mother, none with son) suggests cumbrous despotic Dullness and the servile Grub Street Poet. A slight alteration in these epithets would subvert the humor and turn the lines into pompous eulogy, while the use of indecorous diminutives would result in travesty. Later passages in *The Dunciad*, however, include both "parodies" and mock-epic "imitations"—the "grossness of its images," Dr. Johnson remarked, turns many lines into burlesque[27]—

> Why should I sing, what bards the nightly Muse
> Did slumb'ring visit, and convey to stews; . . .
> How Henley lay inspir'd beside a sink,
> And to mere mortals seem'd a Priest in drink.[28]

"Nightly" is felicitous satire, but most of the rhetoric is indecorous. "Stews," "sink," and "Priest in drink" debase the epic convention; both concept and content become farcical. "But even this fault," Johnson points out, "may be forgiven for the excellence of other passages."[29]

In Thackeray, burlesque, mock-, and heroic epic coexist: his early journalistic comments on Greece, for example, combine farcical derision—"Think of 'filling high a cup of Samian wine' . . . Byron himself always drank gin"; comic diminution—"of the Temple of Jupiter . . . I declare with confidence that not one [column] is taller than our own glorious Monument on Fish Street Hill"; and sober reverence: "You and I could not invent—it even stretches our minds painfully to try and comprehend part of the beauty of the Parthenon—ever so little of it,—the beauty of a single column,—a fragment of a broken shaft lying under the astonishing blue sky there, in the midst of that unrivalled landscape."[30] In Thackeray's early novels, burlesque heroics are progressively revised towards the "agreeable and decorous" mock-epic of *Vanity Fair*. Predictably, Thackeray, like Dr. Johnson, disparages Pope's reliance on farce; *The Dunciad's* abusive rhetoric, "gin, cowheel, tripe," he comments, "is so easy to write."[31] But Johnson's praise of the "stately numbers which dignify the concluding paragraph"[32] is tepid to Thackeray's eulogy of "that wonderful flight with which the 'Dunciad' concludes . . . the loftiest assertion of truth, the most generous wisdom illustrated by the noblest poetic figure."[33]

In comparison with neoclassical genres, Thackeray's epic has no fixed categories. The Augustans distinguished between heroic and mock-epic by rhetorical subject. The "great Argument" of "Eternal Providence" was asserted in *Paradise Lost*; conversely, *The Rape of the Lock* described "What mighty contests rise from trivial things." Mock-epic itself was differentiated from more farcical burlesque only by rhetorical technique. But, though rhetoric is a variable index, *The Dunciad* is not hard to distinguish from *Hudibras*. Thackeray's textures, by contrast, are ambiguous; burlesque, comic, and heroic epic are juxtaposed in novels like *Henry Esmond*—the fluctuating modality expresses an awareness of the multiple aspects of experience. Within this relativistic context, however, Thackeray's epic modes can often be distinguished by the idiomatic variations that indicate a serious or satiric emphasis. Mock-epic is his habitual mode, and instances of his mock-epic manner vary from quasi-burlesque to quasi-heroic, depending on the farcical or decorous quality of the satire. In Thackeray's cursive rhetoric, the language is contemporary and unexceptional—"Miss Newcome has a great look of the huntress Diana"; in semi-farce, it is often colloquial—"Diana and Diana's grandmother"; in decorous satire, the epithet is frequently a compressed allegory—"Diana whose looks were so cold and whose arrows were so keen." Heroic epic is characterized by more oblique, suggestive allusion, often by Greek or Latin quotation—"In Miss Ethel's black hair there was a slight natural ripple, as when a fresh breeze blows over the *melan hudor*"—and by tacit personification —"Ethel, severe nymph with the bright eyes." In more intense moments, the metaphor's immediate dramatic application is often equivocal. Thus, a passage of classical imagery in *The Newcomes* that seems to be a poetic digression, becomes in the event a prophetic emblem of the protagonists' future suffering: "I was looking, of late, at a wall in the Naples Museum, whereon a boy of Herculaneum eighteen hundred years ago had scratched with a nail the figure of a soldier. . . . Which of us that is thirty years old has not had his Pompeii? . . . You open an old letter-box and look at your own childish scrawls, or your mother's letters to you when you were at school; and excavate your heart."[34]

In *The Newcomes*, mock-epic develops into sustained polyphony as does pastoral in *Pendennis*. The mode is most frequently associated with a Diana-motif that characterizes the heroine, and this metaphor sustains one of the novel's major themes—a satiric parable on the Victorian marriage market. The fable begins with the hero's apostrophe to the statues of Venus and Diana at the Louvre: "O Victrix! O lucky Paris! . . . How could he give the apple to any else but this enslaver,—this joy of gods and men? at whose benign presence the flowers spring up, and the smiling

ocean sparkles, and the soft skies beam with serene light!
. . . Did you ever see my pretty young cousin, Miss
Newcome, Sir Brian's daughter? She has a great look of the
huntress Diana. It is sometimes too proud and too cold for
me. The blare of those horns is too shrill, and the rapid
pursuit through bush and bramble too daring."[35]

Ethel Newcome is as yet an innocent, self-centered young
girl. She is not aware of the marital commerce that controls the society in which she lives. But the satiric point is
already implicit in the classical imagery—Venus, the sexual
quarry, is paired with Diana, the virgin huntress, and the
mercenary chase is on. Although mock-epic rhetoric seems
to contrast the two divinities, their conjunction in the
hunt is suggested by Thackeray's substitution of the aggressive epithet "Victrix" in the paraphrase that begins
the quoted passage for Lucretius' original "Genetrix! Delight of Gods and men, sweet Venus" for whom "earth
bears scented flowers . . . oceans smile . . . serene skies glow
with soft radiance."[36] The pride and purity of Diana are
real attributes of the heroine in this early phase of her
experience, but their potential distortion into hostile, predatory qualities is conveyed by echoes of the *Iliad's* Diana-
epithets, "fond of hunting," "piercing, noisy."

As the novel continues, Ethel becomes increasingly
aware of her commercial value in the Victorian market;
she admits it at first with bitter resentment—"when we are
exhibiting, [we] ought to have little green tickets pinned
on our backs, with 'Sold' written on them."[37] Thackeray's
classical imagery, shading from travesty to pathos and recurrently invoking the initial Lucretian allusion, traces the
emotional course of the heroine's career. In Lucretius, the
invocation to Venus is followed by the sacrifice of Iphigenia: "As once at Aulis, the elected chiefs . . . defiled
Diana's altar, virgin queen, with Agamemnon's daughter,
foully slain. . . . A parent felled her on her bridal day,

making his child a sacrificial beast."[38] So, in *The New-comes*, the Diana-motif woven into Thackeray's initial paraphrase of the Venus-metaphor leads, through a series of satiric allusions ("a virgin sold," "funeral pile," "the deadly couch") to a restatement of Lucretius' Iphigenia-image in a passage of pure mock-epic, where the "decorous painter" both elevates and satirizes contemporary codes by introducing delicate fashionable overtones into the classical rhetoric: "let us pity Lady Iphigenia's father when that venerable chief is obliged to offer up his darling child; but it is over *her* part of the business that a decorous painter would throw the veil now. Her ladyship's sacrifice is performed, and the less said about it the better."[39] The heroine's scruples are gradually removed; Victorian beauty ("O Victrix"), under the tutelage of her grandmother, is persuaded to seek a desirable match with the Marquis of Farintosh. As Ethel's participation in the marital chase grows more ardent and purposeful, she comes to resemble the *Odyssey's* "chaste goddess with gentle, lethal arrows"—"other Mayfair nymphs were afraid of this severe Diana, whose looks were so cold, and whose arrows were so keen."[40] Eventually, the Homeric huntress undergoes a further metamorphosis and the imagery suggests a feminine scavenger, searching for marital spoil: "we must compare the Marquis of Farintosh to a lamb for the nonce, and Miss Ethel Newcome to a young eaglet. Is it not a rare provision of nature . . . that the strong-winged bird can soar to the sun and gaze at it, and then come down from heaven and pounce on a piece of carrion?"[41]

At last the scene reverts to Paris, where the hero's original apostrophe to Venus and Diana initiated the heroine's epic personifications. There, Ethel receives a proposal from her eligible Marquis, and the Victorian fable concludes with a diminutive apologue: "I was not present when Diana and Diana's grandmother hunted the noble

Scottish stag of whom we have just been writing; nor care to know how many times Lord Farintosh escaped, and how at last he was brought to bay and taken by his resolute pursuers. Paris, it appears, was the scene of his fall and capture."[42] From the Paris of idealized classical art to a Paris of pseudo-heroic social competition, the mock-epic mode has defined the progress of Thackeray's heroine; the isolated parable of *Vanity Fair* has become a dramatic sequence in *The Newcomes*.

And there is another aspect of Thackeray's expressive integration in *The Newcomes* which is worth considering, since it is a major element in the technique of his mature novels. This is the fusion of his full range of allusive modes —fashionable, romance, pastoral, epic—in passages where the novel's figurative themes meet and intersect. Such a passage occurs in the central part of *The Newcomes*. It opens with a typical instance of Thackeray's rhetorical revision towards true mock-epic decorum—the alteration of an early burlesque of Ariadne, who "consoled herself with drinking,"[43] to the present classical image of the Marquise Ariane, "who had taken to Bacchus as a consolation." The scene is Baden, a continental resort where the hero and heroine meet:

"There was not one woman there who was not the heroine of some discreditable story. It was the Comtesse Calypso who had been jilted by the Duc Ulysse. It was the Marquise Ariane to whom the Prince Thésée had behaved so shamefully, and who had taken to Bacchus as a consolation. It was Madame Médée who had absolutely killed her old father by her conduct regarding Jason; she had done everything for Jason; she had got him the *toison d'or* from the Queen Mother, and now had to meet him every day with his little blonde bride on his arm! J.J. compared Ethel, moving in the midst of these folks, to the Lady amidst the rout of Comus. There they were, the Fauns and Satyrs: there they were, the merry Pagans: drinking and dancing, dicing and sporting. . . . He did not know, in the first place, the mystery of their iniquities. . . . The world was welcome to him; the day a pleasure; all nature a gay feast . . . Clive's happy friendly nature shone out of his face; and almost all who beheld it felt kindly towards him. As those guileless virgins of romance and ballad, who walk smiling through dark forests charming off dragons and confronting lions, the young man as yet went through the world harmless; no giant waylaid him as yet; no robbing ogre fed on him; and (greatest danger of all for one of his ardent nature) no winning enchantress or artful siren coaxed him to her cave, or lured him into her waters— haunts into which we know so many young simpletons are drawn, where their silly bones are picked and their tender flesh devoured."[44]

In this passage, Thackeray's multiple expressive modes create a varied series of imaginative perspectives. Classical reference is modified by fashionable idiom—"jilted," "behaved so shamefully," "absolutely killed her father"—and is rephrased as mock-epic in the pseudo-heroic modern epithets—"Marquise Ariane," "Prince Thésée," "Madame Médée," "toison d'or." The central reference to Comus diffuses pastoral imagery through the passage's mock-classical and fashionable textures—"fauns," "satyrs," "merry Pagans." A free transition evokes the hero's biblical innocence—"He did not know . . . the mystery of their iniquities"—and anticipates, in an ironic image—"nature a gay feast"—the sardonic resolution of the predatory metaphor—"tender flesh devoured." The mode modulates to the chivalric convention—"guileless virgins of romance"— and romance motifs—"dragons," "giants," "ogres"—are fused with classical allusion as the "winning enchantress"

is paired with the "artful siren" in language that rephrases *Vanity Fair's* mock-epic imagery ("marine cannibals," "pickled victims") and resolves the polyphonic
modulations in a prophetic figuration of the hero's marital
tragedy and the heroine's role as scavenging Diana: "no
winning enchantress or artful siren coaxed him to her cave,
or lured him into her waters—haunts into which we know
so many young simpletons are drawn, where their silly
bones are picked and their tender flesh devoured."

Such continuous expressive fusion is the source of the
rich and various allusive content of Thackeray's most
thoughtful novel, *Henry Esmond.* The present stylistic
analysis—a kind of reading which will not often be possible
where thematic development is of primary interest—should
serve as a preparation for *Esmond,* and the wide range of
imaginative perspectives should be remembered in reading
the later novel. Meanwhile, the formal function of Thackeray's allusive themes needs further discussion before their
treatment in *Esmond* can be appreciated; and this formal
aspect of his expressive medium is already evident in the
simpler patterns of *Vanity Fair.* It is important to see how
Vanity Fair's sustained expressive modes—fashionable and
romance textures—combine to create form and event as
well as significance; for the creative integration of *Esmond's* allusive materials is a result of Thackeray's expressive experiments in the earlier novel.

CHAPTER V

FORM, STYLE, AND CONTENT IN

VANITY FAIR

WHEN in *Vanity Fair* Thackeray fused his early, satiric expressive conventions into an integral narrative form, a new kind of novel was in the making. In earlier fiction, content, form, and style were separate elements; they could be considered individually as subjects in their own right. But in Thackeray's major novels, as in the work of many modern writers, these aspects of fiction are inseparable and the language itself is a creative element. The difference is like the familiar contrast between classic and romantic art.

The classic-romantic antithesis involves a fairly clear distinction between two ways of envisioning the form-style-content relationship—ways that may conveniently be called "illustration" and "expression." In classical or "illustrative" art, it is the writer's subject that is of primary importance; style is only a means of communicating, form a way of organizing, content. The classicist begins by defining his subject; then he selects an appropriate style and plans an effective presentation. In romantic or "expressive" art, the writer's style is part of the content of his work; his words create meaning, and patterns develop in the process—the method is thought of as a continuous act of expression. The antithesis is figurative—in practice no writer can begin without words or continue without a plan. But the disparity implies dissimilar creative methods and the results are as different as Proust from Fielding. So, in the classical, illustrative tradition, Horace's *Ars Poetica* defines style as decorous exposition (*locum teneant sortita decentum*), form as appropriate presentation (*sibi coveni-*

entia finge), and both form and style merely as instruments for conveying rational content (*verbaque provisam rem non invita sequentur*).[1] The proto-romantic Longinus, however, considers the expressive medium to be synonymous with the artistic concept ("the expressiveness of the word is the essence of art").[2]

English fiction before Thackeray was in the illustrative tradition. Eighteenth-century writers—Defoe, Smollett, Fielding—equated the novel's subject with rational content; for these novelists, form was identical with plot, an effective arrangement of the narrative materials; and style was an expository or decorative means of communication rather than a creative medium. If Richardson's structures were less controlled, his style less apposite, it was due to technical insufficiency rather than artistic originality, and Sterne is the exception, as he is to all literary rules. Long after the content of the nineteenth-century novel had become "romantic," the illustrative method continued to control the writing of English fiction; the development of new narrative methods does not date from the break between the early romantic poets and the neoclassical tradition. The technique of the novel remained basically unchanged from Fielding to Thackeray, and a look at some examples will show how far this is true.

Classicism found its superlative exponent in Jane Austen, and *Emma* is its most brilliant example. *Emma's* dramatic form is synonymous with narrative fact and, consequently, with its literal "plot." The novel's climaxes coincide with three objective incidents: an abortive marriage proposal, a misguided flirtation, and a successful marriage. The first is a typical instance. Emma attempts to make a match for her friend, Harriet, and her efforts result in Mr. Elton's indecorous proposal for her own hand—the event is logically prepared, Emma's mistake is defined, and

74

the objective outcome of her actions is the rational penalty
for her behavior:

[Preparation] "Depend upon it, Elton will not do . . . he
does not mean to throw himself away."

[Analysis] "Nothing so easy as for a young lady to raise
her expectations too high. . . . Harriet Smith is a girl who
will marry somebody or other."

[Anticipation] "Mr. Elton in love with me!—What an
idea!" ". . . I think your manners to him encouraging."

[Event] "It really was so . . . Mr. Elton, the lover of
Harriet, was professing himself *her* lover."[3]

The literal event is the precise correlative of dramatic
and emotional development, and is sufficient in itself to
convey the author's meaning. Emma's willful distortion
of reality involves her friend, Harriet, in a self-deception,
and the psychological content of the situation is verified by
the actor's rational comments: "a very foolish intimacy . . .
a very unfortunate one for Harriet. . . . Vanity working on
a weak head, produces every sort of mischief."[4] The moral
is explicitly drawn, rather than expressively suggested, by
Emma herself, who is "resolved to do such things no more":
"to take so active a part in bringing any two people together . . . was adventuring too far, assuming too much,
making light of what ought to be serious, a trick of what
ought to be simple."[5] The delicate precision of these last
phrases is the reward of the classical discipline. And every
aspect of the novel is equally felicitous. *Emma's* plot is
exquisitely correlated with dramatic structure, distinct and
iridescent as a Platonic idea: form is an appropriate
harmony (*convenientia finge*); moral insights (*rem provisam*) are essential themes. Nowhere does the novel's
imaginative content supersede its objective structure or
transcend its clear, communicative medium; and this is
both an advantage and a limitation.

The melodic consonance of Jane Austen's style is an

FORM, STYLE, AND CONTENT

instance of decorous illustration (*sortita decentum*); and the illustrative technique excludes the expressive diversity of modern narrative prose. Like Parian marble, the classical novel's diction is a common medium, varying only in the degree of rhetorical precision and the effectiveness of the embellishments. The writer's exercise of individuality is confined to the choice of subject and the manner of ornamentation; for all their differences in creative vision and decorative detail, Fielding, Smollett, and Jane Austen write the same fundamental rhetoric. It is impossible, among novelists of this period, to find such stylistic contrasts as between Hardy, Virginia Woolf, James Joyce; and English novelists continued to write illustrative prose until the middle of the nineteenth century.

This proposition may seem untenable when it includes the Brontës, whose fiction seems so distant from the novels of the eighteenth century; but an analysis of their prose makes it clear that they were practicing traditional techniques. Even so "romantic" a writer as Emily Brontë was limited to the common diction. Although the Brontës' visionary effects are not truly compatible with the neoclassical rhetoric that exquisitely illustrated Jane Austen's luminous insights, at the time they wrote, prose narrative had no other language to express dramatic event, and they adapted, rather than altered, the accepted medium. Thus in *Wuthering Heights*, Emily Brontë represents climaxes of pure emotional content by conventional images of physical action that typify but do not express Heathcliff's agony and Catherine's passion: "He dashed his head against the knotted trunk; and, lifting up his eyes, howled, not like a man, but like a savage beast"; "such senseless, wicked rages! There she lay . . . her hair flying over her shoulders . . . the muscles of her neck and arms standing out."[6]

The point is made clearer by comparing Emily Brontë's language with the eighteenth-century diction of Richardson's *Clarissa*, where the same basic rhetoric is used to describe the very different instance of a prostitute's "squalid" death—the "infamous" Mrs. Sinclair's "wickedness" and "rage": "howling, more like a wolf than a human," "her hair" conventionally "torn," "violence" distending "her muscular features."[7] The common rhetoric's neoclassical abstractions—"savagery," "wickedness," "rage" —preclude the expressive representation of complex emotions, which must be conveyed by the author's or actors' rational comments, as they are in Jane Austen; and when the writer attempts to surmount this restriction, the tradition's invariable equation of subjective experience with generalized behavior ("dashed his head," "lifted his eyes") produces an indecorous but persistently formulaic effect.

In *Vanity Fair*, Thackeray writes another kind of prose; he dispenses with rational analysis, but develops a narrative medium whose expressive images convey the novel's emotional event—Amelia at Waterloo, "her large eyes fixed and without light"; Steyne, "with flame in his eyes," defying retribution.[8] In *Wuthering Heights*, similitudes are confined to explicit comparisons "My love for Linton is like the foliage in the woods . . . my love for Heathcliff resembles the eternal rocks beneath."[9] In *Vanity Fair*, similes are replaced by metaphors whose suggestive range is amplified by allusion to familiar artistic conventions, as when a sequence of romance motifs culminates in imagery that transforms men to oaks and women to doves: "Oh, thou poor little panting soul! The very finest tree in the whole forest, with the straightest stem, and the strongest arms, and the thickest foliage, wherein you choose to build and coo, may be marked, for what you know, and may be down with a crash ere long."[10]

Thackeray's prose, the crucial factor in his narrative experiment, was an unaccustomed harmony ("Nobody in our day wrote, I should say, with such perfection of style,"

Carlyle remarked).[11] Among its precursors were the
rhythms of Sterne, who brought a conversational flexibility
to his narrative style, and the rhetoric of Carlyle, who
revived, in prose, the richness of allegorical figuration.
Sterne's rhythmic range greatly increased the capacity of
the narrative medium to assimilate diverse modes without
losing its expressive unity. His stylistic innovation was
simple and profound: he put Locke's theory of associated
ideas into fictional practice by adapting the informal rhetoric of personal letters or memoirs—cursive punctuations
(dots, dashes, parentheses, semicolons, :—, or —!), conversational inflections ("Fy, Mr. Shandy," "O Thomas!
Thomas!"), inversions, ellipses, and digressions. There are
earlier instances of rhythmic complexity—Swift's "Tale of
a Tub," for example—but none in which a story is simultaneously developed. "The machinery of my work," Sterne
insisted, "is of a species by itself." Digressions are part of his
narration, associations are continuous with statement—"In
a word, my work is digressive, and it is progressive too,—
and at the same time."[12] It was this freedom of rhythmic
movement that permitted Thackeray to integrate diverse
expressive textures in *Vanity Fair*—and if the rhythmic
resources of Sterne's narrative style enabled Thackeray to
assimilate allusive modes, Carlyle's figured rhetoric taught
him to fuse these allusions into cumulative metaphor.
Carlyle combined the biblical tropes of Donne and Milton
with the romanticism of Lamb and De Quincey: "Language is the Flesh-Garment, the Body of Thought," he
intoned in *Sartor*—"Imagination wove this Flesh-Garment," he continued in capitals, "Metaphors are her stuff
. . . it is here that Fantasy with her mystic wonderland
plays into the small prose domain of Sense, and becomes
incorporated therewith."[13]

Sterne and Carlyle are themselves, of course, only particular instances of the complex processes that prefigured

the prose of *Vanity Fair*. Sterne's rhythms were imitated by many writers, including the fashionable novelists that Thackeray parodied; Carlyle's metaphors were derived from Goethe and the German romantics, whose work Thackeray knew, as well as from Milton and Donne. But Thackeray's vigorous version of fashionable syncopations is his tribute to *Tristram Shandy*; and *Sartor* is audible in the resonance of his narrative commentary. *Vanity Fair's* diction combines Sterne's punctuations, inflections, and digressive continuities with satirical modifications of Carlyle's symbolism; and this unprecedented synthesis produces characteristic overtones in passages like the classical-biblical parable that shadows forth Rebecca's fate: "the honest newspaper-fellow . . . can't survive the glare of fashion long. It scorches him up, as the presence of Jupiter in full dress wasted that poor imprudent Semele—a giddy moth of a creature who ruined herself by venturing out of her natural atmosphere. Her myth ought to be taken to heart amongst the Tyburnians, the Belgravians,—her story, and perhaps Becky's too. Ah, ladies!—ask the Reverend Mr. Thurifer if Belgravia is not a sounding brass, and Tyburnia a tinkling cymbal."[14]

Vanity Fair, formed on this flexible, allusive prose, is as different from *Emma* and the "classical" novel as Berlioz is from Mozart. Thackeray's characters are refractions of allusive color rather than instruments of rational insight. They do not think. In *Vanity Fair*, thinking is sometimes an emotional response—"She thought of her long past life, and all the dismal incidents of it"—sometimes a subjective conflict—"how she tries to hide from herself the thought which will return to her, that she ought to part with the boy"—sometimes an intuitive judgment—"He loved her no more, he thought, as he had loved her"—but never intellectual analysis.[15] There is no mutual explication, since the characters never communicate rationally: "poor Amelia

... had no confidante; indeed, she could never have one: as she would not allow to herself the possibility of yielding." These actors represent not intellect deluded but delusion itself. *Emma's* characters often make erroneous choices; in *Vanity Fair*, alternatives are unperceived, and the actors retreat unconsciously from the force of facts: "giving way daily before the enemy with whom she had to battle. One truth after another was marshalling itself silently against her, and keeping its ground."[16] Truth is never confronted in *Vanity Fair*; its inhabitants must be pushed blindfolded over the edge of reality. When Amelia decides at last to relinquish her child, it is in a "burst of anguish": "she was conquered. The sentence was passed."[17] Such characters cannot define or respond to objective event—they hardly recognize it.

The result is that *Vanity Fair's* objective plot-sequence does not control the novel's effective dramatic form. Since the actors respond not to external facts but to inner images represented by allusive motifs and expressive textures, the literal incidents of the novel's "plot" are not correlated with its imaginative events. When Amelia's father loses his fortune, the factual crisis has no effect on dramatic experience. Before the event, distressed by George's negligence, Amelia expects to marry him; after the event, distressed by George's negligence, Amelia marries him. Conversely, when Rawdon dismisses the Marquis of Steyne, Rebecca suffers no literal loss—unlike the social adventuress in *Bleak House*, Lady Dedlock, she has acquired neither wealth nor real prestige; she forfeits nothing but marital security: Rawdon provides her with "a tolerable annuity"[18] and she was always *demi-mondaine*. Again, in the dramatic and central Waterloo episode, literal event is peripheral: malice, jealousy, panic are its subjective phenomena; its only objective incident is dismissed in the last sentence, and is never emotionally or dramatically repre-

FORM, STYLE, AND CONTENT

sented in the narrative context—"Amelia was praying for George, who was lying on his face, dead."[19]

In *Vanity Fair*, factual incident is a convenience for the common reader and the novel's "plot" has no real relationship to dramatic development. Literal event gives no clue to *Vanity Fair's* expressive tensions; thus, the opposition between Becky's and Amelia's fortunes which is felt as a formal principle does not correspond to their objective experiences. A graphic comparison of the heroines' financial and social circumstances, for example, looks like this:

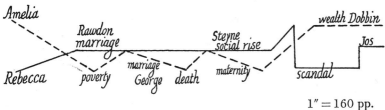

$1'' = 160$ pp.

There is no significant literal relationship between the two fortunes. The heroines' dramatic opposition is not an objective antithesis. Amelia's social status fluctuates erratically, never illustrating the emotional sequence—her prolonged personified journey from amorous confusion to maternal agony. The imaginative pattern of Rebecca's picaresque dramatic progress is not based on financial facts which are statistically monotonous from her marriage to Rawdon through her liaison with Steyne. And Waterloo, since no objective event is represented, has no place in the literal plot, although it is the artistic center of the novel.

Dramatic event in *Vanity Fair* is a very different thing from dramatic event in illustrative novels. Created by the words themselves, the significance of Thackeray's "events" is found in expressive, metaphorical values, not in objective elements. In earlier fiction, narrative incident was an illustration of logical content; *Emma's* final love-scene has no

81

FORM, STYLE, AND CONTENT

expressive importance: it is an affirmation of rational insights: "She had led her friend astray, and it would be a reproach to her for ever; but her judgment was as strong as her feelings, and as strong as it had ever been before, in reprobating any such alliance for him, as most unequal and degrading. Her way was clear, though not quite smooth."[20] In *Vanity Fair*, there are no rational affirmations to illustrate. The final love-scene draws no morals; instead, its allusive textures assemble, in one expressive realization, the successive satiric emblems of Amelia and Dobbin— "fragrant and blooming tenderly in quiet shady places"; "fluttering to Lieutenant George Osborne's heart"; "the prize I had set my life on was not worth the winning":

"The vessel is in port. He has got the prize he has been trying for all his life. The bird has come in at last. There it is with its head on his shoulder, billing and cooing close up to his heart, with soft outstretched fluttering wings. This is what he has asked for every day and hour for eighteen years. This is what he pined after. Here it is—the summit, the end—the last page of the third volume. Goodbye, Colonel.—God bless you, honest William!—Farewell, dear Amelia.—Grow green again, tender little parasite, round the rugged old oak to which you cling!"[21]

The ironic significance of this passage is a purely expressive phenomenon; its textures are a representation of emotional realities, rather than an illustration of rational truths. There is no logical flaw in the premised union—Dobbin is deserving, Amelia is loving, the marriage is appropriate. But dissonance is overt in the writer's satirical allusion to fashionable finales ("the last page of the third volume"), and this central discord governs a sequence of harmonic incongruities. A rhapsody of saccharine infelicities figures the ironic fulfillment of a fantasy: the worthless "prize" of Dobbin's chivalric quest that began with his worship of

George, "the summit" of his pilgrimage—"the end"; Amelia's "feeble remnant" of romance that "clings" to its victim, recalling her role, as George's bride, nesting in "the finest tree in the whole forest" ("Grow green again, tender little parasite")—and the subtly sacrilegious image of Amelia's sentimental ecstasy, the "soft outstretched fluttering wings" of dove-like devotion.

Such narrative event begins with words, and words in *Vanity Fair* are no longer illustration. As Thackeray's writing matures, the pastiches of *Catherine* and the *Legend* are developed into sustained dramatic metaphor: creative prose ("the expressiveness of the word") becomes the novel's effective content. Like poetry, this prose includes the language of emotional event; and it was the dramatic potential of this new expressive medium that transformed the novels of many English writers after Thackeray. The common rhetoric of the heroine's rage in *Wuthering Heights* become creative metaphor in the later novelists— in *Middlemarch*, "Titanic life gazing and struggling on walls and ceilings" of a Roman wedding trip, an image of the heroine's "anger and repulsion"; in *The Egoist*, a "leap for liberty"—"the intellectual halves of her clashed like cymbals, dazing and stunning her"; and in *Tess of the D'Urbervilles*, a reflection of symbolic nature—"The evening sun was now ugly to her, like a great inflamed wound in the sky."[22]

In *Vanity Fair*, expressive realization of emotional event is the novel's effective drama, as in the satirical mating of Dobbin and Amelia. *Vanity Fair's* dramatic "form" depends on allusive continuities—sequences of sentiment and romance—rather than on plot progressions; and these expressive sequences, their entries, their reversals, and their exits, can be graphically visualized in terms of the novel's time-span in such a way as to represent the narrative structure that readers commonly feel in the novel:

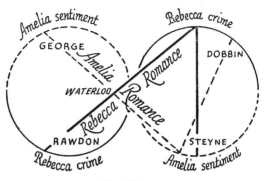

1″ = 265 pp.

These patterns, evolved from expressive continuities, correspond more closely to effective form in *Vanity Fair* than analyses of literal event. The novel's opening scenes are filled with subtle discriminations in fashionable sin and sentiment—Amelia's *"Sehnsucht nach der Liebe,"* Rebecca's "Charming Alnaschar visions." At the first intimation of the heroines' future marriages, the arcs of fashionable parody are intersected by opposing tangents of chivalric satire—Amelia's "little tender heart . . . beating, and longing and trusting" to George, Becky's "barbed shaft" quivering in Rawdon's "dull hide."[23] Waterloo, the satiric paradigm of knightly combat, is *Vanity Fair's* expressive center—a sentimental-chivalric crux: the novel's opposing tangents of romance—Amelia's amorous grail-motifs, Rebecca's magic metaphors—intersect; the heroines' hostilities qualify Amelia's agony, imaged in the blood-red laceration of George's military sash; and Rebecca's victorious visit to her prostrate rival combines picaresque parody (Becky's exploits) with sentimental satire (Amelia's animosity). After the battle, chivalric oppositions are reversed. Rebecca's magical success approaches satirical apotheosis; Amelia's masochism reaches its nadir in the ironies of maternal sacrifice. As Dobbin returns, Amelia's romantic

84

reprieve spans Rebecca's farcical disaster with Steyne; the swift descent of the glittering rogue is crossed by the amorous dove's ascending flight—and the final sequences are suffused with the satirical sentimentality that opened the novel.

Vanity Fair's expressive form is a vast metaphor, an extended figure filled with typifications. If the novel is named from *The Pilgrim's Progress*, its allegory begins in Bunyan's "Town . . . wherein should be sold . . . Lusts, Pleasures, and Delights of all sorts"[24]—"Yes, this is Vanity Fair," the novel's prologue announces, "eating and drinking, making love and jilting . . . not a moral place certainly; nor a merry one, though very noisy." As Thackeray's actors begin to suffer, their subjective world becomes a dramatic scene, and the novel's symbolic psychology revives the *Psychomachia's* generic image of inner strife—a *bellum intestinum* that C. S. Lewis calls "the root of all allegory":[25] "The combat, which we describe in a sentence or two, lasted for many weeks in poor Amelia's heart . . . one by one the outworks of the little citadel were taken, in which the poor soul passionately guarded her only love and treasure."[26] But if Thackeray's initial metaphor is borrowed from Bunyan, his personifications ("behind whom all there lies a dark moral I hope"),[27] unlike the simple symbolism of *The Pilgrim's Progress*, are images of contemporary subjective complexities. Amelia is Love, but delusive love; Dobbin's Faith and Charity are colored by George's Hypocrisy; Rebecca, a moral reprobate, is also a type of Fun and Truth, the artist's persona personified. Thackeray's "Love" becomes an ambivalent quality when the novel's semi-Shakespearian commentary mocks the amorous ingenue ("Perhaps some beloved female subscriber has arrayed an ass in the splendour and glory of her imagination . . . and used him as the brilliant fairy Titania did a certain weaver at Athens.")[28] "Of course you are quite right," Thackeray remarks in a letter, "about Vanity Fair and Amelia being selfish. . . . My object is not to make a perfect character or anything like it."[29] In certain satirical perspectives the ambiguity is intensified—as when Amelia's pathetic poses are ironically reflected in Rebecca's insincerities. Allegory becomes a comic anti-masque when Amelia and Rebecca are beatified—when Amelia's thoughts, "as if they were angels," try "to peep into the barracks where George was"—"the gates were shut, and the sentry allowed no one to pass; so that the poor little white-robed angel could not hear the songs those young fellows were roaring over the whisky-punch."[30]—and when Rebecca, the students' "Angel Engländerin," sobs out her simulated sufferings at Baden: "it was quite evident from hearing her, that if ever there was a white-robed angel escaped from heaven to be subject to the infernal machinations and villainy of fiends here below, that spotless being —that miserable unsullied martyr, was present on the bed before Jos—on the bed, sitting on the brandy-bottle."[31]

Vanity Fair's recension of the allegory of emotional experience is the beginning of a new kind of fiction that includes such disparate exponents as Meredith, Firbank, and Virginia Woolf; it prepares a medium for such a development as *To the Lighthouse*, where drama is interior, experience subjective, fantasy fused with reality in the symbolism of World War I, as it is at Waterloo in *Vanity Fair*. But, unlike Thackeray, Virginia Woolf forces her war-metaphor to function as an objective as well as an emotional event, sacrificing the imaginative suspension of disbelief that is achieved by Thackeray's displacement of literal incident; the symbolic pattern that is sustained in *Vanity Fair* is discredited in *To the Lighthouse* by the intrusion of the realities it symbolizes.

If *Vanity Fair's* expressive method revived the techniques and typifications of Sidney, Spenser, and *The*

Pilgrim's Progress, its content, like Wagner's orchestration, was a radical polyphony. "I think I see in him an intellect profounder and more unique than his contemporaries have yet recognised," Charlotte Brontë wrote. Thackeray's ability to "scrutinise and expose" seemed to her "prophet-like" —"No commentator on his writings has yet found," she insisted, "the terms which rightly characterise his talent."[32]

An aspect of this insight was Thackeray's expressive representation of psychological relativity ("after looking into a microscope how infinite littleness even is"). The glittering allusive tangents of his prose reflected a sustained ambivalent logic—a recognition of the range of possible relationships: "O philosophic reader . . . a distinct universe walks about under your hat and mine—all things are different to each—the woman we look at has not the same features, the dish we eat from has not the same taste to the one and the other—you and I are but a pair of infinite isolations, with some fellow-islands a little more or less near to us."[33] In *Vanity Fair,* perceptions like these fuse bits of human anomaly and fragments of shattered idealisms into eccentric images of psychological truth. "In the passage where Amelia is represented as trying to separate herself from the boy," Thackeray wrote to the critic for *Fraser's Magazine,* " 'as that poor Lady Jane Grey tried the axe that was to separate her slender life' I say that is a fine image whoever wrote it . . . it leaves you to make your own sad pictures."[34] In this sequence, the mother's suffering is mirrored in images that reflect the whole range of her sentimental neurosis—her personified denial of reality and defeat by truth, her chivalric fetishism, her amorous idolatry. The episode is conceived in several dimensions—the mother's possessiveness, her jealousy of the boy's aunt, her obsessive image of George, the child's ironic indifference— "terror is haunting her . . . George's picture and dearest memory. . . . The child must go from her—to others—to

87

forget her. Her heart and her treasure—her joy, hope, love, worship—her God, almost! . . . The mother had not been so well pleased, perhaps, had the rival been better looking . . . preparing him for the change . . . He was longing for it."[35]

Amelia's compulsive fantasies—"her God, almost!"—anticipating religious ironies in the novel's final love-scene, discredit the Victorian image of romantic maternity; and the allegory of Vanity Fair is largely concerned with revealing such emotional compulsions in the elements of accepted conventions. George Henry Lewes, who could accept George Eliot's ambiguities, found Thackeray's too unpleasant ("in *Vanity Fair* . . . how little there is to love") and protested the inclusion of that "detestable passage," rephrased in the prologue to *Esmond*, "wherein [the author] adds from himself this remark:—'And who knows but Rebecca was right in her speculations —and that it was only a question of money and fortune which made the difference between her and an honest woman? . . . An alderman . . . will not step out of his carriage to steal . . . *but put him to starve, and see if he will not purloin a loaf.*' [Lewes' italics] Was it carelessness, or deep misanthropy, distorting an otherwise clear judgment, which allowed such a remark to fall?"[36]

The passage is not personal observation; it is commentary—the rigorous recognition of the relativity of human values that typifies the novel's method. In *Vanity Fair*, the Commentator is a dimension of dissent—"I wonder is it because men are cowards in heart that they admire bravery so much"? " 'Was Rebecca guilty or not?' The Vehmgericht of the servants' hall had pronounced against her"[37]—and, instead of solving dilemmas, asks questions unanswered in the silence at the end: "Ah! *Vanitas, Vanitatum!* which of us is happy in this world? Which of us has his desire? or, having it, is satisfied?" To the *Times'* critic, Thackeray wrote "I want to leave everybody dissatisfied and unhappy at the end"—an image of reality "in that may-be cracked and warped looking glass in which I am always looking."[38] A contingent aspect of Thackeray's insight (his power, Charlotte Brontë put it, "to penetrate the sepulchre, and reveal charnel relics") is expressed in *Vanity Fair's* mock-epic and romance evocations of primitive impulse—an imaginative projection of the hypotheses of contemporary science that became, in *The Newcomes*, a symbolism of creative method:

"Professor Owen or Professor Agassiz takes a fragment of a bone, and builds an enormous forgotten monster out of it, wallowing in primaeval quagmires, tearing down leaves and branches of plants that flourished thousands of years ago, and perhaps may be coal by this time—so the novelist puts this and that together: from the footprint finds the foot; from the foot, the brute who trod on it; from the brute, the plant he browsed on, the marsh in which he swam—and thus, in his humble way a physiologist too, depicts the habits, size, appearance of the beings whereof he has to treat;—traces this slimy reptile through the mud, and describes his habits filthy and rapacious; prods down his butterfly with a pin, and depicts his beautiful coat and embroidered waistcoat; points out the singular structure of yonder more important animal, the megatherium of his history."[39]

The biological analogy is not a casual conceit; it is a newly recognized aspect of human reality that impinges on *Vanity Fair*. In Spenserian allegory, personification illustrates enduring moral fact: Una's truth, Acrasia's artifice, Guyon's discipline. The figurations of *Vanity Fair*, like Spenser's types, personify moral qualities; but Thackeray's characters express other kinds of reality as well—the survival of primitive fantasy, the persistence of the biological past. His actors are not only victims of romance delusions but types of subconscious compulsions. Primal violence is implicit at chivalric Waterloo: "Time out of mind strength and courage have been the theme of bards and romances; and from the story of Troy down to to-day, poetry has always chosen a soldier for a hero . . . there is no end to the so-called glory and shame, and to the alternations of successful and unsuccessful murder, in which two high-spirited nations might engage. Centuries hence, we Frenchmen and Englishmen might be boasting and killing each other still."[40]

The novel's heroines exhibit atavistic symptoms: Amelia acts out archaic obsession—"powerless in the hands of her remorseless little enemy"—Rebecca reveals tribal mores— ("She admired her husband, strong, brave, and victorious.")[41] Under fashionable fantasies, chivalric visions, amorous mystique, lurks the "forgotten monster" of *Vanity Fair*. The actors indulge involuntary urges—George's blood-lust, Dobbin's self-abasement, Amelia's idolatry— and *Vanity Fair's* dramatic structure is partly predicated on these emotional compulsions. Mock-epic imagery reinforces romance motif; ritual fetishes coincide (Amelia worshipping the image of George, Rebecca defacing Miss Pinkerton's doll and piercing Amelia's heart); and racial impulse becomes a sustained expressive metaphor—Sir Pitt is a "hyaena face," Rawdon a rutting bull, Dobbin a Caliban, Amelia a "bleeding heart," and Rebecca a "monster's tail," "writhing and twirling, diabolically hideous and slimy."[42]

This does not mean that *Vanity Fair* is a prototype of Conrad or Kafka; Thackeray is far more concerned with the subtleties of civilized society and the images of idealized convention. His novel is, however, a fable—and a fable with modern as well as traditional implications. Its patterns are unprecedented in English fiction; but they are achieved at a sacrifice. In order to project the internal drama of

90

Vanity Fair, Thackeray has excluded the dimension of objective reality and conceived his characters primarily as types. But the expressive experiment of *Vanity Fair* converges on *Henry Esmond.* The earlier novel's pilgrimage into the human heart leads on to an interpretation of "reality" in *Esmond,* where complex human actors confront both the world of subjective images and the facts of external event.

Esmond's fictional species is a true mutation, without the suggestion of allegorical throw-back that characterizes *Vanity Fair.* Like all mutations, however, its crucial differences are not apparent in themselves, but only in subtle modifications of conventional types—and these traditional types must be recognized in order to grasp the significance of Thackeray's achievement. If *Esmond* is a new interpretation of epic, its difference can be appreciated only by exploring the historical background where theory and practice are evolved and the epic current is submerged in dim documentary seas. The developments that, fusing with Thackeray's expressive medium, produced in *Esmond* a new kind of novel are part of earlier English tradition; and this various and extensive tradition cannot be discussed as part of a critical reading but must be treated as a separate aspect of Thackeray's heritage.

CHAPTER VI

ALLEGORICAL–BIOGRAPHICAL–HISTORICAL

EPIC: *HENRY ESMOND*

ENRY ESMOND is ostensibly historical autobiography. It seems likely that Thackeray also intended the novel to have an epic significance in an explicit, not an impressionistic sense—and this would be a fulfillment rather than a distortion of *Esmond's* ostensible modes. Biography and history were intimately connected with the epic idea in English literature, and the development of these interrelationships is part of *Esmond's* history. This intellectual background does not, of course, "explain" the novel; *Esmond's* historical framework can be reconstructed, but the paradigm will not counterfeit the living form. It will, however, help to define heroic bone beneath the subtle verbal sinews—the epic articulation upon which *Esmond's* vital symmetry depends. And although the heroic concept—the projection of an exemplary cultural image— has persisted throughout literary history, its full span is far beyond the scope of nineteenth-century fiction. For the understanding of Thackeray's novel, heroic experimentation may be said to begin with prose-epic variants— religious and secular allegory, biography, history—and their interrelationships in the eighteenth century.

The eighteenth century, defining epic poetry as the consummate achievement of the human imagination, failed to produce an authentic example. At mid-century the failure was final, and writers began a poignant search for prose forms that might fulfill the epic purpose. At first, fiction was considered too trivial a medium, but by the time Thackeray began to write professionally the novel was thought of as a possible replacement for epic poetry: a

volume of Carlyle's criticism in the 1830's—"a nobler one
does not live in our language," Thackeray wrote, "and one
that will have such an effect on our ways of thought"[1]—
includes a passage that makes the situation darkly clear:
"We have . . . in place of the wholly dead modern Epic,
the partially living modern Novel; to which latter it is
much easier to lend that abovementioned, so essential
'momentary credence' . . . the former being flatly in-
credible."[2] Carlyle's partial, grudging affirmation was a
distinct departure from Johnson's evaluation of "romances" ("artful tales that raise little curiosity"); and
Johnson's judgment was continuous with an historic contempt for fiction ("the trash with which the press now
groans," Jane Austen mimicked in annoyance). The cou-
pling of epic and novel in Carlyle's thought was evidence,
whatever his reservations, of a radical change in the concept of contemporary fiction, and this new attitude was a
point of departure for the writing of *Henry Esmond*.

The nineteenth-century's reluctant recognition of the
novel's expressive potential had behind it the eighteenth-
century search for an epic medium. At the beginning of
the neoclassical era, Dryden, defining current heroic concepts, expressed the fundamental epic purpose—to form
men's minds by consummate example—as it was understood from Milton to Matthew Arnold: "A Heroic Poem,
truly such, is undoubtedly the greatest work which the soul
of man is capable to perform. The design of it is to form
the mind to heroic virtue by example; 'tis conveyed in
verse, that it may delight, while it instructs."[3] In spite of
changing social attitudes, the significance of the epic mode
remained unchanged for Thackeray and his contemporaries. The social and cultural content of the heroic tradition is implicit in Dryden's distinction—"the Epic Poem is
more for the manners, and Tragedy for the passions"[4]—
and his summary of epic patterns is impeccable: "Ulysses

93

travelled; so did Aeneas. . . . But the designs of the two poets were as different as the courses of their heroes; one went home, and the other sought a home."[5] The meaning of the "voyage" cannot be more simply expressed. A national ideal controls the epic search—the hero may recreate his ancestral heritage under new conditions, as in the *Aeneid* or in *Henry Esmond,* or he may enrich his native culture with alien experience, as in the *Odyssey* or in Joyce's *Ulysses.* And Dryden eventually sounded a wistful note that echoes through English epic criticism: "Heroic Poetry is not of the growth of France, as it might be of England, if it were cultivated. Spenser wanted only to have read the rules of Bossu."[6]

Dryden read the rules of Bossu. He wrote *MacFlecknoe.* Pope read the rules of Bossu. He wrote *The Dunciad.* Fielding knew the rules and wrote a "Comic Epic"—*Tom Jones'* true father is Cervantes, not Homer. Although Fielding invokes classical tradition, his novel is not "epic" in the traditional sense; his hero lacks Ulysses' self-knowledge, or even Achilles'; he is aware of society only as an obstacle, and has none of Aeneas' cultural insight. The childlike vision of *Don Quixote* and *Tom Jones* may be a revelation, but it is not an example.

Nevertheless, heroic burlesque was Thackeray's first model ("I imitated Fielding," he wrote in a letter of 1854 —"on looking back lately at some of those early papers I saw whose the original manner was."[7]) *Vanity Fair* is a comic social saga; its actors pursue the delusive chivalric quest. In *The Newcomes* Thackeray introduced a Victorian version of Quixote and Sancho Panza ("I read Don Quixote," he remarked while he was writing the novel. "What a vitality in those two characters!"[8]) But Thackeray never mistook comic for epic heroism—"Tom Jones in my holding is as big a rogue as Blifil," he insisted, "the man is selfish according to his nature as Blifil according to his."[9]

Henry Esmond is a very different matter. When Esmond is in conflict with society, he is conscious of it; when his heroics are foolish, he knows it. There is mock-epic in *Esmond*, but *Esmond* is not mock epic.

The precursors of Thackeray's heroic novel were not novels but anomalous narratives, sharing a representative social purpose. As the epic image after Milton faded from poetry, successive writers tried to express in prose the contemporary moral vision. Religious allegory, secular parable, biography, and history followed in turn. These modes varied in tone and method, but they all included a symbolic hero or a cultural image; their forerunners were the *Odyssey* or Everyman rather than the eccentric Falstaff or Quixote. Throughout the eighteenth and early nineteenth centuries these modes continued to emerge, competing, interacting, and combining with one another.

Religious allegory offered a first significant pattern late in the seventeenth century and is important both for its relevance to the epic idea and for its influence on Thackeray. In Bunyan, the poetic parables of Spenser and Milton, with an infusion of popular polemics, became a new prose-narrative mode; *The Pilgrim's Progress* stamped on English epic narrative a design that has never completely disappeared. Bunyan's dead hero confronted an inner world; his adventures were spiritual, and his surroundings barely typified mundane conditions. But *The Pilgrim's Progress*, despite its lack of "realism," had an emotional relevance that impinged on popular fiction—*Robinson Crusoe* and *Rasselas*, *Sartor Resartus* and *Heartbreak House* redefine Bunyan's emotional valleys and spiritual plains, giant Satanic compulsions and instinctive heavenly helpers; and Bunyan's ghostly protagonist has been recurrently incarnated in his fictional descendants.

While he was writing *Vanity Fair*, Thackeray repeatedly referred to himself as a preacher, a "Satirical-Moralist"—

"Our profession seems to me to be as serious as the Parson's own,"[10] he remarked. The novel reflects his attitude. *Vanity Fair's* actors follow Everyman's erratic track across a semi-Spenserian terrain and meet Bunyan's symbolic Virtues and Vices in modern dress. But *Vanity Fair's* allegorical patterns differ radically from Bunyan's. Thackeray's novel reflected the old structures of religious allegory in the "cracked and warped looking-glass" of his imagination, and the result was an artistic mutation; its orientation was indicated by a critic for the *Quarterly Review* (1848): "there is of course a principal pilgrim in Vanity Fair, as much as in its emblematical original, Bunyan's 'Progress'; only unfortunately this one is travelling the wrong way. . . . The whole course of [Vanity Fair] may be viewed as the *Wander-Jahre* of a far cleverer female *Wilhelm Meister.*"[11]

As important for Thackeray as Bunyan's religious allegory was a second allegorical mode—the ethical epic in prose. This was a special form of the cross between classical epic and Christian allegory that had been under poetic cultivation since Prudentius' fifth-century *Psychomachia*. The allegorical epic was domesticated by neoclassical writers: poetic parable was turned into prose, religious insight became moral precept, and the heroic journey bypassed spiritual highways to explore the secular scene. The process began when the French academicians took to allegorizing classical epics. They made apologues of the Homeric incidents and read Virgil's verse as moral metaphor. Then, not content with glossing the classics, they demanded modern epics that would offer a complete guide to ethical behavior; their speculations progressed from theory to dogma, culminating (too late for Spenser) in the "rules" of LeBossu, who stated categorically that all epic plots "must have an allegorical as well as a literal meaning."[12]

The Abbé Fénelon's *Télémaque*, still so familiar to

Thackeray's readers that he could refer to it casually, put ethical epic into practice at the beginning of the eighteenth century. Fénelon's moral fable, translated into English repeatedly, was as familiar as Freud is today. *Télémaque* was neither vision nor romance. In purposeful prose, this semi-classical allegory turned the voyage of Homer's hero into a foreign tour where Telemachus learned politics and manners, under the guidance of "Mentor" (the *Odyssey's* pseudonym for the goddess of wisdom in disguise). Fénelon's parable had a political purpose; *Télémaque* was an exemplification of the Abbé's favorite kind of kingship, written for his most promising tutee, a hopeful grandson of Louis XIV. Fénelon's hero followed a pattern familiar from religious allegory, encountering a congeries of kings who, like the castles, cities, plains and mounts in Spenser and Bunyan, typified various virtues and vices. But whereas Bunyan's personifications are metaphysical qualities, *Télémaque's* virtues and vices are secular. Fénelon's morality is ethical and political; the hero's experiences mirror man's social life, not his immortal progress; and the fable's scenes combine moral similitude with realistic observation. The heroic-ethical junction is complete in Minerva's farewell: "Fils d'Ulysse . . . je vous ai mené par la main au travers des naufrages, des terres inconnues, des guerres sanglantes, et de tous les maux qui peuvent éprouver le coeur de l'homme. Je vous ai montré, par des expériences sensibles, les vraies et les fausses maximes par lesquelles on peut régner."[13] In *Télémaque* allegorical epic makes contact with contemporary social reality. Combining the classical heroic mode with domestic allegory which represented the practical affairs of modern men, the Abbé translated the epic into genuine narrative prose.

Fénelon was father to one of Thackeray's basic modes— the semi-epic moral parable, affirmative, satiric, or ambivalent, taking its color from disparate contexts and

heterogeneous themes. Two of Thackeray's novels—each
with a chapter called "Rake's Progress," where ethical epic
and Hogarthian fable combine—make *Télémaque* into a
sustained thematic device. In *Pendennis* the parable is a
moral satire. The allusion to Fénelon becomes explicit
when the hero's uncle preempts Minerva's role, the Commentator naming him "Mentor." Thackeray turns this
masculine goddess of wisdom into an emblem of snobbery
—"the world had got hold of Pen in the shape of his selfish
old Mentor."[14] Society's platitudes are discredited when
Mentor connives at callous sexual self-indulgence, indif-
ferent to the injury it inflicts on its object; and the hero
reappraises his secular monitor ("The Major's anger
amused Pen. He studied his uncle's peculiarities with
constant relish . . . his worldly old Mentor . . . Mentor
quitted Telemachus").[15] In *The Virginians*, the Fénelon-
theme becomes a fable burlesquing sentimental love, and
domesticated epic wears the fashionable motley. The
novel's American hero falls in love with his middle-aged
cousin, an "elderly Calypso," and enters a world of devious
amorous imagery where romantic roses are "faded vege-
tables," "amputated and now decomposing greens," seductive eyes are "fish-pools irradiated by a pair of stars,"
and *The Virginians'* epic and ethical parallels are extended
in Homeric ironies: "The last time Ulysses rowed by the
Sirens' bank . . . young Telemachus was for jumping over-
board; but [the crew] were deaf, and could not hear his
bawling nor the sea-nymph's singing. They were dim of
sight, and did not see how lovely the witches were. The
stale, old, leering witches!"[16]

The dual traditions—religious and secular allegory—
play an important part in *Henry Esmond's* epic formulation, though they are not dominant modes. When, in
Esmond's first book, the parable of Jacob and Esau symbolizes subjective relationships that run beneath the ap-

parent drama, or, at the end of the novel, the biblical temptation is reflected in fashionable contexts, Bunyan's allegorical types emerge for the moment from the realistic scene. Esmond's voyage through moral experience is directly related to ethical apologue, as his subjective analysis of political event is in the tradition of Fénelon's heroic morality. But these allegorical concepts are most important for their effect on *Esmond's* primary modes—biography and history—which were practiced concurrently with allegorical epic until they were correlated with the allegorical vision in the nineteenth century.

Biography and history were the major epic efforts of the later eighteenth century. Boswell and Gibbon were the catalysts in this reaction. Gibbon's *Decline and Fall* made past present, and present history, and Boswell's *Life* transformed factual details into an image of human reality. Like miraculous twins, the books appeared simultaneously, and the development of the two modes formed a double sequence that rapidly converged as historians began to analyze men as well as events, and biographers increasingly stressed the historical importance of their subjects. In the end, public fact and personal analysis merged in Carlyle's chaotic conceptions—biography and history, having paused to mate with allegory in *Sartor Resartus*, hesitated on the verge of a new kind of novel and then materialized in *Esmond.*

Biography as it is now known was Dr. Johnson's idea, his practical substitute for poetic epic. Johnson, like his neoclassical colleagues, gave "the first praise of genius" to heroic poetry—"as it requires an assemblage of all the powers which are singly sufficient for other compositions"; the purpose of epic, he said in his Life of Milton, was "to teach the most important truths" by presenting "event in the most affecting manner";[17] and since, for Johnson, art's justification was "the enforcement or decoration of moral or religious truth,"[18] the absence of national epic was a serious problem. Perhaps involuntarily, he attempted to supply the deficiency.

Much of Johnson's genre-criticism is concerned with finding a contemporary medium for moral truth, and the literary definitions in his essay on biography (*Idler*, No. 84) constitute a thoughtful analysis of epic potential. The modes he discusses were still current in Thackeray's time, and many of Johnson's attitudes influenced Thackeray's judgments. Fiction, as it was familiar to Johnson in eighteenth-century "romances," seemed to him a denial of objective reality: "the vicissitudes more sudden, and the events more wonderful; but from the time of life when fancy begins to be overruled by reason . . . the most artful tale raises little curiosity."[19] History had the "weight of truth"—"useless truth." Its "examples and events" were irrelevant to the common reader and produced "the same indifference as the adventures of fabled heroes, or the revolutions of a fairy region."[20] Milton's heroic poetry excluded "the passions," "the changes of the human mind."[21] Adam and Eve, "the man and woman who act and suffer" in *Paradise Lost*, "are in a state which no other man or woman can ever know. The reader finds . . . no condition in which he can, by any effort of the imagination, place himself."[22]

Biography most nearly realized Johnson's epic essentials; it combined the historian's "truth," the poet's "passions in all their combinations," the novelist's "power of diversifying his scenes."[23] Of "the various kinds of narrative," Johnson maintained, "Biography is . . . most eagerly read, and most easily applied to the purposes of life . . . irregular desires and predominant passions, are best discovered. . . . The writer . . . has, at least, the first qualification of an historian, the knowledge of the truth."[24] Johnson illustrated this theory in his Life of Savage; and the vast vitality of Boswell's *Life* presently realized part of his monitor's epic vision. In the nineteenth century the concept was developed by Carlyle, who added an allegorical dimension to the biographical mode—"Fictitious Narratives" are "Biographies," and biographies are "Attempts, here by an inspired Speaker, there by an uninspired Babbler, to deliver himself, more or less ineffectually, of the grand secret wherewith all hearts labour oppressed: The significance of Man's Life."[25] These portentous phrases had their effect on contemporary writers of fiction, who began to interpret their characters' experience in terms of parable. The picaresque structure became in Dickens the allegory of *Oliver Twist* and *Great Expectations*. Novelists began to think of themselves as symbolic biographers—Thackeray saw himself as a biographical archaeologist excavating his characters' emotional past in *The Newcomes*:

"I fancy, for my part, that the speeches attributed to Clive, the Colonel, and the rest, are as authentic as the orations in Sallust or Livy . . . incidents here told, and which passed very probably without witnesses, were either confided to me subsequently as compiler of this biography, or are of such a nature that they must have happened from what we know happened after. For example, when you read such words as QVE ROMANVS on a battered Roman stone, your profound antiquarian knowledge enables you to assert that SENATVS POPVLVS was also inscribed there at some time or other."[26]

Man "everywhere finds himself encompassed with Symbols," Carlyle had written, the "visible record of invisible things."[27] Thackeray applied his mentor's theory.

No one is more eclectic than Carlyle. As the epic substitutes, parable, biography, history cluster in the nineteenth century, it is he who discovers their potential kinships— "Of History, for example, the most honoured if not honourable species of composition, is not the whole purpose biographic?" For Carlyle, biography was both a return to Christian parable and an extension of Boswell's significant realism; and among its analogues, traditional epic was not forgotten. Indeed, Carlyle energetically continued Johnson's search for a national epic mode, and his intellectual synthesis suggested an inclusive approach to the problem— the "class of Fictitious Narratives" which he defined as "Biographies" began with "epic or dramatic Poetry."

Meanwhile history, a major literary mode in the years after Gibbon, was competing with biography for the epic function. Earlier eighteenth-century history, humdrum in Hume and hackneyed in Smollett, was a practical convenience rather than an art. Gibbon's *Decline and Fall* disclosed new imaginative perspectives, and in the nineteenth century history became what it had never been before and has since ceased to be—a dominant intellectual medium, displacing all other kinds of prose. Fiction succumbed in the process, and Scott's novels, in becoming "historical" fiction, were the agency of the most radical extrinsic revision to which the novel has ever submitted.

The new influence was not a subtle one. The cultural cue was given by Carlyle's "On History"; in "On History Again," he pronounced conceptual dogma: "History is not only the fittest study, but the only study, and includes all others whatsoever."[28] All Victorian writers were influenced by this critical attitude. Intellectuals exalted Macaulay and deprecated Dickens. Novelists were on the defensive and their resistance, which began by opposing to Carlyle's "It is the only study" a strident "It is *not*," gathered arguments as it gained momentum.

Thackeray follows correct contemporary form. He pays homage perforce to history in *The Four Georges* and *The English Humourists,* and expresses the requisite reverence in his requiem for Macaulay, citing "the wonderful industry, the honest, humble, previous toil of this great scholar"; Macaulay "reads twenty books to write a sentence; he travels a hundred miles to make a line of description."[29] But Thackeray's pages are covered with protests as well. He defends fiction's expressive validity— "The novelist has a loud, eloquent, instructive language" —and argues that imaginative narratives are "truer than real histories; which are, in fact, mere contemptible catalogues of names and places, that can have no moral effect upon the reader."[30] It is a repetition of Dr. Johnson's argument. "Poetry," Johnson asserted, "by its powers over the imagination," surpasses literal imitation—"this imitation being merely mechanical"; a "genius," he added, shedding sudden critical light, "often arrives at his end, even by being unnatural."[31] In Thackeray, the frequent implicit comparisons often have the effect of pairing epic and history, history and fiction. It was Fielding who first made the epic equation—Thackeray has not forgotten the reference and he cites his neoclassical predecessor to make the premise clear: "a canto of the great comic epic (involving many fables . . . but still having the seeds of truth) . . . Fielding's 'History of Jonathan Wild the Great' [gives] a more curious picture of the manners of those times than any recognised history."[32]

The proponents of history and the defenders of fiction came to grips upon the issue of "truth." History's strategists insisted upon literal truth; the novel's champions, like old Platonic tactitians, stressed the intuitive "seeds of truth." Beginning with Defoe, the contest engaged major English novelists from Fielding to Henry James. Jane Austen entered the lists with *Northanger Abbey* (1818), proclaiming that "while the abilities of the nine-hundredth abridger of the History of England . . . are eulogized [critics are] decrying . . . the novelist [who offers] the most thorough knowledge of human nature, the happiest delineation of its varieties."[33] In the same vein, Dr. Johnson had stressed Richardson's insight into "the recesses of the human heart"; and Thackeray maintained that Addison's sketches were superior to history's compilations—"the fiction carries a greater amount of truth in solution than the volume which purports to be all true."[34] The novelists concurrently strengthened their case by pointing out history's obligation to deal with impersonal events. Public responsibility, they argued, forced the historian to forego vital human data that were the common man's reality— "Few are engaged in such scenes as give them opportunities of growing wiser by the downfal of statesmen or the defeat of generals,"[35] Dr. Johnson had insisted. The novelist, on the other hand, was privileged to recognize anonymity— "to people the old world with its every-day figures," Thackeray wrote, "not so much with heroes fighting immense battles."[36] The unsung hero, the anti-heroic, were the themes of fiction; and novelists constantly reiterated their advantage, as when George Eliot wrote, in conclusion to *Middlemarch*, "the growing good of the world is partly dependent on unhistoric acts, and . . . is half owing to the number who lived faithfully a hidden life, and rest in unvisited tombs."

Gradually the novel's intellectual importance won general recognition. On both critical and fictional fronts, Victorian novelists consolidated their gains, until, at the end of the century, Henry James could blandly assert "The novel is history. That is the only general description . . . which does it justice." "History," he said, is not "expected to apologize": "The subject-matter of fiction is stored up likewise in documents and records, and if it will not give itself away, as they say in California, it must speak with assurance, with the tone of the historian."[37] This "tone of assurance" is one of the voices of Thackeray's commentator, who mimics the historical manner and frequently bases his narrative on fictional documents—"forms it as best he may out of stray papers," he remarks in *The Newcomes*, "as is the case with the most orthodox histories."[38] The purpose of Thackeray's pseudo-historical technique, as old as Homer and as new as Nabokov, is the same as Henry James'. "It is impossible to imagine what a novelist takes himself to be unless he regard himself as an historian," James insists. "As a narrator of fictitious events he is nowhere"; to provide "a backbone of logic, he must relate events that are assumed to be real."[39]

Ultimately, history was itself absorbed by fictive conquests—assimilation was the most insidious and devastating of the novelists' techniques. Bulwer Lytton, Kingsley, Dickens, and most of their colleagues wrote historical fiction; novels dealt with current events; and even when their themes were imaginative, novelists insisted upon essential "human" truth. In addition, the public increasingly demanded drama with its information. As the century progressed, historians were intimidated by the popularity of fiction; and, in the end, it was they who were forced to imitate the novel. One of the ironies of Macaulay's *History of England* was its offer to "cheerfully bear the reproach of having descended below the dignity of history" in giving its readers "a true picture of the life of their ancestors."[40]

Esmond was a major action in fiction's fight for "truth." Scott grasped the historic standard, Fielding raised the epic banner; but both claimed victory before the field was fairly fought. *Tom Jones* had turned epic into comic fable; Scott's novels made history legend—*Waverly* and *Ivanhoe* projected fragments of the past onto a chivalric screen that inflated them to fantasy: "Scott defined romance as 'a fictitious narrative . . . which turns upon marvelous and uncommon incidents,' and the novel as '. . . differing from romance, because the events are ac-

commodated to the ordinary train of human events. . . .'
Classified accordingly, almost all his fictitious narratives
are romances rather than novels."⁴¹ For Thackeray, the
"glorious Scott cycle of romances"⁴² was fabulous legend;
they provided *Esmond* with poetic inspiration rather than
historical method. In *Esmond*, history is substance, not
accident—romance and mock-epic are modes of perception
that qualify but do not efface ordinary human event—the
past is a relevant fact, as well as an artistic image.

Hard on Scott's romantic heels, the Victorian novel's
assimilation of heroic traditions began. The event had been
anticipated. "I wish you could get Carlyle's Miscellaneous
Criticisms, now just published," Thackeray wrote in a
letter of 1839 which stressed the critic's concept of "art for
art's sake. It is Carlyle who has worked more than any
other to give it its independence."⁴³ And it was Carlyle
who, in the course of his *Critical and Miscellaneous Essays*,
projected the hypothetical synthesis of all prose-epic forms
by recurrently suggesting that they are actually the same
thing:

"Consider the whole class of Fictitious narratives; from
the highest category of epic or dramatic Poetry . . . down
to . . . the Fashionable Novel. What are all these but so
many mimic Biographies?"

" 'History,' it has been said, 'is the essence of innumer-
able Biographies.' " [Carlyle, as usual, quotes himself.]

"Fiction [like] the Epic poems of old time, so long as
they continued *epic* . . . were Histories, and understood
to be narratives of *facts*."⁴⁴

In the nineteenth-century critical mind, the heroic experiments of the eighteenth century tended to fuse: parallel forms combined, the epic search converged on contemporary fiction—and, four years before *Henry Esmond*
(1852), a critic in the *Christian Remembrancer* wrote a

facile finale to two centuries of speculation, calmly remarking that "The ground once covered by the Epic and
the Drama is now occupied by the multiform and multitu-
dinous novel."[45] This was what Thackeray's work implied;
and contemporary critics understood his methods. *The
Quarterly Review* (1855) asserted that "eschewing all
hacknied discourses on virtue and vice, he enforces maxims
as serious . . . [as those in] the Spectator, and much more
impressive and profound"; in the tradition of religious
allegory and ethical epic, "his book is in many parts a
discourse upon human nature illustrated by examples."[46]
In *The Edinburgh Review* (1859), the novelist's epic
purpose was premised in an article on Thackeray's *Virginians*: "We desire to see in the hero of a novel our own
ideal, as the Greek saw his own ideal in the heroes of the
Iliad and the Odyssey."[47] Such affirmations were generally
brief, for literary traditions now unnoticed were still so
familiar to nineteenth-century readers that critics took
their identification for granted.

In *The History of Henry Esmond*, history, biography,
and epic coincided. "I've got a better subject for a novel
than any I've yet had," Thackeray wrote in 1850—a subject that fused in a single fiction the diverse modes of
heroic prose. *Esmond* is its hero's autobiography. Its action
is set against the radical English transition from monarchical to constitutional forms under Queen Anne. Its background reflects a realistic English eighteenth century, its
foreground vivifies historic scenes and persons. And its
protagonist writes his narrative in a New World which, at
the novel's end, has become for him, as for "wandering
Aeneas,"[48] to whom he compares himself, a field for the
free development of ancestral traditions—an epic country
where, in Dryden's phrase, he has "sought a home."

To English reviewers, *Henry Esmond* seemed cynical
and sexually indelicate ("Strange are Mr. Thackeray's

notions of human perfection!"[49] *The Times* muttered); but Irish critics saw in the novel suggestions of symbol and saga that were to become explicit in Synge and Joyce. Urging that "the novelist's art . . . be made to exercise a powerful and widely extended influence," a critic for the *Dublin Review* (1853) sensed in *Esmond* the tradition of religious allegory that Thackeray had inherited from Bunyan—beneath the superficies of "the most elaborate novel," *Esmond* developed the method "which is so frequently and effectively employed in the Scriptures of both Testaments;—the concealing a moral . . . under the veil of an apologue or parable."[50] The *Dublin University Magazine* (1853), describing *Esmond* in terms that recall the ethical allegory of *Télémaque*, found "an air, both of reality and importance" in a concept that "serves to connect [the novel's] heroes with events in real history. Although it is the imaginary individual himself who excites our chief interest throughout, yet that interest owes in a great degree its depth . . . to the great political incidents with which his fortunes are associated."[51] This historical context is James' "backbone of logic"—a kind of "truth" in *Esmond* that was absent from *Vanity Fair*. The protagonist, neither heroic clown nor chivalric hero, moves through textures of allegory, mock-epic, and romance, without losing his material substance; the novel is a synthesis of emotional subject and demonstrable object, a technique new to reviewers, many of whom "united in asserting with George Brimley in the *Spectator* . . . '[Esmond's] great charm of reality.' 'All who have *lived* will feel here the pulse of real suffering, so different from "romantic woe," ' wrote George Henry Lewes; 'all who have loved will trace a real affection here.' "[52] *Esmond's* narrative textures convey subjective insights; its language mirrors event in perspectives no more, and no less, real than history's—Thackeray was exploring, through the modes of previous poets, the content of contemporary minds. But in *Esmond*, his allusions, more complex and evocative than in earlier novels, have an added purpose. Instead of projecting personified images, they complement realistic emotional contexts; the novel's metaphors are sharp instruments, and their purpose is to probe the human psyche. *The North British Review* (1855-1856) commented: "We are all of us disciples of that school of the new science of moral anatomy, of which Mr. Thackeray is the master; and it is emphatically true of him, as of all other great writers, that he is only 'outrunning the age in the direction which it is spontaneously taking.' "[53]

ii

Thackeray developed his new kind of epic, as he had other fictional forms, through the creative content of words. "Languages," Dr. Johnson told Boswell, "are the pedigree of nations."[54] In *Henry Esmond*, Thackeray used language itself—the traditional motifs and satirical echoes of allusive prose—to project a metaphorical English pedigree. All the textures of his mature style are here: neoclassical conventions, the rhetoric of chivalry, the intensities of romanticism derived from Carlyle, and the poetic prose of fashionable fiction. In earlier novels, these textures satirized states of mind; the actors, as in *Vanity Fair*, had no existence beyond the attitudes they represented. In *Esmond*, the allusive sequences have a substance of their own; they symbolize the imaginative experiences of English civilization, and the emotional adventures of a hero who is the novel's narrator, rationally evaluating his own perceptions. The narrator's phrases are the reflections of his remembered states of mind; their sequence is the history of a nation whose intuitions were expressed in the verbal modes that are echoed in the narrative.

If *Esmond* represents an epic search for imaginative

truth, unprecedented exigencies were created by its cumulative demands. To find a new means of realizing the epic vision, to turn the writer's new expressive medium into a means of revivifying history, necessitated a creative continuity not possible in the parts-publication technique of Thackeray's earlier novels. Thackeray recognized the difference and followed a procedure he had not used before. *Henry Esmond* is the only novel he conceived and executed in its entirety before publication: "I have given up & only had for a day or two the notion of the book in numbers," he wrote during its composition. "Its much too grave & sad for that & the incident not sufficient."[55] *Esmond* lives as a whole; its themes are dependent on words that create a music not complete until the final phrase.

The novel's formal narrative pattern is a tentative index to its dominant allusive modes. Book I concerns the hero's boyhood in the Castlewood family. The family's rightful heir, Esmond is thought to be illegitimate and is "adopted" by the nominal Lord Castlewood. The boy's devotion to Lady Castlewood and her children, Frank and Beatrix; his loyalty to Lord Castlewood, who is killed at the end of Book I, are accompanied by motifs of pastoral and romance —textures that express a vivid adolescent idealism recalling the lyric modes of Elizabethan England, without interrupting the sequence of classical echoes, often satirical, that characterize the aged narrator's voice. In Book II, satirical modes are dominant; the classical continuity is mainly mock-epic; pastoral and chivalry are burlesqued, for example, in frequent references to *Don Quixote*; and the diction suggests the civilized skepticism of the hero's thwarted young manhood—the neoclassical tone of the historical drama in which he is now an actor. Esmond fights in the English army in France, falls in love with Beatrix, and encounters the great personages of Queen Anne's reign as England wavers between the Stuarts' "divine right" and a confirmation of parliamentary power under the Hanovers. Book III, introducing ironic modifications of the chivalric and mock-epic modes, modulates, through biblical and Miltonic allusion, to lyric insights that herald the romanticism of the approaching age; the hero's maturity is expressed in a somber emergence of classical reminiscence, a rich sonority assimilating the novel's related textures. In this final book, Esmond supports the Stuart cause, is betrayed by the Pretender, ceases to love Beatrix, marries Rachel, Lady Castlewood, and departs for America—a voyage to a new world that enables the aged narrator to present his vision from another perspective. The heroic adventure of the novel is partly, as in Tennyson's "Ulysses," the old Esmond's exploration of his personal and national past.

Esmond's epic theme begins with the motto on the novel's title page:

Servetur ad imum
Qualis ab incepto processerit, et sibi constet.

Taken from the *Ars Poetica*, the phrase has several meanings here. Ethically, it is a variant of "To thine own self be true"; psychologically, it adumbrates the novel's analysis of human behavior ("nature hath fashioned some for ambition and dominion, as it hath formed others for obedience"[56]). Artistically, it refers to the quality of the only novel Thackeray conceived and composed as a whole —*Esmond*, unlike Thackeray's earlier work, would "develop continuously from the beginning and remain consistent with its own first principles." But the full context of the phrase in the *Ars Poetica* (here italicized) also suggests Esmond's epic quality:

. . . si forte reponis Achillem,
impiger, iracundus, inexorabilis . . .
sit Medea ferox invictaque . . .

111

si quid inexpertum scaenae committis et audes
personam formare novam, *servetur ad imum,*
qualis ab incepto processerit, et sibi constet.
"If you should represent Achilles, make him impatient,
ruthless, fierce . . . let Medea be wild and uncontrol-
lable . . . if you bring a new concept to the stage
and boldly form a new character, let his development be
subordinated to his initial personality, and remain self-
consistent."[57]

Medea appears on *Esmond's* first page; Achilles enters
in Book II, where Marlborough figures as "the divine
Achilles"[58]; a new concept *(quid inexpertum)* and an
unfamiliar protagonist *(personam novam)* are the novel's
reason for existence.

Esmond's prologue swiftly sounds the major themes and
motifs. The epic mode is immediately established—the
narrator opens with a satirical invocation to the muse that
heralds the novel's historical purpose: "The actors in the
old tragedies, as we read, piped their iambics to a tune,
speaking from under a mask, and wearing stilts and a great
head-dress. . . . The Muse of History has encumbered
herself with ceremony as well as her Sister of the Theatre."
Having projected the traditional decorum as a frame of
reference, Thackeray inscribes within it an eccentric
pattern: "Why shall History go on kneeling to the end of
time? I am for having her rise up off her knees, and take a
natural posture: not to be forever performing cringes and
congees." If this novel is an experiment in historical epic,
the author's postulates differ radically from Carlyle's formula of heroes and supermen. *Esmond's* prologue supplies
two instances: Louis the Fourteenth ("divested of poetry,
this was but a little wrinkled old man, pock-marked, and
with a great periwig and red heels to make him look tall")
and Queen Anne ("tearing down the Park slopes, after

her stag-hounds, and driving her one-horse chaise—a hot, red-faced woman.") The mock-epic manner is peculiarly appropriate to *Esmond's* early eighteenth-century setting; and even more than in Thackeray's preceding novels it is a significant dissonance as well as a traditional decorum. And mock-epic is supported by a diction that deftly sustains the neoclassical tone throughout the novel: the comma-pause, the rhetorical conjunction, the Latinate tense, the colloquial idiom are deployed with a skill that convincingly mimics eighteenth-century prose. But the narrator's voice is not confined to a pedantic historical realism. The ostensibly archaic style is a verbal convention that never impedes the sinuous interweaving of figures and phrases from very different modes. *Esmond's* integration of contemporary metaphor is characteristic of the stylistic method that has been developing throughout Thackeray's work. It is possible for him, now, to modulate from Augustan mockery in his description of Queen Anne to a phrase whose force derives from satirical experiments with the imagery of nineteenth-century prose: "—a hot, red-faced woman, not in the least resembling that statue of her which turns its back upon St. Paul's and faces the coaches struggling up Ludgate Hill."

Queen Anne and King Louis, figures of actual history, initiate the novel's mock-epic mode; they are sparingly mentioned in the narrative, but they remain implicit symbols of opposing national values, and they recur at crucial moments in the historical fable. Like these contemporary monarchs, the hero's fictional family bow briefly in *Esmond's* prologue, introducing relevant allusive textures. Mock-chivalry represents the Castlewoods' Stuart allegiance: "On that fatal field Eustace Esmond was killed, and Castlewood fled from it once more into exile, and henceforward, and after the Restoration, never was away from the Court of the Monarch (for whose return we offer thanks in the Prayer-Book) who sold his country and who took bribes of the French king." Satirical pastoral suggests the moral disintegration of the Castlewood cavaliers: "What! does a stream rush out of a mountain free and pure, to roll through fair pastures, to feed and throw out bright tributaries, and to end in a village gutter?" The river-image winds through the novel's descriptions of the Castlewood estate, shining and equivocal; the Prayer-Book, with its idolatrous, monarchical implications, reappears at the end of *Esmond* as the *Eikon Basiliké*, sacred to the memory of Charles I.

The rhetoric that characterizes the Stuart Pretender in *Esmond's* prologue mediates between realistic mock-epic (Queen Anne, King Louis) and the novel's sequence of classical motif. Charles Stuart, contrasted with Addison's Cato ("suppose fugitive Cato fuddling himself at a tavern"), is placed in a context of epic machinery that mimics neoclassical imitations of heroic forms: "Such a man as Charles should have had an Ostade or Mieris to paint him. Your Knellers and Le Bruns only deal in clumsy and impossible allegories; and it has always seemed to me blasphemy to claim Olympus for such a wine-drabbled divinity as that." The allegory in which *Esmond* deals is far from clumsy; its classical echoes, intermittently stressed to catch the reader's attention, form the intricate web on which the narrative is woven. The conventional decorum of history—parodied in the portraits of Anne and Louis—is first typified in the prologue by epic images of royalty that mirror these contemporary monarchs and allude to the passage from the *Ars Poetica* that supplied the novel's motto: "Queen Medea slew her children to a slow music: and King Agamemnon perished in a dying fall (to use Mr. Dryden's words): the Chorus standing by in a set attitude, and rhythmically and decorously bewailing the fates of those great crowned persons." The passage echoes Dryden's description of the "lamentation" made over Hector "when his body was redeemed by Priam; and the same persons again bewail his death, with a chorus of others to help the cry."[59] This indirect allusion reinforces the epic implications of the motto; and the Homeric reference that was suggested in the initial image of Agamemnon is supported by the Stuarts' epithet—a "thankless and thriftless race" (later likened to "the Atridae of old"[60]), recalling the *Iliad's* "folk-devouring king."

The decorum that has been ironically defined in *Esmond's* prologue is discredited by the narrator ("Why shall History go on kneeling to the end of time?"). Echoes from the *Ars Poetica* recur—"I would have history familiar rather than heroic" (*ex noto fictum carmen sequar*[61]). And the resonance of Juvenal's Eighth Satire on the worthlessness of inherited honors (*Stemmata quid faciunt*) accompanies mock-epic instances in the prologue as it does throughout the novel: Juvenal's cloddish Lateranus, driving, like Queen Anne, his "rapid car" past the remains of his ancestors; Ponticus, boasting of his family with its "squalid dictators and Masters of the Horse," like old Lord Castlewood, prizing "his dignity (as Warden of the Butteries and Groom of the King's Posset)"; the Consul at his all-night tavern greeted by a perfumed sycophant and an accommodating prostitute—the prototype of Charles Stuart, "fuddling himself at a tavern with a wench on each knee, a dozen faithful and tipsy companions of defeat." The overture ends with a return to the Horatian theme, now made explicit by direct quotation (a characteristic device in *Esmond*); Thackeray's original running-head— "*de te fabula*"[62]—glosses a coda that recalls a similar passage in *Vanity Fair*: "I look into my heart and think I am as good as my Lord Mayor, and know I am as bad as Tyburn Jack . . . I can't but accept the world as I find it, including a rope's end, as long as it is in fashion."

So, *Esmond's* prologue formulates the pattern of the novel's classical reference. A traditional theme is sounded over a dubious harmony that develops dissonant satirical echoes. Beginning with epic reminiscence—the first chapter introduces a crucial reference to the *Aeneid*—the novel's modes develop contemporary discords without forfeiting heroic insight. The classical allusions range from Martial to Herodotus, but the major references are to Homer, Virgil, Horace, Juvenal, and eventually Lucretius. Aspects of Aeneas and Ulysses are reflected in Henry Esmond; Horatian motifs culminate in an image of the artist examining illusion, art questioning art; and the varying sonorities of the Latin satirists are a commentary on the vanity of human wishes. Nevertheless, *Esmond's* protagonist is not Aeneas nor Ulysses nor a compound of the two; he is a modern man, exploring universal epic patterns with the mind and insights of today. *The History of Henry Esmond* neither parallels literal Homeric structure like Joyce's *Ulysses* nor presents a simple, comic inversion like *Tom Jones. Esmond's* classical parallels represent imaginative experience, and the quality of this experience is suggestively modified in the context of Thackeray's prose. Pastoral, mock-epic, and chivalric modes reinterpret heroic adventure in the perspective of past idealisms (the Miltonic shepherd, the Addisonian gentleman, the Quixotic adventurer) and in satirical inversions of these ideals (the Augustan Corydon, the heroics of *The Dunciad*, the Restoration cavalier). A still more potent catalyst, the intuitive insight of romanticism, transforms the heroic tradition; and Thackeray's distillate of nineteenth-century lyricism becomes an introspective medium in which conventional images acquire an unfamiliar chiaroscuro—the rhythmic and rhetorical flexibility of his style enables him to write a language that projects a history of the English mind from

116

its classical background to its romantic present within the limited scope of an eighteenth-century memoir.

To appreciate the richness of *Esmond's* imaginative patterns the novel's prose must be examined in detail; but the most meticulous examination will omit more than it includes. Subtle correlations too continuous to be followed in analysis unify Thackeray's multiple insights. Details like the significant name of a hero who is the true but unrecognized heir to a title that he generously forgoes (*Haimrich*, head of the house; *Estmund*, gracious protector) are perhaps peripheral. But *Esmond's* subtle modulation of integral phrases is of the novel's essence. The opening lines of the prologue, for example, phrase the archaic formulae of heroic decorum with quiet irony:

"The actors in the old tragedies, as we read, piped their iambics to a tune . . . the Chorus standing by in a set attitude, and rhythmically and decorously bewailing the fates of those great crowned persons."

The same figure, however, becomes a vehement satire on artistic convention when the hero argues with Addison at the center of the novel:

" 'I admire your art: the murder of the campaign is done to military musick, like a battle at the opera, and the virgins shriek in harmony, as our victorious grenadiers march into their villages.' "[63]

The music of *Henry Esmond* is developed from the interplay of such delicate figurations. "Theres a great deal of pains in it that goes for nothing," Thackeray wrote[64]; and *Esmond's* expressive interrelationships can be fully explored only by reading and rereading the novel. The present critical analysis is no more than a suggestive resource, and is confined to identifying fundamental harmonies and establishing their primary progressions.

CHAPTER VII

ESMOND AS EPIC

i. SUBJECTIVE EXPERIENCE

IN VERBAL FORM

IN *Henry Esmond,* the epic process is closer to the method of Tennyson (*In Memoriam* was published almost simultaneously) than to the technique of earlier novelists who had never developed a medium for presenting subjective experience. Thackeray's conception of the recording narrator incapsulates the novel's content in a mental world that is itself a protracted observation of thoughts and feelings. The crucial dramatic tension in this world is the interplay between the old narrator's perceptions and those of his younger self. The use of "commentary" in Thackeray's earlier novels is a precursor of this treatment of the narrator; but the earlier undifferentiated persona of the Commentator could exploit multiple points of view without distinction of voices. *Esmond's* narrator is not an amorphous presence but a dramatic individual; his contemporary voice must be differentiated from the voices of his remembered selves.

In *Esmond,* narrative counterpoint acts as an index of the hero's development. Book I's clear distinction between the child's mind and the narrator's—between the imaginative images of remembered youth and the corrective insights of experienced objectivity—creates a sustained duality. In Book II, this alternation of disparate perspectives is subordinated to the dominate voice of the hero's maturity, reporting, analyzing, judging, sporadically interrupted by the sombre or mellow perceptions of the old man.

118

In Book III, the peremptory analytics of young manhood disintegrate, and the diminishing temporal distance between the narrator and his recorded persona leads to the synthesis of interpretive perspectives with which the novel ends. This progressive characterization of Esmond's various voices depends on Thackeray's use of verbal modes and allusive textures, most of them familiar from his earlier prose. But the writer's peculiar problem of differentiating multiple voices within a single subject leads him to develop special harmonies for this novel.

Throughout the book, the contemporary, recording voice of the old narrator must be distinguished from his dramatic mode. Since Esmond, in the tradition of memoirs of the period, habitually refers to himself in the third person, reserving the "I" for moments of special intensity, his reflective comment can be marked only by its stylistic quality. One aspect of this differentiation is the exercise of a deliberately "artful" rhetoric—the neoclassical narrator performing in his "singing robes": passages of formal figurative elaboration (such as the opening lines of the novel) are built on the balanced rhythmic progressions that would have been inappropriate in the "conversational" asides of the earlier Commentator. A consonant device is the narrator's pervasive use of classical allusion. In Thackeray's earlier novels, classical echoes were suggestive rather than definitive. In *Esmond*, the narrator uses classical quotation as a means of intellectual reference; his phrases and paraphrases are intended to call to mind the original context, both like and unlike the modern instance; and the sometimes intrusive quality of these allusions comes to convey the strenuous mental world of the narrator with his acute sense of the intersection of past and present.

Again, the child Esmond's intuitive perceptions must be distinguished both from the reflective comments of his

119

recording self and from the analytic insights of Esmond, the young man. For this purpose, Thackeray introduces a modification of his earlier romance textures. The echoes of Scott and Dumas that typified his chivalric parody are diversified by a new, poetic quality—the quality of "fairy-tale" as it became familiar to the later nineteenth century. Thackeray's "fairy-tale" textures are only partly derived from traditional legends, although he was familiar with collections like those of Perrault;[1] there was the work of Hans Christian Andersen, whose stories Thackeray had read a few years before he wrote *Esmond* ("I am wild about him, having only just discovered that delightful delicate fanciful creature"[2]); and the oriental tale that had always been part of his expressive resources. But it was the poetry of Tennyson that animated this new mode. In Thackeray's letter of appreciation for the *Idylls of the King*, the quality of Tennyson's influence is made clear, as well as its relationship to oriental fable. Reading some familiar lines from "The Princess," Thackeray says, in a *Fraser's Magazine* of 1850, "I thought about the other horns of Elfland blowing in full strength, and Arthur in gold armour, and Guinevere in gold hair, and all those knights and heroes and beauties and purple landscapes and misty gray lakes. . . . You have made me as happy as I was as a child with the *Arabian Nights*."[3]

The first book of *Henry Esmond* is the novel's clearest locus for contrasting narrative textures that differentiate the hero's recorded selves. Later, the fairy-tale texture disappears, the age-span between the narrator and his dramatic protagonist is diminished, and the contrast between voices becomes more complex and less emphatic. Here, where the child is correlative to the old man and the dual equilibrium is the crux of the narrative, the novel's distinct but inseparable harmonies receive their clearest expression.

120

Book I: *"The Early Youth of Henry Esmond, up to the Time of His Leaving Trinity College, in Cambridge"*

Esmond's opening scene, suffused with Virgilian motifs, is a typical instance of the purpose and expressive method of epic reference in the novel. The hero, not yet adolescent, orphaned by the death of his father, Lord Castlewood, abandoned by his stepmother, the Viscountess, supposes himself illegitimate; he is discovered on the Esmonds' hereditary estate by the new Castlewood family. The first episode mainly concerns the meeting between Esmond and Rachel, Lady Castlewood (their union ends the novel); its Virgilian allusions refer primarily to the encounter between Aeneas and his goddess-mother in the first book of the *Aeneid*.

A reference to "Sir Peter Lely's" emblematic portrait of the old Viscountess "in which her ladyship was represented as a huntress of Diana's court"[4] begins the sequence—with a comic parallel to Aeneas' first impression of Venus, disguised as a huntress (*an Phoebi soror?*[5]). Esmond, the "sad lonely little occupant"[6] of Castlewood's gallery (*ipse ignotus, egens*[7]), identifies himself—"My name is Henry Esmond"[8] (*sum pius Aeneas*[9])—and is transfixed by a vision of Rachel in which the qualities of Venus (*rosea cervice refulsit, ambrosiaeque comae divinum vertice odorem spiravere*[10]) combine with the recognition of divinity (*o—quam te memorem, virgo? . . . o dea certe!*[11]): "she had come upon him as a *Dea certè*, and appeared the most charming object he had ever looked on. Her golden hair was shining in the gold of the sun; her complexion was of a dazzling bloom. . . . To the very last hour of his life, Esmond remembered . . . the very scent of her robe."[12] A further allusion, complementing the effect of the satiric Diana-image, casts a shadow on this refulgence. Rachel, holding out her hand to Esmond—

"when was it that that hand would not stretch out to do an act of kindness, or to protect grief and ill-fortune?"[13]— mirrors the response of the Virgilian Dido (*non ignara mali miseris succurrere*[14] later quoted directly[15]), and Dido's romantic pathos will eventually be reflected in Rachel's emotional experience; in the *Aeneid*, it is to Dido that Venus is leading the hero.

This first scene in *Esmond* evokes both a traditional epic event (the hero's response to maternal divinity) and a fundamental psychological experience but it provides no parallels with Virgil's plot. Nothing in the episode offers an explicit reference to literal events in the *Aeneid*: the hero, rather than narrating heroic adventures, is about to undergo the painful, private experience of adolescence; his introduction to the Castlewood family prefaces not a royal romance, but a tense domestic conflict in which he is more spectator than participant. The Virgilian reminiscence depends upon verbal figuration and the epic patterns are suggestive rather than imitative. The scene's epic images—maternal confrontation, the intuition of divinity— recur climactically in the novel; but the contexts and perspectives are widely and meaningfully divergent from historical tradition. The nonclassical choice of the child's mind as a context for this imaginative response is significant—the novel is, in a major sense, a dramatization of the displacement of such naive, idealized responses; when Rachel, the goddess, becomes for Esmond an erring woman he compulsively transfers his early images to her daughter who in turn disillusions him. Even in this brief passage, the epic motifs include suggestive variations—the implicit confrontation of an innocent Venus with a seductive Diana, the hinted identification between the maternal idea, the divinity of love, and the passionate, pathetic Dido. As these images diffuse through the novel their significance alters radically but their initial truth is never lost. It is in this interplay between the remembered and the real, between image, event, and interpretation, that *Esmond* constitutes an experiment in epic for the novel.

Having begun *in medias res*, the narrator recapitulates events that have preceded the opening scene—establishing, in this initial flashback, the multiple time levels that intersect throughout the novel. A first, brief image of Castlewood, with its "darkling woods," its "cloud of rooks," its "purple hills,"[16] phrases the visionary motif of Tennysonian romance. Fairy-tale images define the child's perspective; half-memories of the French town where his mother had been seduced by old Lord Castlewood and of the family of emigrant weavers with whom he first lived in England culminate in the sharp detail of the "noverca, or unjust stepmother, who had neglected him for her own two children."[17] His impression of his father, who is "adopting" him as a page, recalls the story-book panoply of an oriental potentate—"a grand languid nobleman in a great cap and flowered morning-gown, sucking oranges."[18] The witch-figure is reflected in his initial vision of the Viscountess, Castlewood's wife, complete with wicked wand and familiar spirit: "She wore a dress of black velvet, and a petticoat of flame-coloured brocade . . . with great gold clocks to her stockings, and white pantofles with red heels: and an odour of musk was shook out of her garments whenever she moved or quitted the room, leaning on her tortoiseshell stick, little Fury barking at her heels."[19]

This childhood fantasy on the parental Esmonds is followed by the old narrator's satirical analysis of the debauched father, who, having spent his fortune, repairs it by marriage ("to show how great his appetite was, Mr. Wycherley said, he ended by swallowing that fly-blown rank old morsel his cousin"[20]); and of Isabella, his Viscountess, a former royal mistress, lampooned by a reference to the Virgilian seer in comic conjunction with Herodotus'

Egypt and medieval ritual—"Mr. Killigrew called her the
Sybil, the death's-head put up at the King's feast as a
memento mori."²¹ The emergence of the old narrator's
voice modifies the Castlewood image; his reference to
Virgil is a reminder of his present distance from the scene,
at the end of the epic voyage: "Esmond saw the same sun
setting, that he now looks on thousands of miles away across
the great ocean,—in a new Castlewood by another stream,
that bears, like the new country of wandering Aeneas, the
fond names of the land of his youth."²²

At the English Castlewood, the boy is tutored by Father
Holt, the Catholic chaplain of the parental Esmonds who,
in contrast to the younger generation, have kept the
Pretender's faith. Religious mysticism is combined with
romance motif in the child's mind—Lord Castlewood joins
a loyalist conspiracy, a Commonwealth soldier is shot
("The wine is drawn," Father Holt says, "we must drink
it"²³—turning chivalry to facile sacrament); the insurrec-
tion fails, Castlewood escapes to Ireland and dies there.

The death of his father elicits from Esmond a self-
appraisal that is the first of three major heroic evocations
in the novel, and this expression of the boy's imaginative
trauma concludes the recapitulation. Here the plasticity of
Esmond's epic technique is evident, as Homeric reminiscence diversifies earlier Virgilian allusion. The scene is
intensified by memories of Telemachus alone in his tower
room; telling Athene of his father ("he has left me grief
and tears"; "My mother says I am his child but I do not
know"); thinking "through the immortal night" of "the
journey Athene had suggested" to find news of Odysseus:²⁴

"That night, as he lay in his little room which he still
occupied, the boy thought with many a pang of shame and
grief of his strange and solitary condition:—how he had a
father and no father; a nameless mother. . . . The soul of

the boy was full of love, and he longed as he lay in the darkness there for some one upon whom he could bestow it. He remembers, and must to his dying day, the thoughts and tears of that long night, the hours tolling through it. Who was he and what? Why here rather than elsewhere? I have a mind, he thought, to . . . find out what my father said . . . on his death-bed. . . . Shall I get up and quit this place, and run to Ireland?"[25]

This is the novel's first statement of the crucial epic search for identity. The question is compelled, here and later, by Esmond's loss of parental orientation—the death of his father, his rejection by Rachel, the death of his mother. The hero's self-assertion (*eim' Odysseus Laertiades, sum pius Aeneas,* My name is Henry Esmond) is concurrent with his quest for assurance (Telemachus' journey, the underworld quests of Aeneas and Odysseus). But the conversion of this traditional theme to creative metaphor is an effect of Thackeray's expressive technique. The crux of the passage is a purely romantic insight—"the boy's heart was full of love"; it might be Tennyson's phrase. That this insight can be realized in the epic context is an instance of the resources of a prose that has assimilated the rhythmic, figurative, and lyric textures of Sterne, Carlyle, and "fashionable fiction." The writer's communication of emotional content is achieved by a series of expressive nuances—the balanced metrical stress and rhythmic expansion of "a father and no father; a nameless mother," the alliterative lilt of "he longed as he lay in the darkness," the figurative emphasis in "the hours tolling" are part of a suggestive intensification that never disrupts the novel's narrative decorum. Thackeray's peculiar skill is demonstrated in a simplicity of language with hints of rhetorical formality ("He remembers, and must to his dying day, the thoughts") permitting the assimilation of this expressive prose into the neoclassical manner of the narrator and his casual return to a quasi-idiomatic mode at the end. Through the writer's stylistic resources a new perspective on traditional experience is achieved; the traditional epic event is transmuted into a vital contemporary reality.

After the detection of the Stuart conspiracy, Commonwealth troops occupy Lord Castlewood's estate; it is during their tenure that Esmond learns of his father's death. The military interlude provides a transition to the dramatic present, during which Esmond's response to external event is dominated by the presence of Richard Steele—a corporal in the occupying forces. Steele later takes his place with Addison and Swift as an emblem of the enigmatic relationship between art and reality; here, his creative vision already offers a divergent perspective on conventional experience, as when he describes for Esmond, after the news of Castlewood's death, his memory of his own father's funeral ("I had my battledore in my hand, and fell a-beating on the coffin"[26]).

The old Viscountess, dispossessed of the family estate by her husband's death, returns to London, and is succeeded by the younger Castlewoods with whose arrival the novel opens. As the soldiers prepare to leave, Steele's characteristic aphorism—he "would stop their jokes with a *maxima debetur pueris reverentia*"[27]—echoes Juvenal's astringent satire on dissolute paternity (*nec tu pueri contempseris annos*[28]). The phrase is a classical prelude to subsequent narrative event, hinting at the hidden incompatibilities belied by the idyllic image of the new Castlewood family that are to distort the development of their own children as well as of Esmond himself.

The Juvenalian resonance is first combined with mock-epic when the narrator, in his satirical mode, characterizes Rachel's family-idolatry—"first and foremost, Jove and supreme ruler, was her lord"[29]; the writer then modulates to a correlative of fairy-tale imagery (as in "Monsieur Galland's ingenious Arabian tales"[30]) reflecting the child's perspective while it retains, for the moment, the narrator's mocking tone: "As they say the Grand Lama of Thibet is very much fatigued by his character of divinity, and yawns on his altar as his bonzes kneel and worship him, many a home-god grows heartily sick of the reverence with which his family-devotees . . . ply him with flowers, and hymns, and incense, and flattery."[31] This boredom becomes reciprocal—"the woman perceives that the god of the honeymoon is a god no more; only a mortal like the rest of us,— and so she looks into her heart, and lo! *vacuae sedes et inania arcana.*"[32] The phrase from Tacitus' description of the Roman entry into the temple at Jerusalem, its "shrine vacant, the secret chamber empty," is later reflected in thematic ceremonial images of desecrated pastoral rite.

An epidemic of smallpox acts as catalyst in this passive conflict. The boy Esmond contracts the disease at the local blacksmith's, whose daughter has been his partner in an adolescent romance. The discovery of his flirtation reveals Rachel's incipient passion for this pseudo-son in a violent image whose sexual content is a rubric on her marriage: "Let him go—let him go, I say, tonight, and pollute the place no more."[33] Lady Castlewood's compulsive revulsion is annotated by her husband—" 'She was always so,' my lord said; 'the very notion of a woman drives her mad' "[34] —and the phrase recalls Dido's jealous rage (*saevit inops animi*),[35] a reminiscence that will characterize Rachel's later relations with Esmond.

The revelation of sexual jealousy is not further stressed here; but it is the end of Esmond's idealization of maternal divinity. The novel's initial evocation of the Virgilian Venus recurs; and, as the image fades, the boy is deprived of his beatific vision. *Esmond's* contemporary hero has outgrown an established epic tradition; the insight becomes, now, only an aspect of remembered experience. The symbolic disappearance of the goddess, on which the narrator will eventually make his comment, is figured in a passage that recalls Aeneas' vision of his mother, luminous and rosy-lipped, at the fall of Troy (*in luce refulsit alma parens . . . roseoque haec insuper addidit ore*[36]): Esmond "scarce seemed to see until she was gone; and then her image was impressed upon him, and remained for ever fixed upon his memory. He saw her retreating, the taper lighting up her marble face, her scarlet lip quivering, and her shining golden hair."[37]

To avoid contagion, Lord Castlewood leaves the estate. Beatrix goes with her father; his son, Frank, contracts the disease from Esmond, and the boys remain at Castlewood under the care of Rachel, who eventually succumbs to the illness, and recovers with the partial loss of her beauty. When Castlewood returns, the marital conflict is intensified. Rachel condemns her husband's desertion; he resents her altered appearance.

This painful sequence of emotional antagonisms is explored both realistically and subjectively in swiftly modulating expressive textures. The empty shrine of Tacitus' Jerusalem is recalled as pastoral motifs emerge, first in the neoclassical mode of the old narrator—"that poor lamp whereof I speak that lights at first the nuptial chamber is extinguished by a hundred winds and draughts down the chimney, or sputters out for want of feeding"[38] (Ovidian memories of Hymen's ineffectual torch—*fax quoque, quam tenuit, lacrimoso stridula fumo usque fuit nullosque invenit motibus ignes*[39]—recall the ineffectual wedding of Orpheus and prelude the image of Eurydice that will etherealize Rachel's pathos). The ritual flame-emblem is sustained and acquires sexual significance—"the flame shines no more," "the love-lamp is put out," "my lord's fire for his wife disappeared"[40]—and the pastoral motif is

modified into a lyric evocation of the boy Esmond's perceptive fantasies; again, the impressionistic sequence of metaphor, materializing "love" as blossom, branch, stick, crook,
exemplifies the potential of romantic, even "fashionable"
textures: Love "has its course, like all mortal things—its
beginning, progress, and decay. It buds, and it blooms out
into sunshine, and it withers and ends. Strephon and
Chloe languish apart; join in a rapture: and presently you
hear that Chloe is crying, and that Strephon has broken
his crook across her back."[41] The sexual content of this
imagery is developed in contrapuntal textures. The boy's
imaginative reaction to Rachel's unhappiness is reflected
in romance motifs, a princess imprisoned by an ogre:
"sweet fancies and images of beauty that would grow and
unfold themselves into flower; bright wit that would shine
like diamonds could it be brought into the sun: and the
tyrant in possession crushes the outbreak of all these, drives
them back like slaves into the dungeon."[42] The narrator
rephrases the sexual antagonism in mock-epic terms: "It
was my lord's custom to fling out many . . . clumsy sarcasms
which my lady turned . . . or which again worked her up to
anger and retort when, in answer to one of these heavy
bolts, she would flash back with a quivering reply."[43]

The alternation between these perspectives, with their
delicate, transitional gradations, expresses multiple and
simultaneous insight into these complex relationships.
Lord Castlewood, angered by his wife's resentment, becomes openly unfaithful—"my lady found not only that
her reign was over, but that her successor was appointed
. . . *pudet haec opprobria dicere nobis.*"[44] The Latin, from
Ovid's dramatization of the Phaeton legend ("It is hu-
miliating," says Phaeton, whose friends insinuate his
mother's frailty and will not believe that Phoebus is his
father, "to have them circulate such ugly rumors about
us") reinforces the epic theme: the essential heroic resist-

ance to anonymity that requires Phaeton's irrational act is reflected in Esmond's tortured awareness of illegitimacy ("What matters . . . whether a poor bastard dies as unknown as he is now?" "His birth was a source of shame to him"[45]).

As the first book approaches conclusion, the hero's early, idealized images begin to lose their vitality. Esmond is enrolled at Cambridge in preparation for taking clerical orders, and he accepts the arrangement from necessity rather than conviction. After his loss of confidence in Father Holt and the Catholic faith, his first religious fervor has never returned—the narrator analyzes the change in a brief passage that reflects a modification in the novel's expressive textures as Olympian allusion becomes satirical rather than lyric: "When his early credulity was disturbed, and his saints and virgins taken out of his worship, to rank little higher than the divinities of Olympus, his belief became acquiescence rather than ardour."[46] But the boy's last image of Castlewood as he leaves for Cambridge rephrases the fairy-tale motif. Prefaced by the narrator in a moment of mock-chivalry ("my knight longs for a dragon this instant"[47]), the scene is set in textures of impressionistic romance: "It lay before him with its grey familiar towers, a pinnacle or two shining in the sun, the buttresses and terrace walls casting great blue shades on the grass . . . he saw his mistress at the window looking out on him, in a white robe, the little Beatrix's chestnut curls resting at her mother's side."[48]

When Esmond returns from the university, the "little Beatrix" of this virginal vision has become an incipient force in his emotional experience; her new role is heralded by Diana-imagery, recurring from the novel's figuration of Rachel as Venus. On his journey, Esmond has visited the old Viscountess of Castlewood, who persists in displaying the improbable portrait of her youth, "a virgin huntress armed with a gilt bow and arrow, and encumbered only with that small quantity of drapery which it would seem the virgins in King Charles's day were accustomed to wear."[49] The thematic significance of the painted fetish (a parody, at once, of romantic idealization and neoclassical pomp) begins to emerge when the adolescent Beatrix, half-child, half-coquette, is mirrored in prismatic allusive fragments, each a traditional personification of enigmatic divinity—a phantasmagoria of appealing and sinister aspects that culminate in an allusion to Horace's image of seductive fatality: "Harry watched and wondered at this young creature, and likened her in his mind to Artemis with the ringing bow and shafts flashing death upon the children of Niobe; at another time she was coy and melting as Luna shining tenderly upon Endymion. This fair creature, this lustrous Phoebe, was only young as yet, nor had nearly reached her full splendour: but crescent and brilliant. . . . She was *saevo laeta negotio*, like that fickle goddess Horace describes, and of whose 'malicious joy' a great poet of our own has written."[50] Beatrix assumes many masks—Dulcinea, Circe, Eve, Venus—but this motif of pseudo-Olympian chastity, inherited from the debauched old Viscountess, pursues her to the end of the novel.

The tension between Rachel and Castlewood is unchanged on Esmond's return, but the entrance of a new actor—Lord Mohun, the famous, historical Augustan rake—leads to a swift denouement in this bitter domestic drama. For the boy Esmond, Mohun is a figure from chivalric romance—"a person of a handsome presence, with the *bel air*, and a bright daring warlike aspect."[51] His role is characterized by the atypical appearance of epic parallels in dramatic situations. Like Penelope's Homeric suitors, Mohun depletes Castlewood's estate and attempts to seduce his wife. Castlewood challenges him to a duel. Telemachus supports Ulysses; the hero seconds his pseudo-father. But

the significant epic reference is allegorical: Esmond, defending Castlewood, is wounded in the hand—the allusion
to Telemachus' identical injury recalls also Odysseus' symbolic boar-wound—and the parable of the primitive initiation ritual is developed at the beginning of Book ɪɪ. The
apparently incidental reminiscence becomes a crucial
motif in the novel; the image of initiation reinforces the
theme of discarded illusion; the literal wound is translated
into a scar-metaphor that becomes a symbol for psychological experience.

Lord Castlewood is killed in the duel with Mohun; as
he dies, Virgilian imagery ("The blood rushed from his
mouth, deluging the young man"[52]) is a sardonic reminder
of the epic reality. With the foster father's death, the
hero's early history is finished; Book ɪ ends with Esmond's
imprisonment. But the dramatic textures are diversified
by a variant motif; Castlewood has confessed to a knowledge of the hero's legitimacy on his deathbed—Esmond's
father had been legally married to his French mother—
and the content of the confession is figured in a primitivis-
tic biblical image that reflects the incongruity of the setting: "On the Dutch tiles at the Bagnio was a rude picture
representing Jacob in hairy gloves, cheating Isaac of Esau's
birthright."[53] The allusion foreshadows the role of a hero
who will resign his birthright to his foster-father's son and
will always retain the onus of a dubious birth. And the
religious motif is sustained by a phrase in the minister's
benediction over Castlewood's body—the culmination of
a sequence that, at crucial moments in the first book, has
replaced classical allusion with church Latin[54]—in the boy's
imagined lament for the death of married love; in Rachel's
illusion of a reconciliation between Mohun and her husband; in Esmond's memory of the inscription on a sun-dial
as Castlewood leaves to fight his duel;—and now, in the

formalities of his pseudo-father's death: *abi in pace; Beati pacifici; memento mori; Benedicti benedicentes.*

BOOK II: *"Mr. Esmond's Military Life, and Other Matters Appertaining to the Esmond Family"*

In the second book of *Henry Esmond,* the voice of the narrator is less sharply distinguished than before from that of the alter-ego whose perceptions are no longer a child's. The earlier modal alternation is replaced by a thematic counterpoint between war and love, aggression and passion, objective and subjective violence. The expressive textures are modified: fairy-tale motifs disappear, romance and chivalry are subordinated or burlesqued, pastoral loses its lyric quality; the neoclassical modes, satirical or formal, are dominant.

Book II begins with Rachel's impassioned rejection of Esmond after the death of her husband. Esmond has voluntarily submitted to the imprisonment that is the legal consequence of the duel with Mohun, and the prison-scene reflects, through deviant emotions, the Hades-sequences of the classical epics—the second of the novel's crucial heroic instances. The ritual death-and-purgation image of the traditional underworld descent is interwoven with the motif of torture and initiation; and it is balanced, near the end of Book II, by a symbolic evocation of re-birth. Both episodes express the hero's relation to a maternal image; and both are related to the psychological insights of Book I's epic search for identity.

When Lord Castlewood dies, Rachel, tortured by her sense of spiritual infidelity, instinctively seeks to escape self-accusation by substituting Esmond as an objective culprit. Her punitive visit to the hero's prison is qualified by images that evoke the blood-rites preceding the classical descents to Hades. The duel's "midnight scene of blood and homicide" is recalled. Esmond, striking his hand, feels "the blood rushing again from the wound," and lies "in a pool of blood."[55] Lady Castlewood, inverting the heroic matriarch's role and altering the sacrificial blood-symbolism that permits maternal communication in the *Odyssey*, echoes the Ovidian Dido's accusation—"Take back your hand . . . there's blood on it" (*est etiam frater, cuius manus inpia possit respergi nostro, sparsa cruore viri*).[56] Rachel's half-conscious passion for her foster son intensifies her feeling of guilt toward her dead husband. She tries to project her agony in a compulsive condemnation of Esmond for his part in the duel; but the condemnation is erratically interspersed with admissions of complicity, recalling the confessions of Virgil's Dido: "my husband's heart went from me: and I lost him through you" (*non servata fides cineri promissa Sychaeo*);[57] "All that has happened since, was a just judgment on my wicked heart— my wicked jealous heart. O, I am punished, awfully punished!" (*infelix Dido, nunc te facta impia tangunt*).[58]

The essence of the scene, however, lies not in the transposition or adaptation of epic instance to modern circumstance, but in the figuration of the hero's subjective response to archetypal event. The child's fantasies that found their expression in the lyric modes of Book I culminate in Esmond's hallucinatory image of Rachel—a symbol of the ghostly conflict between devilish and divine in this Hades of the mind, echoing the Miltonic Satan's encounter with Michael ("rushing from aspect maligne Of fiercest opposition")—"Her words as she spoke struck the chords of all his memory, and the whole of his boyhood and youth passed within him, whilst this lady, so fond and gentle but yesterday,—this good angel whom he had loved and worshipped,—stood before him, pursuing him with keen words and aspect malign."[59]

The significance of the image is sustained and extended in phrases that echo the Horatian irony—"The blow had been struck, and he had borne it. His cruel Goddess had shaken her wings and fled" (*rapax Fortuna cum stridore acuto sustulit*)[60] —and the episode is resolved in a metaphor of initiation derived from the symbolic wounding at the end of Book I. Here, the epic insight dispenses with the romanticism of rhythms and figures that characterized the heroic stretto of Book I. The metaphors are severe, universalized Augustan conventions, the rhetoric has the parallelisms and inversions of neoclassical prose. The old narrator's point of view is dominant, and the Latin tag— *reficimus rates quassas*—is an intellectual reference-point, linking Esmond's present disillusionment and recognition of reality with Rachel's earlier emotional crisis after her husband's defection—"When Lady Castlewood found that her great ship had gone down, she began . . . to put out small ventures of happiness; and hope for little gains and returns, as a merchant on 'Change, *indocilis pauperiem pati*" (*reficit rates quassas, indocilis pauperiem pati*).[61] To express Esmond's experience, the timorous mercantile image of Rachel's emotional convalescence becomes a metaphor of epic voyage, the incisive final lines stressing the narrator's distant presence in an America that represents the Hesperides of this internal journey: "O, dark months of grief and rage! of wrong and cruel endurance! He is old now who recals you. Long ago he has forgiven and blest the soft hand that wounded him: but the mark is there, and the wound is cicatrized only—no time, tears, caresses, or repentance, can obliterate the scar. We are indocile to put up with grief, however. *Reficimus rates quassas*: we tempt the ocean again and again, and try upon new ventures. Esmond thought of his early time as a noviciate, and of this past trial as an initiation before entering into life,—as our young Indians undergo tortures silently before they pass to the rank of warriors in the tribe."[62]

135

On Esmond's release from prison, the old Viscountess of
Castlewood, finding that he has learned of his claim to the
Castlewood succession, buys him a commission in the
English army as a tacit reward for his forebearance. The
Viscountess's Diana-image (" 'Twas painted about the
time when royal Endymions were said to find favour with
this virgin huntress"[63]) flickers again about the figure of
Beatrix, whose eulogy by Richard Steele ("sure her famous
namesake of Florence was never half so beautiful"[64]) suggests how the change in a final consonant has distorted
Dante's ideal heroine. The Viscountess parades the cavalier
Esmonds' royalist commitments (shared by Rachel and her
children, from whose society Esmond is, for the moment,
excluded), and the Stuart motif, with its echoes of Odysseus
taunting Agamemnon ("folk-devouring king . . . we followed you for your profit . . . this you ignore"[65]) is followed
by three Greek lines from the *Odyssey*—a sudden incur-
sion of alien sound at the quiet center of the novel:

" 'Tis a wonder to any one who looks back at the history
of the Stuart family, to think how they kicked their crowns
away from them; how they flung away chances after
chances; what treasures of loyalty they dissipated, and how
fatally they were bent on consummating their own ruin
. . . of all the enemies they had, they themselves were the
most fatal.

Ω ποποι, οιον δη νυ θεους βροτοι αιτιοωνται
εξ ἡμεων γαρ φασι κακ᾽ εμμεναι, οι δε και αυτοι
σφησιν ατασθαλιησιν ὑπερ μορον αλγε᾽ εχουσιν.[66]

The sombre words of Zeus ("O how pitiably humans
blame the gods, pretending they are the cause of evil; men
injure themselves, beyond fate, and suffer pain") diffuse
back, through the narrator's comment on Esmond's suffering and endurance in prison ("Who hath not found himself
surprised into revenge, or action, or passion, for good or

evil; whereof the seeds lay within him, latent and un-suspected until the occasion called them forth?")[67] to the novel's Horatian motto (*Servetur ad imum Qualis ab incepto processerit*); and forward through the mock-Homeric battle sequences of Book II to the hero's pseudo-heroic self-jeopardy when he joins the Stuart cause to propitiate Beatrix.

Esmond now, receiving his army commission, takes part in a series of military engagements directed mainly against France. The first campaign is climaxed by an action at Vigo Bay—"a bad business, though Mr. Addison did sing its praises in Latin. That honest gentleman's muse had an eye to the main chance."[68] The novel's sardonic analysis of national gallantry has begun; the theme of art versus reality that is to be developed through Addison's celebration of British prowess is initiated. The campaign concluded, Esmond returns to England and visits Castlewood.

The Castlewood family—Rachel, her son Frank, her daughter Beatrix—are seen in altered perspective after the hero's absence. Esmond meets Lady Castlewood and her son at evening service in the Cathedral. Frank has acquired the charm of "a pretty picture such as Vandyke might have painted," and the provenance of his later portrait "done at Paris" refers the boy's attributes, "his mother's eyes," and "his father's curling brown hair," to Diomede's mockery of Paris in the *Iliad* ("curly-locks, girl-eyes")[69]—one of a cluster of devious images that play about this pretty anti-hero. Rachel is now neither the poetic divinity of the hero's childhood nor the angel-fury of his prison fantasy; the narrator adumbrates her metamorphosis—"goddess now no more, for he knew of her weaknesses . . . but more fondly cherished as woman perhaps than ever she had been adored as divinity."[70]

This recognition of reality preludes a reconciliation scene in which, for the first time, Rachel and Esmond meet

as responsive adults, and Lady Castlewood's sexual love is
acknowledged. The Cathedral's music is still sounding for
Rachel, and her passion expresses itself in the imagery of
the final hymn—" 'we were like them that dream,' I
thought, yes, like them that dream."[71] The parable of her
desire echoes the psalm's final verse, and recalls the narrator's earlier comment on the hero's potential "for good
or evil; whereof the seeds lay within him, latent and
unsuspected" ("He that goeth forth and weepeth, bearing
precious seed, shall doubtless come again with rejoic-
ing").[72] The sober objectivity of the hero's altered vision
is indicated by his unwonted juxtaposition of lyric and
realistic perceptions—"The moon was up by this time,
glittering keen in the frosty sky. He could see, for the first
time now clearly, her sweet care-worn face"—and Rachel's
idealized roles are discarded as she expresses her emotion
in poignantly sexual phrases from the psalm—"she laughed
and sobbed on the young man's heart, crying out wildly,
'bringing your sheaves with you—your sheaves with
you!' "[73] The celestial imagery that accompanied Esmond's
recognition of Rachel's faded beauty is developed in a passage whose "romantic" figuration confirms the emotional
significance of the event, the sequence culminating in a
cluster of classical echoes:

"As he had sometimes felt, gazing up from the deck at
midnight into the boundless starlit depths overhead, in a
rapture of devout wonder at that endless brightness and
beauty—in some such a way now, the depth of this pure
devotion (which was, for the first time, revealed to him
quite) smote upon him, and filled his heart with thanks-
giving. . . . To be rich, to be famous? What do these profit
a year hence, when other names sound louder than yours,
when you lie hidden away under ground, along with the
idle titles engraven on your coffin? But only true love lives

after you,—follows your memory with secret blessing,—or
precedes you, and intercedes for you. *Non omnis moriar.*"⁷⁴

Biblical echoes have modulated to Horatian and Virgilian allusion; the coffin-image recalls Horace's apostrophe
to Archytas, the measurer of heaven and earth (*pulveris
exigui prope litus parva Matinum*—the "handful of
dust" will recur when the Duke of Hamilton dies).⁷⁵ Accompanied by motifs of Christian blessing and intercession,
Virgil's *omnia vincit Amor*,⁷⁶ a dominant theme at the end
of the novel, is distantly heard, and Horace is pronounced
in his own tongue, the reference assimilating in a single
phrase the motto's sense of identity—*servetur ad imum*,
the symbolism of the "seed," and the epic theme of immortality ("I shall not wholly die . . . I shall grow continuously, acquiring later fame").

Esmond, deeply moved by Rachel's love, asks her to
join him in a voyage to America: Book I's parable of the
"wandering Aeneas" illuminates the image of a land both
new and ancestral (*est locus, Hesperiam Grai cognomine
dicunt, terra antiqua*⁷⁷) in which the dubious past may be
discarded—"Begin a new life in a new world . . . that land
in Virginia which King Charles gave us—gave his ancestor.
. . . No man there will ask if there is a blot on my name"⁷⁸
—but Lady Castlewood, realizing that his emotion is gratitude rather than passion, demurs. A Beatrix who has now
"reached her full splendour" is about to intervene.

Esmond returns with Frank and Rachel to the family
estate; and his first vision of Beatrix, suffused with suggestions of the earlier Venus and Diana motifs, effaces the
remembered refulgence of an idealized Rachel—"Love
seemed to radiate from her. Harry eyed her with such a
rapture as the first lover is described as having by Milton."⁷⁹
The echo of Lucretius, with its sinister sensuality (*Veneris
membris vis omnibus exoriatur*) suggests, through the

139

pristine Miltonic allusion, later, less innocent images from *Paradise Lost*;[80] and the two allusive sources continue their interaction throughout the novel's presentation of Beatrix. The objective commentary of the old narrator, phrased in forceful Augustan rhetoric, sustains the Lucretian reference in a context of classical psychology—"What is the fond love of dearest friends compared to this treasure? Is memory as strong as expectancy? fruition, as hunger? gratitude, as desire?" (*unaque res haec est, cuius quom plurima habemus, tum magis ardescit dira cuppedine pectus*).[81] The theme of passion has received its initial definition, and Miltonic epic, with its divergent perspective on man, has begun to modify the heroic vision. The narrator turns to the alternate theme of the second book, the other violence of war while the Castlewood episode closes with a whisper of the earlier romance motif, Esmond momentarily resuming his role as a young Telemachus "looking out from his window towards the city, and the great grey towers of the Cathedral lying under the frosty sky, with the keen stars shining above."[82]

The campaign of 1704 opens with a festive military progress through the Netherlands. Reality intrudes: devastation, brutality, death—and the epic invocation of the prologue recurs, its decorous mockery intensified to dissonance: "Why does the stately Muse of history, that delights in describing the valour of heroes and the grandeur of conquest, leave out these scenes, so brutal, mean, and degrading, that yet form by far the greater part of the drama of war?"[83]

The emphatic distortion of Virgilian convention (*Vos, o Calliope, precor, adspirate canenti, quas ibi tum ferro strages, quae funera*[84]) heralds a new treatment of classical reference where epic allusion becomes anti-heroic satire, and rhetorical parody, mocking the glorification of war, deflates the pretentious convention defined by Addison's

sophistic defense of neoclassical poetry. A critical dramatic
instance of epic diminution is the novel's analysis of
Marlborough, who, like Achilles ("a god is always by his
side, guarding him"), "had this of the god-like in him, that
he was impassible before victory, before danger, before
defeat."[85] The narrator's analysis of this "chief, whom
England . . . worshipped almost," its classical imagery
foreshadowing the Homeric prototype, characteristically
exploits the sardonic parallel constructions and calculated
verbal intensifications of eighteenth-century satire: "He
took a mistress, and left her; he betrayed his benefactor,
and supported him, or would have murdered him, with the
same calmness always, and having no more remorse than
Clotho, when she weaves the thread, or Lachesis, when she
cuts it."[86] Parody predominates in the portrait of Marlborough's rival, General Webb, who is introduced in
banal contemporary verses ("Propitious Heaven must sure
a hero save, Like Paris handsome, and like Hector brave").
The ruthlessness of Marlborough is complemented by the
vanity of Webb—"to be Hector à la mode de Paris, was a
part of this gallant gentleman's ambition"[87]—and their
hostilities form a sardonic anti-masque on the *Iliad's* epic
competition. Romance textures are correlatively modified,
the satirical purpose controlling their chivalrous images;
Beatrix, her beauty mimicking Milton's fallen Eve ("whose
eye darted contagious Fire"), is figured in a passage of
comic gallantry where the themes of war and passion intersect—"Mr. Amadis presented himself to Madam Gloriana.
Was the fire of the French lines half so murderous as the
killing glances from her ladyship's eyes?"[88]

But the pathos of Rachel's relinquishment is phrased
in the novel's lyric mode. Earlier suggestions of amorous
parallels—Dido's death, Eurydice's dissolution—are realized in a passage that deftly adapts the swell and fall of
Carlyle's undulating rhythms and develops the alliterative

effects of "fashionable" prose through soft, sibilant sequences of "s" and "f": "And as, before the blazing sun of morning, the moon fades away in the sky almost invisible;—Esmond thought, with a blush perhaps, of another sweet pale face, sad and faint, and fading out of sight, with its sweet fond gaze of affection; such a last look it seemed to cast as Eurydice might have given, yearning after her lover, when fate and Pluto summoned her, and she passed away into the shades."[89] The maternal mistress, her divinity discarded, has entered an underworld in which the hero will discover her prototype at the end of Book II, when he visits his own mother's grave in Flanders.

Frank Esmond, now about to enter the army, is a new actor in the novel's military anti-masque, a Harlequin hero who parodies Prince Charming—"young Castlewood, in his new uniform, and looking like a prince out of a fairytale."[90] "A hundred songs" are written about him, their fulsome flattery—"my young lord was praised . . . as warmly as Bathyllus"—reflecting the Horatian lines on Anacreon's effeminate lover, whose imputed resemblance to Paris (*non pulchrior ignis accendit obsessam Ilion*)[91] recalls the earlier Paris-parallel that defined this gallant Pierrot. Frank is a comic finale to the narcissistic romance heroes of Thackeray's earlier fiction; after a term in military service, he marries a fading Belgian beauty whom he has compromised ("She is the cleverest woman in all Bruxelles," he writes to Esmond, "understanding painting, musick, poetry, and perfect *at cookery and puddens*"[92]) and returns to head the Castlewood estate with a degree of bourgeous probity.

In London, Esmond meets Joseph Addison, the prototype of Augustan decorum. The significance of artistic deviation from reality—the distinction between meaningful and meretricious illusion—is implicit in the hero's courteous quotation from Addison's own Latin verses (*"O, qui canoro blandius Orpheo vocale ducis carmen"*[93]); and the Orpheus allusion preludes a pastoral irony that pervades the poet's impersonation. Esmond bitterly attacks the "military music" of Addison's *Campaign* poem, his impassioned outbreak recalling the *Aeneid's* lines on the fetish in the Temple of War (*Furor impius intus saeva sedens super arma*)—"You hew out of your polished verses a stately image of smiling victory; I tell you 'tis an uncouth, distorted, savage idol; hideous, bloody, and barbarous."[94] Motifs from the novel's prologue—the mourning chorus, the decorous bloodshed of Agamemnon and Medea—are integrated with satiric pastoralities (a "bout of bucolick cudgelling"; "the leader cared no more for bleating flocks than he did for infants' cries").[95] Addison's reply is a pastiche of Horatian and Virgilian allusions—the pastoral image is again invoked in his reference to the death of Orpheus ("Were I to sing as you would have me, the town would tear the poet in pieces"), and the novel's cumulative allusions to the fourth *Georgic,* continued here and in Addison's typical tag, *Si parva licet* (the poet's motives are implicated in satirical memories of the Virgilian bees' "innate love of gain"), will culminate in Hamilton's death-scene, with its reminiscence of Virgil's ironic battle of the bees.[96] Horace's poetic rules are cited—"it hath been, time out of mind, part of the poet's profession to celebrate the actions of heroes in verse, and to sing the deeds which you men of war perform" (*Res gestae regumque ducumque et tristia bella*), and Addison's peroration rises, by way of cultural decline, to a jingoistic Latin quotation from the second-rate pompositiesof Claudian.[97] In response, Esmond objects to the poet's glorification of Marlborough, and is answered by an argument that defines the dubious Homeric parallel—"War and carnage flee before him to ravage other parts of the field, as Hector from before the divine Achilles. You say he hath no pity; no more have the gods, who are above it, and superhuman."⁹⁸ After this grandiose apostrophe, Addison returns to the business of obtaining information from Esmond about the battle of Blenheim which he is celebrating in his profitable poem—" 'here is the plan,' says he, 'on the table: *hac ibat Simois*, here ran the little river Nebel, *hic est Sigeia tellus*, here are Tallard's quarters' "⁹⁹; and with his sentimental Ovidian quotation, the European battlefield is reduced to a comic projection of the *Iliad*—an epic burlesque that will characterize the narrator's image of Esmond's later campaigns.

Rejoining the army, Esmond meets Father Holt, his father's Catholic chaplain, in Brussels, and learns the details of his mother's marriage. Gertrude Maes, seduced by the hero's father, had become pregnant. Lord Castlewood, wounded in a brawl and expecting to die, married, and deserted her when he recovered. After the birth of Esmond, who was adopted by a French family of weavers, Gertrude entered a convent in Brussels, and died a nun. Esmond visits his mother's grave.

This episode which, characteristically, is not an action but a purely subjective experience, and which finds its classical parallels solely in the textures of its language, is the third and last of the novel's epic climaxes. It is an answer to the prison scene at the beginning of Book II—the descent to Hades, the agony of rejection and initiation. Here, maternal reconciliation and voluntary relinquishment are expressed in symbolisms of submersion and rebirth. Esmond's image of his mother "in tears and darkness," his "pity for the pangs" she had suffered, reflect the meeting between Odysseus and Anticleia in the Homeric underworld ("moaning she spoke to me"; "seeing her I wept"¹⁰⁰). Biblical imagery is invoked, as in earlier passages, but here the writer achieves a perfect fusion between religious and epic motif. The bird that appears and bears away a leaf reflects not only the biblical dove but the birds ("columbae") of Venus guiding Aeneas to golden foliage, his safe-conduct in the underworld.[101] The beginning of the writer's peroration—"the earth is the Lord's as the heaven is"—echoes Virgil's vision of pervasive divinity in the fourth *Georgic* (*deum namque ire per omnia, terrasque tractusque maris caelumque*);[102] and the reminiscence of the biblical flood in the final lines—"walking below the sea," "treading amid bones"—recalls both Odysseus' mother's description of the underworld ("between are great rivers and dread streams, Oceanus first") and Telemachus' fantasy of a dead Odysseus ("whose white bones, perhaps, rot in the rain . . . or waves roll them in the sea"):[103]

"Esmond came to this spot in one sunny evening of spring, and saw, amidst a thousand black crosses, casting their shadows across the grassy mounds, that particular one which marked his mother's resting-place. . . . He fancied her, in tears and darkness, kneeling at the foot of her cross, under which her cares were buried. Surely he knelt . . . in pity for the pangs which the gentle soul in life had been made to suffer . . . beyond the cemetery walls you had glimpses of life and the world, and the spires and gables of the city. A bird came down from a roof opposite, and lit first on a cross, and then on the grass below it, whence it flew away presently with a leaf in its mouth: . . . might she sleep in peace; and we, too, when our struggles and pains are over! But the earth is the Lord's, as the heaven is; we are alike His creatures, here and yonder. I took a little flower off the hillock, and kissed it, and went on my way like the bird that had just lighted on the cross by me, back into the world again. Silent receptacle of death! tranquil depth of calm, out of reach of tempest and trouble! I felt as one who had been walking below the sea, and treading amidst the bones of shipwrecks."[104]

The resonance of "romantic" prose—here, the impressionistic imagery of Carlyle and of "fashionable" fiction— a subtle harmony enriching the lucidity of eighteenth-century religious rhetoric, is simultaneous, now, with classical reminiscence, and foreshadows the ultimate synthesis of the narrator's expressive modes. The delicate contrasts implied in "sunny evening," "spring," and "shadows"; the quiet juxtaposition of "the spires and gables of the city"; the deft, rhythmic rendering of the bird's sporadic flight ("came down . . . lit first . . . flew away") are skillful refinements of the lyric resources that nineteenth-century prose had borrowed from romantic poetry. The ultimate transition to the "I" of first-person narrative, defensible in the tradition of the English memoir, has the effect of a sudden self-recognition, as in Coleridge or Byron; and, with this narrative transition, the writer introduces an image that has the impact of a final, intuitive symbol.

After this crucial insight, Book II is swiftly completed. The military theme becomes a swaggering burlesque, figured in altercations between General Webb and the Duke of Marlborough. Like the Homeric Paris ("brandishing two spears . . . he challenged all the best of the Argives"[105]), Webb makes a vainglorious parade of his achievements "and, mighty man of valour as he was, shook his great spear, and blustered before the army too fiercely."[106] The inflated epithets of Webb's neoclassical eulogist become, in the facile sarcasm of self-satisfied youth, a parody on the General's pretensions: " 'Like Hector, handsome, and like Paris, brave!' whispers Frank Castlewood. 'A Venus, an elderly Venus, couldn't refuse him a pippin.' "[107] This pseudo-Homeric hero confronts his neoclassical Achilles over an issue of the *London Gazette*. Marlborough has authorized an inaccurate report of the battle of Wynendael which slights Webb's victorious command. The *Gazette*, arriving during a banquet at which both generals are present, is the occasion of a bloodless mock-duel; Webb, unable to reach Marlborough, is determined to show him the offensive news item—"with a perfect courtesy, drawing his sword, he ran the 'Gazette' through with the point, and said, 'Permit me to hand it to your Grace.' "[108] The officers' postured heroics are pursued on the battleground of London prestige; and in this modern conflict, Hector is, perhaps, the winner.

As the image of military glory blurs to burlesque, the reflection of civilian suffering is more sharply focussed. The great classical poets, with all their admiration for wartime valor, had recorded the realities of human suffering; Virgil described the tragedy of domestic bereavement, Juvenal the ravages of Roman colonization.[109] Their compassionate insights are implicit in the narrator's record of English tactics during the siege of Lille: "The wretched towns of the defenceless provinces, whose young men had been drafted away into the French armies, which year after year the insatiable war devoured, were left at our mercy; and our orders were to show them none."[110] Esmond's military experience is nearly over. Reality has reduced the significance of heroic textures from decorous satire to skeptical farce.

The alternate theme of personal passion concludes Book II, as Esmond's love for Beatrix begins to dominate his actions. The virginal goddess has become an enchantress, and Circe lends her traditional epithets to a "smiling young temptress, who had bewitched more hearts than his in her thrall"[111]—beginning a series of metamorphoses that will end with the dubious transformation of the seductress herself. The hero's initial divinification of Rachel is being re-enacted with her daughter, but Esmond has begun to analyze his own delusion. Once more, reminiscences of Lucretius[112] sharpen the writer's insight into his alter-ego's compulsive ardor; and again the temporal distance of the narrator is recalled:

"When the writer's descendants come to read this memoir, I wonder will they have lived to experience a similar defeat and shame? Will they ever have knelt to a woman, who has listened to them, and played with them, and laughed at them,—who beckoning them with lures and caresses, and with Yes, smiling from her eyes, has tricked them on to their knees, and turned her back, and left them? All this shame, Mr. Esmond had to undergo; and he submitted, and revolted, and presently came crouching back for more."[113]

BOOK III: *"The End of Mr. Esmond's Adventures in England"*

In the last book of Henry Esmond, fantasy again directs the hero's life. Modifying the patterns of Book I, however, where the perceptions of the child are shaped by his fantasy, the protagonist now sees his motives with rigorous clarity—his actions, not his intelligence, are controlled by irrelevant emotion. His insights coincide with the narrator's—commentary is not an astringent analysis but a temporal perspective. Since Esmond is aware of the fantasy-impulses on which he acts, the thematic counterpoint is not between abstractions like illusion and reality but between intuitive aspects of compulsion and free will.

Motifs of compulsion dominate Book III. The symbolic figure of the artist is now not the mask of a willful illusionist but the projection of an obsessive imagination. Wickedness, even virtue, are only partly voluntary qualities— perception is insufficient without the ability to act. Esmond's love for Beatrix cripples his volition, not his awareness—he "bound his good sense, and reason, and independence, hand and foot; and submitted them to her."[114] Reality is not a rational alternative but an emotional discipline. Esmond suffers as he submits to "the depth and intensity of that love" Rachel bears him[115]; as in *Emma* (where the same paradox is confronted), the recognition of reality involves self-abnegation; in both novels, the consummation of reciprocal love requires a relinquishment of emotional idealisms.

The altered relationship between fantasy and reality subtly modifies the expressive textures. If, in Book III, the lyric modes of Book I sometimes represent satirically discredited states of mind (the Miltonic Fall is re-enacted as ironic comedy: Esmond rejects Beatrix, Eve elopes with the serpent), pastoral, chivalric, romantic textures, fused with classical and biblical allusion, also reflect real values —poetic intensity, responsive love—their polyphony expressing the enigmatic identities between truth and illusion. In Book I, variant allusive textures were identified with lyric or satirical modes and Book II was dominated by textures associated with satire; in Book III the same textures are no longer distinguished by rhetorical kind— their persuasive or derogatory force is determined only by expressive relationships. Depending on context and emphasis, romance may represent the pursuit of a sterile fantasy or the realization of an enduring value; romanticism may combine with Miltonic allusion to satirize a meretricious denouement; *Paradise Lost* may pair with Virgilian pastoral in metaphors of emotional fruition. Illusion and reality are perceived, now, as aspects of an integral subjective experience, their validity depending not on objective absolutes but on their affinities with compulsion and sterility or with fruition and freedom.

Esmond's war-sequence ends at the beginning of Book III. The prologue's emblematic image of Louis XIV recurs in a context of Homeric nostalgia for Priam's golden age— "Despot as he was, the French monarch was yet the chief

149

of European civilization, more venerable in his age and misfortunes than at the period of his most splendid successes."[116] It is an instance of altered perspective; decorum, however insufficient, has another, venerable face. At Malplaquet, the last battle in which the hero takes part, the French defend their own frontiers with "an heroick ardour of resistance"[117] that exacts from the victorious English a staggering penalty in death and losses; the final phrase of the military theme revives the first Book's rubric of religious Latin—" 'Twas the most gloomy pageant I ever looked on; and the 'Te Deum', sung by our chaplains, the most woeful and dreary satyre."[118]

Esmond, having sold his commission, returns to London; he takes a desultory interest in politics and meets some of the great contemporary statesmen. The prologue's alternate emblem of royalty, Queen Anne, reappears in this context, reversing the French King's profile—a symbol of power without pride, regal prerogative without the discipline of decorum: Esmond accuses St. John Bolingbroke of worshipping an unworthy idol—"how humbly will you kneel down to present a despatch—you, the proudest man in the world, that has not knelt to God since you were a boy, and in that posture whisper, flatter, adore almost, a stupid woman, that's often boozy with too much meat and drink."[119] Bolingbroke's rebuttal, citing Cervantes' chivalric farce, draws the implicit parallel between his own compulsion and Esmond's, and begins a series of images that define the hero's pursuit of Beatrix in terms of outworn clichés that were still alive for him at the beginning of the novel: " 'But Dulcinea del Toboso is peerless, eh?' says the other. 'Well, honest Harry, go and attack windmills—perhaps thou art not more mad than other people.' "[120]

Homeric metaphor is satirized in a passage that foreshadows Beatrix's ultimate mutation: "for a much longer period than Ulysses (another middle-aged officer, who had travelled much, and been in the foreign wars), Esmond felt himself enthralled and besotted by the wiles of this enchantress. . . . She had but to raise her finger . . . and the poor infatuated wretch would be sure to come and *rôder* about her mother's house."[121] And the imaginative precision of the writer's language amplifies the Circe image: "*rôder*," which, in French, means "prowl," also counterfeits the English "root," and the degradation of the Circean swine mirrors the hero's emotional condition. The mock-epic mode of the Ulysses-reference is significant; Homeric allusion, with its emphasis on objective adventure and primal emotion, has less relevance to the subtle subjective insights of Book III than the lyric evocations of Virgil's *Georgics* or the spiritual iconography of Milton. Virgilian pastoral, too, replaces neoclassical Arcadia; the Dresden image dissolves in the caustic allusions of the disenchanted hero—" 'I'm a dismal shepherd, to be sure . . . and require a nymph that can tuck my bed-clothes up, and make me water-gruel.' "[122]

Routine Augustan conventions cannot contain the pressure of the emotions that are to be expressed in Book III. The aesthetic dilemma projects a vision of Jonathan Swift, the artist tortured by his own compulsions, whose intrinsic greatness derives from his agony. Ovidian allusion pairs him with Virgil ("for the famous Dr. Swift, I can say of him, 'vidi tantum' "[123]), as Addison was coupled with Claudian, and a simultaneous tribute to Marlborough stresses the multiplication of altered perspectives: "He writ their lampoons, fought their enemies, flogged and bullied in their service, and it must be owned with a consummate skill and fierceness. 'Tis said he hath lost his intellect now, and forgotten his wrongs and his rage against mankind. I have always thought of him and of Marlborough as the two greatest men of that age."[124] The narrator's epic distance is re-emphasized in an apostrophe whose biblical language recalls the *Aeneid's* premise (*causa mali tanti coniunx iterum*) and harshly sounds the formal theme of this final book—"my years are past the Hebrew poet's limit, and I say unto thee, all my troubles and joys too for that matter, have come from a woman."[125]

The semi-chivalric ritual of Esmond's amorous servitude is interrupted by the Duke of Hamilton, who makes an offer of marriage to Beatrix. Hamilton is a type of the ideal chevalier—"one of the most splendid gentlemen of Europe . . . so high in stature, accomplished in wit, and favoured in person, that he might pretend to the hand of any Princess in Europe."[126] He personifies prestige and wealth, attributes that interest Beatrix more than Esmond's adoration (" 'All the time you are worshipping and singing hymns to me,' " she tells him, " 'I know very well I am no goddess, and grow weary of the incense' "—recalling her father's discomfort when, like "the Grand Lama of Thibet," he was worshipped by Lady Castlewood[127]). Hamilton's "ducal coach-and-six" effectively whisks Beatrix out of Esmond's reach, while neoclassical rhetoric emits a complacent creak and outworn idealisms disintegrate: "As you have seen the nymph in the opera-machine go up to the clouds at the end of the piece where Mars, Bacchus, Apollo, and all the divine company of Olympians are seated, and quaver out her last song as a goddess."[128]

Hamilton is an ephemeral apotheosis of the romance idealism. He is assassinated for political reasons by Lord Mohun with a group of hired confederates; and Mohun's re-entry introduces an expressive mode that has not yet been exploited—the conventions of fashionable fiction, the rhetoric of romantic crime. Beginning as a chivalric cliché, Mohun has already assumed the melodramatic mask when he fights his duel with Castlewood ("My lord's dark face grew darker at this taunt, and wore a mischievous fatal look"[129]). He reappears during the French campaigns of Book II, his "hateful handsome face . . . degraded with crime and passion";[130] and, by the time of Hamilton's death, he exemplifies the farcical fate of the Marquis of Steyne, his malignancy reduced to inept brutality; he dies, wounded in the duel—"That party to which Lord Mohun belonged had the benefit of his service, and now were well rid of such a ruffian."[131]

Esmond brings Beatrix the news of Hamilton's assassination. Surrounded by tradesmen, she is examining a decorative chalice displayed by a modish jeweller. In the carving of this sumptuous fetish, Lucretian imagery that has intermittently figured the sexual phases of Esmond's relation to Beatrix culminates in a parable of subjugation and sterility, adapting the description of Mars and Venus in *De Rerum Natura*, where the supine war-god draws his indolent breath from the goddess's lips: "I think Mars and Venus were lying in the golden bower, that one gilt Cupid carried off the war-god's casque—another his sword— another his great buckler . . . Beatrix . . . pointed out the arch graces of the Cupids, and the fine carving of the languid prostrate Mars."[132] Hamilton has illustrated the finest idealism of the romance tradition, and it proves an insufficient formula for the ambiguities of reality. His vulnerability to the violence of Mohun, the emblem of fashionable crime, is a dramatic symbol of the tradition's inadequacy, and a further allusive irony—the reduction of great things to small—relates this insight to the Virgilian deflation of Addison's heroic decorum in Book II; the narrator's comment on Hamilton's death fuses Horatian fatalism (*pulveris exigui prope litus*) with an exquisite echo of Virgil's minuscule battle of bees (*hi motus animorum atque haec certamina tanta pulveris exigui iactu compressa quiescunt*): "Esmond thought of the courier, now galloping on the north road to inform him, who was

Earl of Arran yesterday, that he was Duke of Hamilton
to-day, and of a thousand great schemes, hopes, ambitions,
that were alive in the gallant heart, beating a few hours
since, and now in a little dust quiescent."[133]

Hamilton's conquest is the last of Beatrix's Circean
victories. Having exploited the sensual to its consummation in the metaphorical emasculation of the Duke's semi-
Martian virility, she is transformed by her own enchant-
ments, assuming the image of a magnificent beast of prey:
"The leopard follows his nature as the lamb does, and acts
after leopard-law: she can neither help her beauty, nor her
courage, nor her cruelty; nor a single spot on her shining
coat; nor the conquering spirit which impels her, nor the
shot which brings her down."[134]

With this last metamorphosis of imagined divinity, the
idealized conventions of Book 1 have disintegrated. In her
final exploit, Beatrix will trap herself, and the allusive
motifs that have reflected her triumphs will congeal into
brittle, distorting fragments from the fashionable mirror.

But the lyric modes survive their discredited conventions. Esmond sees Rachel at Castlewood, where Beatrix
has retreated after Hamilton's death, and the novel's expressive motifs merge in a shimmering polyphony that will
be quietly recapitulated in the coda. Rachel's persisting
love is figured in reminiscences of the Virgilian Spring
(fecund divinity dispensing rain, the song of birds, par-
turient pastoral fields) with its pre-Miltonic image of
Eden (*non alios prima crescentis origine mundi*).[135] These
pastoral motifs are succeeded by Castlewood's familiar
image, the emblem of fairy-tale and romance—a symbol,
now, of memory and the permanence of poetic insight—
and this image, in turn, by metaphors of natural fertility.
The sublimation of Esmond's early fantasy-relationships
is suggested by a visual transposition, from the figure of a
boy looking up at a lady in a chivalric dream-castle to the

representation of a man and woman walking together on the ground; and the writer's remarkable control is again evident in the perfection of the eighteenth-century idiom: balanced rhythmic progressions, generalized epithets— "delicious choruses," "blushing sky," "pearly hills"—which have a peculiar propriety in this evocation of the ideal world:

"They walked out, hand-in-hand through the old court, and to the terrace-walk, where the grass was glistening with dew, and the birds in the green woods above were singing their delicious choruses under the blushing morning sky. How well all things were remembered! The antient towers and gables of the hall darkling against the east, the purple shadows on the green slopes, the quaint devices and carvings of the dial, the forest-crowned heights, the fair yellow plain cheerful with crops and corn, the shining river rolling through it towards the pearly hills beyond; all these were before us, along with a thousand beautiful memories of our youth, beautiful and sad, but as real and vivid in our minds as that fair and always-remembered scene our eyes beheld once more."[136]

The delicate ambiguities of this passage contrast suggestively with the simple, primal insight of earlier epic climaxes; this is the expression of a subtler subjective response, the reflection of a perceptual relativity. The allusion to Milton's lost Paradise—"They hand in hand with wandring steps and slow, Through *Eden* took their solitarie way"[137]—fuses with the Virgilian image of original innocence as the fantasy-motif of romance qualifies, through the metaphor of memory, the realities of nature. Dramatic irony is implicit—the partners in this idyllic scene are not childlike lovers but complex adults; the pathetic Rachel, not Eve's surrogate, Beatrix, comforts the hero; the scene preludes not a mystical temptation and redemption but Eve's frivolous Fall in a farcical Eden.

After Hamilton's death, the hero becomes protagonist in a self-created fantasy that quietly parodies the melodramatic intrigues of popular plots. The actor is conscious of his emotional compulsion—"he was eager for some outward excitement to counteract that gnawing malady which he was inwardly enduring"—as the writer is aware of his delusive dependence on historical event—"Nor should it be called a game, save perhaps with the chief player"[138]; it is a satirical climax, mocking the outward forms of art and emotion, and implicitly contrasting them with the expressive realization of inner reality.

Esmond contrives a plot to re-establish the Stuart pretender on the English throne; it is a maneuver in his pursuit of Beatrix, but his conscience is unconvinced. The prologue's tacit Homeric reference is defined, sardonically identifying this prince "whose race seemed to be doomed like the Atridae of old,"[139] and the hero harbors "skeptick doubts as to the benefit which might accrue to the country by bringing a tipsy young monarch back to it."[140] With some embarrassment, Esmond, a neoclassical Ulysses stealing the Palladium ("disguised as a beggar, he entered Troy"), visits Paris "stealthily and like a spy."[141] He brings back a portrait of Charles Stuart dressed as young Lord Castlewood—a passport to impersonation, suggested by the Pretender's resemblance to Frank, who has not been home since his Belgian marriage. The Stuart Agamemnon, alias Lord Castlewood, comes to London with Frank as his titular attendant and is domiciled at the Esmonds' town house. Rachel and Beatrix, hypnotized by dubious chivalry —"kneeling down at the bedside and kissing the sheets out of respect for the web that was to hold the sacred person of a King"—prepare an ironic shrine for the Homeric misfit: "there was a copy of Eikon-Basilike laid on the writing-table; a portrait of the martyred King, hung always over the mantel."[142] The fetish of the *Eikon Basilike*—Charles I's mystic Image of a King—is a recurrent motif, deviously mirroring the ineffective real presence.

While Esmond prepares for a coup-d'état, the nominal Lord Castlewood makes love to Frank's sister. The Pretender's first reaction to Beatrix diffuses textures of fashionable sentiment through the romantic sequence—" 'qui est cette nymphe, cet astre qui brille, cette Diane qui descend sur nous?' "[143] The French gallantries recall Thackeray's early burlesques of "silver-fork" fiction; and the Diana-fetish that satirized the old Viscountess returns to haunt her successor. Diana is swiftly transformed to a modish Venus; the suggestion of fashionable cliché marks the distance between the parallel apotheosis of Rachel at the beginning of the novel and this facile divinification of Beatrix—"A light shone out of her eyes; a gleam bright enough to kindle passion in any breast. There were times when this creature was so handsome, that she seemed, as it were, like Venus revealing herself a goddess in a flash of brightness."[144] The hero's childhood vision of maternal love has been transferred to the unattainable mistress. As the royal flirtation progresses, Esmond's jealous suspicions are shared by Frank and Rachel, who cooperate in consigning Venus to Castlewood; confronted by her family, the heroine resembles an outlaw at bay—"attack," "feint," "sally," "hemming in poor Beatrix"—recalling the animal-metaphor that defined her earlier frustration—"a special malignant fate watched and pursued her, tearing her prize out of her hand."[145]

In appropriate decorative banalities, the heroine's absence is deplored: "Where is that charming nymph, and why doth she not adorn your ladyship's tea-table with her bright eyes?"[146] Finding that Beatrix has gone to Castlewood and suspecting the reason, the quasi-monarch is incensed, leaves the Esmond house, and takes refuge with another eminent loyalist. The projected coup-d'état is at the point of execution; the hero assembles his confederates, but pseudo-Agamemnon is amusing himself with the nymph whom he has followed into the country. Esmond and Frank ride after him, and the succeeding scene deviously resolves this artificial intrigue. The double significance of the epithet "Pretender" becomes clear as the guileful serpent emerges from rhetorical foliage—"Esmond darkly thought, how Hamilton, Ashburnham, had before been masters of those roses that the young Prince's lips were now feeding on"—and ironic echoes of Milton ("Defac't, deflourd, and now to Death devote") sharpen the harmonies of the familiar melodrama—"Her cheek was desecrated, her beauty tarnished; shame and honor stood between it and him."[147] Fashionable motifs burlesque the scene; Esmond finds a sheet of sentimental verses addressed to Beatrix—"Here is 'Madame' and 'Flamme,' 'Cruelle' and 'Rebelle,' and 'Amour' and 'Jour,' in the Royal writing and spelling. Had the Gracious lover been happy, he had not passed his time in sighing."[148] The hero fights a mock-duel with the Pretender, who, finding that the political intrigue has been jeopardized by his folly, agrees to return to London. Beatrix appears; a reminiscence of her Miltonic prototype ("From his slack hand the Garland wreath'd for *Eve* Down dropd, and all the faded Roses shed") is filed to a sardonic point—"The roses had shuddered out of her cheeks; her eyes were glaring; she looked quite old."[149] A final flicker of the animal-motif parodies *Paradise Lost* ("he would have spoke, But hiss for hiss returnd"), insinuating the improbable serpentine metamorphosis of Eve herself— "She came up to Esmond and hissed out a word or two"— and the scene ends with a farcical return of the mock-epic Diana-motif, discredited divinity in the shape of an impotent huntress:

"If words could stab, no doubt she would have killed Esmond; she looked at him as if she could.

"But her keen words gave no wound to Mr. Esmond; his heart was too hard."[150]

The heroic pursuit of Venus has ended. After Eve's fashionable delinquencies with her pseudo-Satan, Esmond turns to the reality of Rachel's love in the fertile but disenchanted Eden that is the antithesis to a desultory Paradise in this final book of the novel. But the relinquishment of fantasy requires a sacrifice; the vision of Beatrix must now remain a memory, the hero's deprivation re-emphasizing the significance of the scar-metaphor, with its symbolism of severance and initiation: "such a passion once felt . . . becomes a portion of the man of to-day, just as any great faith or conviction, the discovery of poetry, the awakening of religion, ever afterward influence him; just as the wound I had at Blenheim, and of which I wear the scar, hath become part of my frame."[151]

The enigma of illusion and reality—the problem of their relative truth—is posed, not resolved. The memory-motif, with its suggestion of synthesis, is a tentative interpretation; the loss is real—its thematic significance is expressed in recurrent melodic metaphors: the fairy-tale motif of Castlewood—"There was the fountain in the court babbling its familiar musick"—the sound of Beatrix's laughter—"years afterwards I hear that delightful musick"—the ambiguous harmonies of the novel's coda: "With the sound of King George's trumpets, all the vain hopes of the weak and foolish young Pretender were blown away; and with that musick, too, I may say, the drama of my own life was ended."[152]

The sentence expresses precisely the paradox of this final book. The "music" of the hero's life has accompanied the meretricious "drama" of his infatuation—the "glorious chance of winning the game."[153] The "drama" has ended, not his life; the "music" has ceased, not its sound—"We forget nothing. The memory sleeps, but wakens again."[154] *Esmond's* coda, filled with biblical, Virgilian, and Miltonic reminiscences that interfuse and resolve, rephrases, in prosaic eighteenth-century idiom, the image of a natural Eden, now identified with the American Hesperides of this epic exploration: "Sure, love *vincit omnia*; is immeasurably above all ambition, more precious than wealth, more noble than name. He knows not life who knows not that: he hath not felt the highest faculty of the soul who hath not enjoyed it."[155] Virgil's phrase sustains the coda's enigmatic motif of realization and loss, evoking the poet's pastoral lament for the cruelty of the love-god, who cannot be altered by human pain (*non illum nostri possunt mutare labores . . . omnia vincit Amor: et nos cedamus Amori*), and fusing with the Miltonic vision of redemption beyond the reach of human wealth or wisdom, surviving the exile from Paradise—"add Love, By name to come calld Charitie, the soul Of all the rest."[156] The final image of Rachel—"as beautiful in her autumn, and as pure as virgins in their spring, with blushes of love and 'eyes of meek surrender' "—associates the personification of Eve with the Miltonic metaphor of fruition ("with eyes Of conjugal attraction unreprov'd, And meek surrender, half-imbracing leand On our first Father . . . hee in delight . . . as *Jupiter* On *Juno* smiles, when he impregns the Clouds That shed *May* Flowers").[157] The motif of America—"In our transatlantick country we have a season, the calmest and most delightful of the year, which we call the Indian summer"[158]—recalls the classical Atlantis, and a biblical reminiscence—"Our diamonds are turned into ploughs and axes for our plantations"—reverses the Virgilian parallel (*curvae rigidum falces conflantur in ensem*).[159] The novel's final image touches a tenuous thread reaching back to the prison scene of severance and initiation: after Esmond's confrontation with Rachel he had missed a button from his coat; the cryptic emblem, like the golden buckle by which Penelope identifies Ulysses, recurs and is explained—"the only jewel by which my wife sets any store, and from which she hath never parted, is that gold button she took from my arm on the day when she visited me in prison"—it is "the old old story of the wishing-ring," the talisman of the traditional fairy-tale.[160]

ii. HISTORY IN FICTIONAL FORM

Bulwer Lytton wrote a novel of the English eighteenth century. His dedication reads: "In 'Devereux,' I wished to portray a man flourishing in the last century, with the train of mind and sentiment peculiar to the present . . . the historical characters introduced are not closely woven with the main plot, like those in the fictions of Sir Walter Scott —but . . . give a greater air of truth and actuality to the supposed memoir."[161]

Thackeray, reading his rival's clever, shallow novel, would have realized how much better it could be done. Perhaps *Devereux* was the irritant that initiated *Esmond*, perhaps it was only an incidental stimulus, but its protean author was expressing an idea implicit in contemporary thought. Whatever Bulwer meant, it was more than a formula for reading the present into the past. Carlyle saw history as a sequence of symbolic typifications in an omnipresent allegory, Macaulay as an organic cause—and this was a new development; before the nineteenth century, history had been only a record from which interesting facts and useful lessons could be drawn, not an aspect of contemporary reality.

In *Esmond*, history is both cause and symbol. Events observed by a modern intelligence, self-conscious and introspective, are experienced by an imagination which is in the process of cultural development. The hero's mind grows with his civilization, its evolution reflected in the expressive textures of his language. As the writer's ornamental decorums are discarded, they are replaced by analytic neoclassical satire; when they return, at the end of the novel, they have become modern symbolisms—romantic insights, sustained by the motif of memory.

Esmond's historical events are sociological causes. The novel is set in an England that was rapidly discarding monarchial aristocracy for parliamentary government. The change continued for over a century, but the replacement of the divinely appointed Stuarts with the contractual Hanoverians is a crucial instance. Historical significance is not the novel's crux, but it is a forceful theme; political evolution in *Esmond* is an objective illustration of the cultural process that is reflected in the hero's subjective experience. The new social philosophy's ethical viewpoint is curtly signified in a brief exchange that affixes Thackeray's signature at the center of the novel. The old Viscountess compliments the hero on his unselfishness in foregoing the Castlewood succession: " '*Noblesse oblige*,' says Mr. Esmond, making her a low bow." The French phrase is, surprisingly, a "maxim" of the nineteenth-century Duc de Lévis, and was not widely known until it supplied the title of a popular play after *Esmond's* publication. Its original meaning—"nobility entails responsibility"—paraphrases Juvenal's republican slogan "*nobilitas sola est atque unica virtus*"—and at the same time slyly echoes the Thackeray family motto, "*Nobilitas sola virtus*."[162] It is a trivial, though cunning instance; but the Juvenalian reference is pertinent.

The resonance of Juvenal's eighth satire pervades the novel's political comment. The iconoclastic motifs of the prologue—"I look into my heart and think I am as good as my Lord Mayor, and know I am as bad as Tyburn Jack"[163]—are muted during the first two books but return as an organic theme in the commentary of Book III, where the mystique of Stuart legitimacy—"that monstrous pedigree which the Tories chose to consider divine"[164]— mirrors, in historical perspective, the irrationality of the hero's emotional obsession. The romantic melodrama of which Esmond is compulsive architect, in ironic parody of fashionable fiction, is paralleled by the political intrigue in which he is a self-convicted illusionist: " 'twas a scheme of personal ambition, a daring stroke for a selfish end,—he knew it. What cared he, in his heart, who was King?"[165] The satirical theme is developed through the personification of the Pretender, who, mimicking Juvenal's decadent dictator, "was often content to lay the dignity of his birth and grief at the wooden shoes of a French chamber-maid, and to repent afterwards (for he was very devout), in ashes taken from the dust-pan."[166] Like the fantasy of amorous divinity, "the old doctrine of divine right" is discredited in Book III: the conviction that "Parliament and people consecrate the Sovereign, not Bishops nor genealogies, nor oils, nor coronations"[167] becomes insistent. The hero's rejection of the Stuart mystique, like his relinquishment of romantic delusions, is symbolized by the exposure of Beatrix and the Pretender in the novel's satirical Eden.

In his concept of a narrator with a dramatic alter ego, Thackeray exquisitely realized Bulwer's idea of "a man flourishing in the last century, with the train of mind and sentiment peculiar to the present." The heroic actor, experiencing the novel's political events as they occur, responds as a perceptive contemporary; the distant narrator analyzes the historical sequence in detachment and *Esmond's* commentary supplies a quizzical modern perspective: "Will we of the new world submit much longer, even nominally, to this antient British superstition? There are signs of the times which make me think that ere long we shall care as little about King George here, and peers temporal and peers spiritual, as we do for King Canute or the Druids."[168] This creative synthesis of history and fiction— a sequence of expressive modes figuring cultural development, public events mirroring a private experience, a double perspective correlating past and present—was a significant break with the illustrative tradition. *Esmond's* method has reappeared in radically different forms—in *Romola, Orlando, Ulysses,* in Tolstoy, Proust, and Dos Passos. The techniques vary from Joyce's parodies to Dos Passos' pastiches, from George Eliot's psychological commentary to Virginia Woolf's fantastic psychology, from Tolstoy's essays to Proust's metaphors; and each, perhaps, is an independent discovery. But the aesthetic significance of history in these later novels is strictly comparable with Thackeray's achievement. It is a concept without parallel in Scott or Cooper, Bulwer Lytton or *The Tale of Two Cities.*

Esmond's political sequence shares with its epic theme the opposition of England to America, reactionary to progressive—the heroic antithesis of archaic homeland to Atlantis or Hesperides; and it is through epic or traditional symbolism that history is converted into imaginative symbol. Again, the crucial distinction is between illustration and expression; Fielding's heroic similes, Voltaire's epic satire offer rational modern parallels, not universal intuitions. When Thackeray expresses Castlewood's abortive relationship with Rachel in pastoral convention, as a branch that buds, blooms, withers, and becomes a punitive masculine crook, his parable is a brief instance of D. H. Lawrence's extended biblical allegory in *Aaron's Rod;* when he images the Castlewoods' sexual antagonism, his mock-epic evocation of Jove's thunder and Juno's quivering reply anticipates Virginia Woolf's allusive method in

164

To the Lighthouse, where Mrs. Ramsay, reassuring her husband, seems to "pour erect into the air a rain of energy . . . and into this delicious fecundity . . . the fatal sterility of the male plunged itself, like a beak of brass."[169] When, in *Esmond*, Lord Castlewood becomes a Grand Lama worshipped by his bonzes, or Marlborough is seen triumphant in battle and "the god is confessed," the technique is the same as E. M. Forster's in *A Passage to India*: "The Collector had watched the arrest from the interior of the waiting-room, and throwing open its perforated doors of zinc, he was now revealed like a god in a shrine."[170] These allusive metaphors share a purpose in which they differ from the fictional tradition before Thackeray. They not only document the narrative with traditional instances of marital intercourse or arbitrary power, they suggest universal sexual or social insights; their significance disseminates through the whole of human experience, synthesizing past and present.

Esmond's integral form, too, depends on this expressive method. The major epic metaphors of quest, severance, initiation, submersion, and rebirth, the Miltonic symbolism of fall and redemption with its antithetical Edens, generate forms that convert historical experience into a recurrent allegory of human event. The writer's expressive technique communicates this event as subjective response or intuitive perception; and the union of past and present takes place. This is the common purpose of the recurrent mythology in Proust, of the Homeric parallels in *Ulysses*. George Eliot's *Middlemarch*, Meredith's *Egoist* are more proximate successors; but it is not the question of literal derivation that is important—it is the occurrence of an artistic mutation that produced new qualities in the novel.

Esmond is the first effective response to the critical demand for novels that would count intellectually in the same way as history, imaginatively as epic, and emotionally as a representation of the subjective truths that had become a reality for the nineteenth century. Illustrative fiction excluded subjective experience; nothing substantial was gained by Bulwer's flashes of inspiration; and the anomalous splendor of *Wuthering Heights* was unproductive because it depended on the personal intensity of its author's vision rather than on a practicable narrative technique. There are pages in other novels that anticipate Thackeray's effects, and there are other works, like *Sartor*, that develop a similar method in another medium; but the infinitely demanding process of integrating these contemporary experiments into an organic fictional form was deferred until *Esmond*. The novel was a remarkable achievement, and Thackeray knew it—"Here is the *very* best I can do," he told an American friend. "I stand by this book, and am willing to leave it, when I go, as my card."[171]

CHAPTER VIII

STYLE AND FORM IN *ESMOND*

THE style-form relationship in *Henry Esmond* is a more critical equilibrium than the expressive interplay of *Vanity Fair*; a new component has entered the earlier pattern—the element of objective reality. Literal event is part of *Esmond's* texture—a nexus of intransigeant fact, not truth as such but an indispensable part of it, sometimes generating, sometimes resisting subjective experience, partly illuminated and partly refuted by imaginative reality, and always an integral factor in the creative equation.

Vanity Fair is a parody of objective reality, an image in a distorting mirror, revealing an unfamiliar truth, but one that is dependent upon the mirrored object for its existence. The textures of romance and sentiment that express subjective experience in *Vanity Fair* are derivative idealizations; they may be modified, satirized, or disoriented, but premise no truths beyond those which, however obliquely, they reflect. The structure evolved from these imaginative textures cannot admit realistic criteria; objective event must be excluded or deactivated if it is not to discredit the fantasy-world, as the movements of everyday life, dressing or eating, are not admissible in classical ballet.

In *Esmond*, although objective event is an integral aspect of narrative experience, imaginative reality is not disqualified. This is possible because the writer's language can now express intuitive truths that have a validity of their own, surviving the intrusion of objective data. Intuitions coexist with literal event—the fusion of figurative textures with factual and formal premises is too intri-

167

cate to be diagrammed, despite the novel's historical framework and neat tripartite structure. *Esmond's* expressive metaphors no longer depend on parodic textures; they can evoke universal perceptions, aspects of human experience so fundamental that they cannot be discounted as unreal. The fantasy-motifs remain—sentimental, decorous, melodramatic—and are discredited by realistic data, a process which is part of the narrator's subjective experience. But fantasy is only an aspect of *Esmond's* expressive metaphor; insights as valid as literal reality coexist with objective event.

In their simplest form, such expressive insights occur as single metaphors that transcend physical or temporal data. Characteristically, these metaphors are independent of the dramatic context, rising spontaneously out of a generalization, an action, a memory or a visual image. In Book I, after Castlewood's infidelity, when Rachel and Esmond are isolated, she in a shadowy underworld of jealousy and passion, he in an adolescent dream of beauty and horror, a pair of images whispers through the commentary, transmuting their pain:

"As you have seen the awkward fingers and clumsy tools of a prisoner cut and fashion the most delicate little pieces of carved work; or achieve the most prodigious underground labours."

"holiday musick from withinside a prison wall—or sunshine seen through the bars; more prized because unattainable."[1]

These images amplify the characters' literal experience. They are conceits that would be indecorous, inappropriate to the object, in illustrative art. But because they suggest fundamental human realities—oppression, aspiration, memory—they are more persistent than fantasy and intensify rather than obscure the objective crisis of Esmond's imprisonment with its glimpse of the "poor wretches" at Newgate ("his insensibility to their misery . . . hath struck with a kind of shame since—as proving how selfish during his imprisonment, his own particular grief was") and its melodic image of Rachel's cruelty—"Her words as she spoke struck the chords of all his memory."[2]

Similarly, a sequence of metaphor that begins in simile may end in symbol—so, the celestial figures that accompany Beatrix's incarnation as Diana—"crescent and brilliant," a "bright particular star"—become, when Esmond is reconciled with Rachel, a memory of his returning voyage—"stars of solemn midnight," "endless brightness and beauty"—preluding an image that evokes the evanescent dream-like quality of all romantic love—"the great grey towers of the Cathedral lying under the frosty sky, with the keen stars shining above."[3] A dramatic situation, too, may suggest an image that transfigures the event, as when Esmond confesses to Rachel his abortive passion for Beatrix and the metaphor of Rachel's pathos becomes a symbol of ineffective beauty, an instance of inconsequent destruction: "She had in her hand the stalk of one of the flowers, a pink, that he had torn to pieces."[4] A visual image may transform the actor into an intuitive emblem, as Beatrix, bargaining for the chalice that is to represent her triumph over Hamilton, becomes, momentarily, a type of enigmatic sensual splendor: "there were flambeaux in the room lighting up the brilliant mistress of it. She lifted up the great gold salver with her fair arms."[5]

Again, a sequence deriving from dramatic event may involve dissimilar actors in a pattern whose implications extend beyond their behavior. The sustained metaphor of Esmond's political artifice in the last book of the novel is intersected by an imagery of ironic games played by fatalistic characters—the compulsive ambition of Marlborough, "who was no more moved by the game of war than that of billiards, and pushed forward his squadrons, and drove his red battalions hither and thither as calmly as he would combine a stroke or make a cannon with the balls,"[6] impinging on the hero's desperate attempt to win Beatrix by military prestige—"he had no suit to play but the red one, and he played it"—and travestied when the old Viscountess orders Esmond's portrait "in his red coat, and smiling upon a bomb-shell, which was bursting at a corner of the piece." Like the prison-metaphor of Book I, these motifs reinforce a literal event. When Esmond leaves for his last campaign, the Viscountess parts from him "with perfect alacrity" and resumes her habitual pastime of piquet: " 'Tierce to a king,' were the last words he ever heard her say: the game of life was pretty nearly over for the good lady, and three months afterwards she took to her bed, where she flickered out without any pain."[7] A thematic narrative sequence may be summed up in a single, apparently peripheral image. The compulsive drama of Book III, in which the Stuarts' self-destructive folly, Rachel's jealousy, Beatrix's resentment, and Esmond's passion, are refracted through metaphors of anger and pain ("leaving her with only rage and grief for her portion," "the cruel wound which fortune had inflicted"[8]) is concentrated in the commentary's digression on Swift: "I have read his books, (who doth not know them?) here in our calm woods, and imagine a giant to myself as I think of him, a lonely fallen Prometheus, groaning as the vulture tears him."[9] And this theme of compulsion is resolved at the end of Book III in a parenthetic elegy for Father Holt, the shadowy Jesuit priest who tutored Esmond in his early years at Castlewood, and who is dead, now, in America—"a cross over him, and a mound of earth above him; under which that unquiet spirit is for ever at peace."[10]

Time itself is suspended in verbal patterns of changeless intensity, while the incidents accompanying the vision are confused or obliterated. Thus, the image of sudden lucidity before Lord Castlewood's duel with Mohun: "the scene remained long in Esmond's memory:—the sky bright over-head: the buttresses of the building, and the sun-dial casting shadow over the gilt *memento mori* inscribed underneath: the two dogs, a black greyhound and a spaniel nearly white, the one with his face up to the sun, and the other snuffing amongst the grass and stones, and my lord leaning over the fountain, which was plashing audibly."[11] So, time recedes in the novel's crucial epic passages. The questions of Book I—"Who was he and what? Why here rather than elsewhere?"—the emotional severance in prison —"Esmond thought of his early time as a noviciate, and of this past trial as an initiation before entering into life"— prelude the hero's symbolic submersion near the end of Book II: "I felt as one who had been walking below the sea, and treading amidst the bones of shipwrecks."[12] So, too, metaphor fuses with objective reality when, in Book III, Esmond and Rachel walk through a newly procreant landscape that is also an instance of the recurrent Castlewood images that sustain the novel's memory-motif. These images alter with the hero's emotions; the "grand house" is an emblem of fantasy in childhood—"many grey towers and vanes on them, and windows flaming in the sunshine"[13]— a pastoral harmony before the idyllic meeting with Rachel: "the dawn was rising over Castlewood village; he could hear the clinking at the blacksmith's forge yonder among the trees, across the green, and past the river, on which a mist still lay sleeping"[14]—a morbid figure in the final drama, when Esmond, pursuing Beatrix and the Pretender, enters "the court, over which the dawn was now reddening, and where the fountain plashed in silence."[15] But these modalities are all aspects of permanence—the persistent recurrence of the image is as timeless as memory itself.

Such images are intrinsically creative; they do not depend upon parodic convention. In *Esmond*, motifs of parody, too, form fantasy-sequences, but their continuity differs from the allegorical patterns of *Vanity Fair*; here, the sequences are not pre-determined by the fable—the angel is both a parody and a person, the witch is Diana and dies in bed, the lascivious siren is a "beautiful spirit" or a stricken prey—reality intrudes, fragmenting, but not dissipating, the intuition.

In *Aspects of the Novel*, E. M. Forster, discussing one of the most meaningful phases of expressive form, wrote, "this seems to me the function of rhythm in fiction; not to be there all the time like a pattern, but by its lovely waxing and waning to fill us with surprise and freshness and hope."[16] It is this effect of fluctuating continuity that is realized in *Esmond's* expressive insights. Thematic motifs, sometimes extended metaphors, sometimes suggestive fragments, are reintroduced, rephrased, reinterpreted, their figurative modulations developing rhythms that integrate the dramatic substance of the novel. The materials of this rhythmic recurrence may be philosophical, allusive, symbolic as in the Castlewood sequence, or comic—as when the prologue's portrait of old Lord Castlewood, proud of "his dignity (as Lord of the Butteries and Groom of the King's Posset)" is burlesqued in the Viscountess's loyalist protestations—"the Esmond that would have served your Majesty will never be groom to a traitor's posset"—and reflected in the ironic afterglow of romance, as Frank Esmond compares his lineage with the Churchills'—"Where were they, when our ancestor rode with King Henry at Agincourt, and filled up the French king's cup after Poictiers?"[17] The image persists, its shading changes—the prologue's emblem of historical hypocrisy, the melodic slaughter of Agamemnon and Medea, becomes a symbol of aesthetic artifice in Addison's dispassionate Horatian homily. The rhythmic effects vary from the chordal strophes of the Stuart dirge

172

with its central Greek resonance to the single, emblematic recurrence in Book III of the prologue's profiles of King Louis and Queen Anne.

From modulating rhythmic continuities the novel's forms emerge, nebulous but perceptible like intermittent arcs in rippling water, the inner related but distinct from the outer. The figurative relationships are oblique but unmistakable—as in the changing thematic metaphor of deified humanity. The initial divinification of Rachel as Venus, reformulated in the final ironic apotheosis of Beatrix, generates lesser correspondences throughout the course of the narrative, each figuratively reflecting the others: a sequence of idol-imagery, beginning with Rachel's adoration of her husband, recurring in the "savage idol" of war that satirizes Addison's poetic decorum, and sustained in the commentary on Esmond's passion for Beatrix— "Who, in the course of his life, hath not been so bewitched, and worshipped some idol or another?"[18]—the motif of Marlborough's power, personified in "the divine Achilles" and Addison's victorious angel, spanning Book II; the brief sequence at the center of the novel where images of aetherial wings mirror the personal aspirations of the youthful actors in moments of dubious magic. First, the narrator's evanescent vision of Frank and Beatrix: "This brother and sister were the most beautiful couple ever seen: though after he winged away from the maternal nest this pair were seldom together."[19] Next, the hero's Icarus-travesty, a metaphysical caricature of Cupid and Psyche: "What a fool am I to be dallying about this passion, and singeing my wings in this foolish flame. Wings!—why not say crutches?"[20] Then, the legendary symbol of Beatrix's transcendent ambition: " 'I want my wings and to use them, sir.' And she spread out her beautiful arms, as if indeed she could fly off like the pretty 'Gawrie,' whom the man in the story was enamoured of."[21]

These figurative sequences—the visionary Venus-motif, the satirical idol-imagery, the sinister war-god symbolism, the evocation of imaginative flight—share the thematic metaphor of superhuman aspiration and their successive correlations are one aspect of Esmond's expressive synthesis. The brilliant personifications of Rachel and Beatrix stand in radiant counterpoise at the extremes of the novel, spanning, like a ray of light, the obverse sequence of idolatrous self-abasement, within which the imagery of a deified Marlborough surrounds the charming, intimate figurations of Frank and Beatrix, exuberantly soaring about the comic anti-masque of the hero's descent. These intimations are recurrent and evanescent, fading into the novel's substance of drama or history and reappearing, altered but familiar—rhythmic correlations, cumulative rather than sustained.

Esmond's epic theme, too, is a flickering, rhythmic continuity. The early Aeneas-metaphor merges with the recurrent image of America—the epic vision of "a new life in a new world."[22] The hero's personification as Ulysses enthralled by Circe foreshadows Hamilton's amorous surrender, its reminiscence of Mars enslaved by Venus rephrasing the Achilles-motif of Marlborough and prefiguring the final beatification of Beatrix. So, Rachel's Venus-persona becomes, through the image of Beatrix as Diana ("flashing death upon the children of Niobe") and Steele's sentimental idealization—"Niobe in tears"—a type of mythic deprivation—Euridice fading away "before the blazing sun of morning."[23] So, too, Esmond passes through variant heroic phases—Aeneas, Telemachus, Ulysses, Adam —the successive figurations swiftly phrased and resolving into a complex harmony, their rhythmic values emerging again with each recurrent epic typification.

As these expressive rhythms coexist and fuse with objective reality, the literal and imaginative aspects of experience separate, intersect, pursue each other, and are resolved in a sustained polyphony. Literal events, in *Esmond,* are like rocks from which a stream of water takes its shape—the liquid forms expand and alter beyond the limits of the object, as *Esmond's* expressive textures amplify and change the shape of event. In *Vanity Fair,* subjective experience is unqualified; part of the novel's irony is the ineffectiveness of objective event—the Sedley's sudden poverty makes no perceptible difference in Amelia's relationship with George. In *Esmond,* a parallel event—the smallpox epidemic—has an immediate effect and a subsequent expressive development. The literal crisis separates Castlewood from his wife, and confirms Rachel's attachment to Esmond; this situation is recurrently amplified in the hero's imagination, and it is not until after he has left and returned to Castlewood more than once that the estrangement of husband and wife assumes its full emotional significance. Nevertheless, neither the Castlewoods' experience nor the hero's subjective response can be dissociated from the smallpox incident itself, which is recalled again and again as present emotions are revealed or past experiences confessed—when Esmond tries to bring about a reconciliation between Rachel and her husband—" 'Why did you bring back the small-pox,' she added after a pause, 'from Castlewood village? You could not help it, could you? Which of us knows whither Fate leads us? But we were all happy, Henry, till then.' "[24]

The accusation is hysterically intensified in the prison-scene—"Why did you not die when you had the small-pox" —and its psychological meaning is indicated when Rachel refuses Esmond's offer of marriage after her first confession of love: "You could not see me, Harry, when you were in the small-pox, and I came and sate by you. . . . You never loved me, dear Henry—no, you do not now, and I thank

Heaven for it. I used to watch you, and knew by a thousand signs that it was so."[25]

The contrast between *Esmond* and *Vanity Fair* is even clearer in their disparate treatment of the war-motif. In *Vanity Fair*, the battle-sequence is a brilliant background for self-generating emotions; Amelia's jealousy and fear of losing George, Becky's aggressive coquetry, George's narcissism, would have followed without Waterloo; the war appears in the novel as a symbolism of violence, not as an objective fact—its literal climax, George's death, occurs off-stage. In *Esmond*, however, the war-sequence is the effective instrument of the hero's separation from the Castlewood family—if the prison-scene at the beginning of Book II is a parable of severance and initiation, the Vigo campaign is its objective realization; and Esmond's effort to win military prestige is the literal equivalent of his emotional compulsion. Without the experience of human suffering during the campaigns, the delusive idealism of Addison's heroic decorum would lose its point. The hero's epic confrontation with primal realities at his mother's grave would have neither preparation, explanation, nor antithesis—and this climactic insight intensifies the paradox of vacuous violence and needless suffering in the succeeding battle scenes. As in earlier event, the imaginative culmination of *Esmond's* war-sequence is a subsequent expressive development; Hamilton's epic personification completes the theme of heroic gallantry, as Mars succeeds Achilles, and it is in the Duke's death, with its ironic reminiscence of the pigmy violence of Virgil's bees and its sombre echo of Horatian paradox—the man of infinite genius reduced to dust—that the hero's new perspective on human reality finds its consummation.

The dramatic placement of the novel's epic climaxes involves a similar counterpoint between event and response. *Esmond's* major insights are always related to a literal event—the death of the hero's father; his rejection by Rachel; the death of his mother; his reunion with Rachel. The response and the event may be nearly simultaneous or there may be a considerable time-lapse between the two. But in each epic instance, the literal plot-progression momentarily ceases, and the crucial expressive sequence is developed in a context devoid of narrative action. The first of these episodes occurs during the occupation of Castlewood by government troops, when the child is isolated from normal personal relationships; the second takes place in prison; the third, the hero's symbolic response to his mother's death, occurs in a period of winter inactivity between two continental campaigns; the ultimate instance, his emotional reunion with Rachel is realized in a tenuous interval between Hamilton's death and the ensuing preparations for the Stuart intrigue. In each case, the interruption of the conventional plot-movement suggests an aspect of timelessness; but the expressive correspondences between these climactic episodes and the novel's dramatic continuities preclude a dissociation of objective and imaginative reality.

It is the absence of this correspondence between subjective experience and objective event that limits Virginia Woolf's expressive triumph in *To the Lighthouse*. The deficiency is partly due to a failure to prepare for the literal event and relate it to imaginative response—a fault betrayed by the weakness of the war-sequence that is introduced toward the end of the novel and by the author's mechanical device of bracketing objective material within a faltering context of expressive textures:

"night after night, and sometimes in plain mid-day when the roses were bright and light turned on the wall its shape clearly there seemed to drop into this silence this indifference, this integrity, the thud of something falling.

"[A shell exploded. Twenty or thirty young men were blown up in France, among them Andrew Ramsay, whose death, mercifully, was instantaneous.]"[26]

The failure in preparation and interrelationship is symptomatic of the disparity between the novel's figurative language and the content of objective reality. In *To the Lighthouse*, as in *Esmond*, the war-sequence includes the data of external event. Yet the creative metaphors of *To the Lighthouse*, like the fantasy-motifs of *Vanity Fair* (where literal incident is deactivated or treated as symbol) cannot sustain the intrusion of objective reality; these metaphors express the characters' private experience— distorted reflections of objective event, rather than evocations of a different reality. The orientation is indicated at the beginning of the novel: "The wheelbarrow, the lawn-mower, the sound of poplar trees, leaves whitening before rain, rooks cawing, brooms knocking, dresses rustling—all these were so coloured and distinguished in his mind that he had already his private code, his secret language."[27]

In *Esmond* the motifs of idolatry, the celestial metaphors, even the image of a broken flower, preserve their traditional symbolisms; in *To the Lighthouse*, the novel's central emblem is idiosyncratically transformed into a sexual metaphor, which, however, is also a symbol of some unexpressed aetherial vision: "She saw the light again . . . as if it were stroking with its silver fingers some sealed vessel in her brain whose bursting would flood her with delight . . . and she felt, It is enough!"[28] This is a beautiful and convincing image of the private mysticism of a sensitive mind; but it has no symbolic tradition to reinforce its fusion with literal event.

So, too, when an allusive metaphor appears in *To the Lighthouse*, as in the recurrent, lyric reminiscence of Leda and the Swan, the traditional symbolism is inverted:

178

"James felt all her strength flaring up to be drunk and quenched by the beak of brass, the arid scimitar of the male, which smote mercilessly, again and again, demanding sympathy."²⁹ It is a classical refrain that expresses not the conventional parable—quiescent feminity encountering seminal masculine force—but an antithetic vision that is part of the heroine's personal, emotional response. This is the reverse of *Esmond's* method where, for example, the Horatian image of Fortune, reflecting the hero's fantasy of Rachel as an angel-fury, also preserves its ancient "luck"-significance, an intuition so familiar that it is accepted as an aspect of literal reality—"His cruel Goddess had shaken her wings and fled: and left him alone and friendless, but *virtute suâ*."³⁰ Because the image retains its conventional symbolism, it can be reinterpreted to express a more "realistic" content in a passage that is both a figurative comment on the hero's loss of Beatrix and a link (through the mention of Vigo) with the objective events of the military campaigns: "my bankrupt walks into Mr. Esmond's lodging . . . as jolly and careless as when they had sailed from Southampton ten years before for Vigo. . . . So it was that when Fortune shook her wings and left him, honest Tom cuddled himself up in his ragged virtue, and fell asleep."³¹ *Esmond's* procedure is not prescriptive, but the maintenance of imaginative decorum is essential. The convincing evocation of subjective response is a magnificent achievement, but if a novel's significance depends upon this evocation, the assimilation of a competing reality requires expressive continuities that can intermediate between them. When literal event is intruded upon fantasy-textures without becoming symbol and without such figurative intermediation, the objective reality is unconvincing and the expressive continuity is violated. It is the flaw in *Mrs. Dalloway's* episode of "insanity and suicide," a failure which Virginia Woolf herself suspected:

"The reviewers will say that it is disjointed because of the mad scenes not connecting with the Dalloway scenes. And I suppose there is some superficial glittery writing. But is it 'unreal'?"[32] This dissociation of texture and content is always a danger in the expressive novel. But the problem has various answers—it finds, for example, a brilliant solution in E. M. Forster's *A Passage to India*.

Forster, surveying the shadowy field of English fiction, saw two lucid apparitions—"Miss Austen with the figure of Emma by her side, and Thackeray holding up Esmond."[33] The coincidence is significant—it is a literary emblem of end and beginning. Both novels explore the ambiguous relationship between fact and fantasy and resolve the paradox in a conclusion that suggests imaginative loss as well as emotional gain; each is an exquisite realization of creative resources. Their content and emphasis inevitably differ, but the critical contrast is in narrative method. In *Emma*, fantasy is never explicit; translated into action and dialogue, it is simultaneous with dramatic fact, differentiated only by objective effect and discursive analysis. In *Esmond*, fantasy is realized in narrative textures; it diffuses around dramatic event, influenced, initiated, restricted by factual data but creating, within the limits of the objective correlative, its own expressive forms.

It is *Esmond's* figurative counterpoint that Forster develops so brilliantly in *A Passage to India*. Literal events —Aziz's meeting with Mrs. Moore, the visit to the caves, Mrs. Moore's death, Fielding's marriage—are objective reference points around which the major symbolisms— Mosque, Caves, Temple—develop their expressive parabolas. Mrs. Moore's death and Fielding's marriage are not dramatized—it is only their figurative radiance reflected in the intuitive responses of the actors that gives them meaning; the meeting with Aziz is realized expressively at the end of the novel. As in *Esmond*, this alternation between subject and object is interconnected by recurrent rhythms, recalling the symbolic musical phrase that Forster cited from *The Remembrance of Things Past*: "It is almost an actor, but not quite, and that 'not quite' means that its power has gone towards stitching Proust's book together from the inside, and towards the establishment of beauty and the ravishing of the reader's memory."[34] Rhythmic motifs persist and modulate throughout *A Passage to India*, from the delicate image of the wasp with its evocation of infinite love and the dramatic horseback scenes with their symbolism of union and severance to the major metaphors of earth, sun, water, stars—all preserving, as in *Esmond*, the conventional meanings that relate them to fundamental human intuitions and enable them to coexist and fuse with objective reality.

If this expressive counterpoint is like *Esmond's*, however, the formal principles of *A Passage to India* are of a different kind. Decisive structural elements of a purely classical order shape the rhythmic progressions. The critical instance is the trial-sequence at the center of the novel. It is a realistic episode, its imaginative dimension, as in the novels of the eighteenth century, mainly implicit in objective incident and dramatic behavior; and this integral, self-evident event provides a climax for the novel's classical triangular effect of rising and falling action.

In *Esmond*, by contrast, the central resonance develops in Addison's delusive evocations—a figurative episode which divides its objective correlatives, diffuses through the hero's antithetic experience at his mother's grave, and is not resolved until the expressive sequence of Hamilton's death. Again, in *A Passage to India*, the central climax is reinforced by a conclusive tripartite structure: the first section, an exploration of conventional rapprochements between the races, ends with the last of the entertainments that bring Indians and English together in a social context.

The second section begins a new plot-sequence—the visit to the caves—and develops into a drama of dissociation during the climactic trial. The final section, representing a tentative racial reunion, is separated from the preceding sequence by a definitive time-interval.

Esmond, too, has a triple plot-structure: Book I concerns the domestic incidents of the hero's childhood; Book II, his army career; Book III, his compulsive pursuit of Beatrix. But these literal divisions, like the novel's objective events, exist only as ineluctable aspects of reality in an expressive polyphony that transcends, without discrediting them. After the first book the hero never returns to his early life at Castlewood; but the prison-sequence that typifies this break with the past is only adumbrated, its development deferred to the beginning of Book II. The last words of Book I are characteristic of the confidence with which the writer disappoints conventional expectation and deflects the climax beyond the limits of literal form: "Esmond writ a hasty note on his table-book to my lord's man, bidding him get the horses for Mr. Atterbury, and ride with him, and send Esmond's own valise to the Gatehouse prison, whither he resolved to go and give himself up."[35] Similarly, the second book ends with Beatrix's engagement to Ashburnham, a peripheral incident that is only a prelude to the conquest of Hamilton; the concluding phrases barely indicate the quality of the event: "my young lord had made his offer, half-an-hour after Esmond went away that morning, and in the very room where the song lay yet on the harpsichord, which Esmond had writ, and they had sung together."[36]

It is not until Book III that Esmond's ensuing decision to quit the army and his new relationship to Beatrix are explored; and this beginning is both a conclusion to Book II and a preparation for the final sequences. *Esmond's* apparently conventional structure is, in fact, no more definitive than its unstressed literal events; the expressive development transforms it, dissolving predictable climaxes in a figurative relativity that dispenses with classical patterns. The subordination of literal divisions is a formal reflection of the novel's imaginative shape.

In *Esmond*, thematic continuities find their unity in the narrator's point of view, as in Forster's novel they are integrated by a formal structure. The perceptual arc, where past and present, proximity and distance intersect, correlates partial patterns of action and imagination, color and shadow, that recurrently "ravish the reader's memory." *Esmond's* point of view is reflected in the novel's eighteenth-century decorum—an exquisite idiomatic surface that mirrors an intelligence both typical and unique, of its time and timeless. The narrator's mind is an enigmatic medium; its archaic conventions, its conscious rhetoric, its traditional formulas make it difficult of access for modern readers. But it is against this background of neoclassical abstraction and analysis that the intuitive realizations and expressive intensities of this marvelously imagined personality achieve their emotional force and interpretive significance; in this lucid perceptual medium an imaginative *discordia concors* takes place—the cumulative insights become a single vision.

History is the objective aspect of *Esmond's* point of view, as dramatic event is the literal aspect of the narrative sequence. And history has two dimensions—a vertical axis of development in time, and a horizontal axis of correlation and synthesis. Along the temporal axis, there is social change and political evolution: powder succeeds wigs, Hanovers succeed Stuarts, and America outgrows the English system. On the horizontal axis, historical time is subsumed in perceptual relativity; the narrator's present is the reader's past, as today is both yesterday and part of tomorrow—as "Esmond's verses" have passed into an oblivion that repeats itself with each generation: "Have you never read them? They were thought pretty poems, and attributed by some to Mr. Prior."[37] In the same way, the narrator's symbolic distance telescopes literal event; in the expanded trajectory of his American perspective, historical data is contemporary with current experience and disparate actions intersect: "A little river, the Canihe, I think 'twas called (but this is writ away from books and Europe; and the only map the writer hath of these scenes of his youth, bears no mark of this little stream), divided our picquets from the enemy's."[38] Epic continuities, too, reinforce the historical synthesis; the reminiscence of the Trojan battlefield—"hac ibat Simois"—diminishes time to a perceptual point.

The narrator's mind is like an optic lens from which a luminous cone of vision diffuses over a field of fact and fantasy whose emanations are correlated and reabsorbed into the integral source. History, with its complementary aspects of extension and synthesis, provides the formal pattern for this perspective; the dual axis is reflected in the expressive synthesis of the narrator's point of view. If the perceptual cone is taken as a unifying image, it clarifies the artistic organization of the novel as a whole.

At the base of this expressive cone, corresponding to *Esmond's* dramatic sequence, is the development of the protagonist's imagination during the course of the novel. It is part of what the old man sees—the emotional progress of his earlier self, now subsumed in an inclusive identity. This development is an intermittent, cumulative process, exemplified in the hero's exploration of the human condition. Qualifying a kind of initial determinism—"as those tender twigs are bent the trees grow afterward"— are successive insights into the complexity of individuals —"How each has a story in a dispute, and a true one, too, and both are right, or wrong, as you will!" "There's pity and love, as well as envy, in the same heart and towards the same person." These insights modulate through images of emotional antithesis—"there are some moments when the tenderest women are cruel, and some triumphs which angels can't forego"—to a recognition of the compulsive drives that govern human behavior:

"There's some particular prize we all of us value, and that, every man of spirit, will venture his life for. With this it may be to achieve a great reputation for learning; with that, to be a man of fashion, and the admiration of the town; with another, to consummate a great work of art or poetry, and go to immortality that way; and with another, for a certain time of his life, the sole object and aim is a woman."[39]

This vision of compulsion, dominating the last part of the novel, is itself qualified as Esmond accepts Rachel's love—"thankful to have been endowed with a heart capable of feeling and knowing the immense beauty and value of the gift." It is this ability to respond to other realities that permits the individual to transcend the limitations of personal fantasy as childhood passes into maturity; the insight is suggested in the narrator's comment at the beginning of the novel: "I think no persons are more hypocritical, and have a more affected behaviour to one another, than the young. They deceive themselves and each other with artifices that do not impose upon men of the world; and so we get to understand truth better, and grow simpler as we grow older."[40]

This theme of intuitive simplification is sustained throughout the novel in the expressive textures that figure the counterpoint between fact and fantasy and is the key to the ultimate synthesis of objective and imaginative truth. It is the image projected by the writer's modulating style, the purpose of his changing, allusive evocations.

The novel's expressive correlations along this fictional field begin to fuse into the single cone of vision as the writer recurrently interprets narrative event *sub specie aeternitatis*—from the sardonic apostrophe, "Where are those jewels now that beamed under Cleopatra's forehead, or shone in the sockets of Helen?" to the neo-Horatian *memento mori*: "To be rich, to be famous? What do these profit a year hence . . . when you lie hidden away under ground, along with the idle titles engraven on your coffin?" These traditional annotations are amplified in the magnificent rhetoric of Hamilton's death-dirge—"The world was going to its business again, although dukes lay dead and ladies mourned for them; and kings, very likely, lost their chances."[41] It is a thematic synthesis of great and little, tragic and comic, existence and annihilation that is consummated in the novel's major epic insights—interrupting time, displacing identity, following the hero through an underworld of pre-conscious experience or an idyll of original innocence.

The fusion is completed in the narrator's memory. At the apex of the perceptual cone is the intersection of timelessness with time—an evocation of the intuitive unity of truth expressed in the transcendence of imagination over temporal sequence: "Our great thoughts, our great affections, the Truths of our life, never leave us. Surely, they cannot separate from our consciousness; shall follow it whithersoever that shall go; and are of their nature divine and immortal."[42] This intuition is the crux of the artistic vision, the focal point where realistic, fantastic, and imaginative textures are integrated into an expressive whole. Historical continuity and emotional development—the temporal aspects of the narrator's point of view—are intersected by the timeless metaphors of distance and equivalence; their cumulative correlation is the essence of the novel's form.

STYLE AND FORM IN *ESMOND*

Esmond's symbolic fusion of time and memory rises from the narrative's recurrent rhythms, is realized in the writer's expressive synthesis, and gives the novel its characteristic shape—the resolution of thematic motifs in a transcendent perception—the visual cone, its dramatic field in the modulation of the fictional sequence, its apex in the interpretive point of view. But this fusion is also an aspect of the novel's content; and in *Esmond* content is inseparable from style and form.

CHAPTER IX

STYLE AND CONTENT IN *ESMOND*

STYLE and content in Thackeray are so intimately related that each in a sense creates the other. Style is a source of content when Thackeray uses it to mirror his characters' emotions, the richly mimetic language evoking, through metaphor and allusion, intuitive realities that escape the discursive analysis and objective illustration of earlier novelists. Content determines style when the representation of a new kind of insight requires new expressive techniques—when Thackeray transposes diverse realities into a prose that seems to reflect simultaneously the multiple facets of subjective truth. In practice, these are only different aspects of a single style-content relationship; but the distinction illustrates the richness of Thackeray's narrative medium. The relevance of style to content, for example, is amply demonstrated in Thackeray's treatment of civilized sexuality; the effect of content on style is best exemplified in his development of the fictional "point of view."

i

Thackeray's representations of the complex interaction between sexuality and emotions differ both from the "realism" of the eighteenth century and from the "romanticism" of his own age. Eighteenth-century writers treated intimate relationships between men and women either as sentimental love-relationships, where sexuality was excluded, or as social relationships, where sex was comic or melodramatic. The dissociation between love and physical desire made sexual frankness easy—as it has, in a different way, for contemporary writers. Nineteenth-century romanticism, on the other hand, idealized all emotional relationships between men and women; sex became a dirty word.

Dickens and Tennyson, spokesmen of their age, consecrated the image of spiritual love. Thackeray accepted the mystic attribution—"The Maker has linked together the whole race of man with this chain of love," he wrote. "It joins heaven and earth together"[1]—but this is only a partial expression of his attitude. The difference between Thackeray's insight and the "romantic" interpretation is apparent in a passage from one of his letters: " ' 'Tis better to have loved & lost than never to have loved at all.' I said the same thing before I read it in Tennyson. . . . It gives the keenest tortures of jealousy and disappointed yearning to my dearest old mother (who's as beautiful now as ever) that she can't be all in all to me. . . . When I was a boy at Larkbeare, I thought her an Angel & worshipped her. I see but a woman now, O so tender so loving so cruel."[2] This is a kind of psychological speculation beyond the reach of writers contemporary with Thackeray; and the insight is developed in *Pendennis*, where the commentator remarks of the hero's resistance to maternal domination, "I have no doubt there is a sexual jealousy on the mother's part, and a secret pang."[3]

It is consonant with Thackeray's relativistic approach to the human condition that he can value the idealisms of romantic love while he insists on the realities of a passion that "sports with rich and poor, wicked and virtuous alike."[4] Civilization's sexual ambiguities are thematic in his novels—often, as in the familiar *Vanity Fair's* mermaid-sequence, expressed in pre-Freudian metaphor. It is not necessary to suppose that Thackeray always had sexual symbolisms in mind when he developed these metaphors, but the consistency with which he sustains their implications makes it clear that he was thoroughly in control of their cumulative significance. It is risky to attribute verbal naïveté to Thackeray. When, for example, he parodies historical analogies in a piece for *Punch*, his salacious image is certainly intentional: "it couples the brethren of Watt and Cobden with the dusky family of Pharaoh and Sesostris; it fuses Herodotus with Thomas Babington Macaulay; it intertwines the piston of the blond Anglo-Saxon steam-engine with the needle of the Abyssinian Cleopatra."[5] This is not the language of a writer whose suggestive imagery is involuntary or imprecise.

In *Henry Esmond*, Thackeray's sensitive control of language permits him to represent the intimate personal relationships of the Castlewood family on a series of expressive levels. The surface convention is thoroughly plausible: Esmond's chivalric devotion to Lady Castlewood; his romantic passion for her daughter; Rachel's self-denying love; Castlewood's promiscuity and repentance; Beatrix's role as "belle dame"—these tableaux, though traditional, are not improbable. But beneath the idealized attitudes, without discrediting their reality, Thackeray's language reflects less poetic motivations.[6] Psychological conflicts appear mainly in dramatic situations; sequences of metaphor suggest subtler, symbolic interrelationships.

In *Esmond's* early chapters, the Castlewoods' ingratiating domesticity, replacing the decadence of an older generation, seems idyllic, if precarious. It is when this conventional equilibrium is disrupted by the smallpox epidemic that the family's latent tensions become dynamic. In a decisive episode, Rachel's sexual jealousy shatters the decorum of her angelic behavior as she accuses Esmond of "polluting" the house with his adolescent flirtation. The sexual motif recurs when Lord Castlewood returns to his family after the epidemic. Greeting Esmond, he joins his wife for the first time since her illness, and ironic echoes of the marriage night (climbing the stairs, passing through the curtains) anticipate the carnal crisis occasioned by Rachel's physical misfortune—

> " 'What, Harry, boy!' my lord said, good-naturedly,
> '. . . The small-pox hasn't improved your beauty . . .'
> " 'Fie! how yellow you look,' . . . [Beatrix] said . . .
> "My Lord laughed again, in high good humour.
> " 'D— it!' he said, with one of his usual oaths, 'the little slut sees everything . . .'
> " 'And now for my lady,' said my lord, going up the stairs, and passing under the tapestry curtain that hung before the drawing-room door. Esmond remembered that noble figure. . . . Within the last few months he himself had grown from a boy to be a man, and with his figure, his thoughts had shot up, and grown manly."[7]

The preoccupation with physical appearance, the stigmata of disease, the epithet "little slut," the recognition of Esmond's recent maturity, place a cumulative emphasis on the sexual content of the situation which is reinforced in the sequel—"My lady's countenance . . . wore a sad and depressed look for many weeks after her lord's return."[8] If Esmond's thoughts have "shot up and grown manly," it is clear what he is thinking as he watches Lord Castlewood's ascent.

Esmond's condemnation of Castlewood's infidelity is implicit from the time of the Lord's return to his family; Castlewood conceals until the night before his death a jealousy of Rachel's pseudo-son that partly explains his own promiscuity—"when you was but a boy of fifteen I could hear you two together talking your poetry and your books till I was in such a rage that I was fit to strangle you."[9] The marital tension is increased by Lady Castlewood's habitually repressed but strenuous emotional life. Her passion, guilt, and penance find expression only after Castlewood's death, in the fervent phrases of her reconciliation with Esmond: "it is your birthday! But last year we did not drink it—no, no. My lord was cold, and my Harry was likely to die; and my brain was in a fever; and we had no wine. But now—now you are come again, bringing your sheaves with you."[10] "My lord was cold"; "we had no wine"; "bringing your sheaves"—the images briefly epitomize the sexual continuity. After the loss of her marital prerogative, Lady Castlewood turns to an idealized romance with her foster son, while her husband consoles himself with open infidelity, hiding his jealousy of the boy. Esmond, bewildered by adolescent desires, the obligations of loyalty, and a precocious awareness of the implications of adult behavior, fashions in defense a mask of decorum and devotion. In the course of the novel, however, this mask is intermittently belied by phrases that melt the narrator's eighteenth-century rhetoric, as when Esmond confesses to Rachel his passion for Beatrix—"returning again and again to the theme, pacing the room, tearing up the flowers on the table, twisting and breaking into bits the wax out of the stand-dish."[11]

Beatrix herself figures in the marital conflict as a capricious child, whose barbed remarks conceal her emotional reactions. The result of these early domestic tensions in the unresponsive, beautiful woman is suggested by the combination of yearning and defiance that characterizes her relationship with Esmond—"I think I have no heart; at least, I have never seen the man that could touch it; and had I found him, I would have followed him in rags."[12] Her opposing compulsions—to refuse and submit, to dominate and be possessed—are the outcome of early frustrations. Ultimately, Beatrix confesses to Esmond the distress that attended her mother's intense emotional involvements: "I would have had her all to myself; but she wouldn't. In my childhood, it was my father she loved. . . . And, then, it was Frank; and now, it is Heaven and the clergyman. How I would have loved her! From a child I used to be in a rage that she loved anybody but me."[13]

It is this resentment of her parents' neglect during a traumatic personal conflict that has produced the hostilities of Beatrix's maturity. The child's jealousy of the masculine rivals for her mother's love is expressed in the woman's emotional frigidity ("the old chill came over me, Henry, and the old fear of you"[14]); her desire for affection is reflected in fantasies of infinite submission, her defiance in images of sexual power ("You were ever too much of a slave to win my heart, even my Lord Duke could not command it"[15]); and her mother, who figures sometimes as an unattainable desire, is also a threatening competitor ("you never loved me, never, and were jealous of me from the time I sat on my father's knee."[16]). The sense of isolation, of unresolved conflicts and unrealized desires, is summed up in Beatrix's harsh and inclusive denunciation—"You are a hypocrite, too, Henry, with your grave airs and your glum face. We are all hypocrites. O dear me! We are all alone, alone, alone."[17]

Accompanying this dramatic sequence, one of the novel's subtler, ironic continuities is the expressive recurrence of the symbolic "red," the color of joy, violence, carnality. The motif enters with the old Viscountess—"all the red and white in all the toyshops of London could not make a beauty of her"—and the personification of this coquettish *"memento mori"* whose child succumbs to "tainted blood" (his life, the wits quipped, was "nothing but corruption") initiates a thematic imagery—"my Lady Viscountess . . . persisted in blooming up to the very midst of winter, painting roses on her cheeks long after their natural season".— that recurs at the death of the village girl whose flirtation with Esmond brings smallpox to Castlewood (her "buxom purple cheeks . . . had shared the fate of roses.")[18] The motif is intensified when Lord Castlewood returns after the epidemic. Chivalry is epitomized in his entrance—"My lord came riding over the bridge . . . clad in scarlet"—satirized in his approach—"looking handsome and red . . . like a beef-eater"—and perverted in Beatrix's comment on the ancestral Viscountess—"She saw the Dowager's paint t'other day, and asked her why she wore that red stuff." A memory-motif transforms the knightly figure into an image of ironic romance—" 'And now for my lady,' said my lord, going up the stairs. . . . Esmond remembered that noble figure handsomely arrayed in scarlet."[19] It is an anti-masque of consummation; the symbolic red, with its festive and sensual implications, recalls classical images of love and marriage (Ovid's "purpureus Amor," the red-gold robe of Hymen, Milton's "Celestial rosie red, Loves proper hue"). The chivalric-amorous irony is consummated as Lord Castlewood complains to Esmond of Rachel's subsequent hostility, the images evoking a semi-Spenserian allegory of knightly siege (attendant blushes, flags of passion, the amorous King) and rephrasing the motif of pollution that qualifies the Viscountess and orients the smallpox episode: "She keeps off from me as if I was a pestilence. By George! she was fond enough of her pestilence once. And when I came a-courting, you would see miss blush—blush red, by George! for joy. Why what do you think she said to me, Harry? She said herself, when I joked with her about her d—d smiling red cheeks: ' 'Tis as they do at Saint James's; I put up my red flag when my king comes.' "[20]

The color-motif is transposed to war-imagery when Esmond makes his first appearance in his "laced scarlet coat"; the Viscountess recognizes the emblem of cavalier fantasy: " 'Red,' says she, tossing up her old head, 'hath always been the colour worn by the Esmonds.' And so her ladyship wore it on her own cheeks very faithfully to the last."[21]

The hero's passion for Beatrix intersects the military violence when Esmond first sees her after the Vigo campaign—"the light falling indeed upon the scarlet ribbon which she wore"; and images of Beatrix—"white as snow in sunshine; except her cheeks, which were bright red, and her lips, which were of a still deeper crimson"—interact with references to her ominous avatar, the Viscountess—"Rouge Dragon"; "She's not so—so red as she's painted."[22] The dual themes of passion and violence are sustained in images of war with its "red battalions" and fused in Esmond's compulsive behavior—"he had no suit to play but the red one, and he played it."[23] Throughout the sequence, the emblem of the Viscountess persists, undergoing a gradual metamorphosis—"As the sky grows redder and redder towards sunset, so, in the decline of her years, the cheeks of my Lady Dowager blushed more deeply"; "those wrinkled old roses which Esmond had just been allowed to salute"—and it is this transformation of the Viscountess that is reflected in the final, ironic metamorphosis of Beatrix in a travestied Eden, as the Pretender becomes serpent, feeding on Eve's "roses," and Beatrix personifies factitious virginity—"The roses had shuddered out of her cheeks."[24]

This figurative continuity integrates *Esmond's* sexual insights with expressive sequences that impart a deeper meaning to the psychological drama. The pollution-motif of the smallpox episode is related through metaphors of chromatic red to the spiritual desiccation of the Castlewoods' chivalric heritage—personal neurosis becomes an emblem of the degeneration of an imaginative tradition; the satirical distortion of military glory, with its heroic conventions, is assimilated as the fusion of sexual and military violence becomes a thematic symbolism, the red ranks of battle, the red flags of passion, modulating to the spurious red of fading roses—an outworn romance fetish that links the chivalric futility of the old Viscountess with Beatrix's desultory travesty of original sin at the end of the novel.

From the interaction of figurative and dramatic sequences, *Esmond's* narrative style evolves an expressive content beyond the intellectual facilities of Victorian culture. The sexual significance of social behavior, the psychological implications of sexual response, are realized through a metaphorical intensification of dramatic episodes that suggests profounder figurative meanings in individual narrative instances. And, like translucent designs, each visible and coordinate with the first, the sequences of psychological and expressive insight are juxtaposed with an evocation of classical myth—a world of primitive intuition, of sadistic and masochistic impulses and metaphors of annihilation and rebirth, its imagery of nymphs, ogres, angels, gods, goddesses, submersion, and initiation reviving a traditional symbolism of intuitive experience and creating, in the neoclassical context of the narrator's eighteenth-century decorum, an iconography of the persistent subconscious.

ii

The second aspect of the expressive relationship—how content creates style—is remarkably illustrated in Thackeray's development of the "point of view." Like Henry James, Thackeray recorded a range of subjective experience that was rapidly becoming modern reality. This new content required new expressive techniques. In Thackeray's later novels, subjective insight gave rise to a narrative method that, conditioned by the same necessities, anticipated the characteristics of James' later work.

The fictional "point of view" admirably reflected the relativity of objective values to individual experience—a concept that was increasingly explored by Victorian writers.

196

A contemporary of Tennyson's wrote of *In Memoriam*, "the points where I am most affected are where a certain *retour sur soi-même* occurs"; Matthew Arnold saw perceptual relativity as a crucial dilemma—in *Empedocles on Etna*, we are "prisoners of our consciousness."[25] Novelists developed a similar interpretation; the rejection of ethical absolutes is a central theme in Eliot and Hardy.

Thackeray was thoroughly in sympathy with this new attitude. His letters reiterate the validity of the individual response: "What is sublime to one, appears odious or puerile to another; what is religion superstition—Nothing tastes alike, nothing sounds quite alike, looks quite alike to one person and another."[26] This personal conviction became in the later novels a principle of artistic composition. In *Esmond*, it determines the narrative method, and the hero's analysis of relative truth provides a paradigm for the novel's artistic procedure: "A word of kindness or acknowledgment, or a single glance of approbation, might have changed Esmond's opinion of the great man; and instead of a satire, which his pen cannot help writing, who knows but that the humble historian might have taken the other side of panegyrick?"[27] The novel's juxtaposition of conflicting realities is thematic, from the extended treatment of the Castlewoods' marriage to the miniatures of Swift and Bolingbroke; narrative event is constantly referred to personal viewpoint.

Progressively through his novels Thackeray came to write with a "point of view" in mind—the observers interchanging freely, except in *Esmond*, where the narrator is constant (although he contains many "selves" or perspectives). In most of the other novels, the voice that corresponds to Esmond's is that of the commentator—not Thackeray, but sometimes the narrating persona, sometimes a dramatic observer. In *Vanity Fair*, the commentary is entirely supplied by the author's persona, and the

STYLE AND CONTENT IN *ESMOND*

actors' own imaginative responses are only implied. In
later novels, the narrative darts in and out of the psyche
not only of characters but of whole social groups, always
interpreting fictional event through a characteristic viewpoint with its particular distortions and insights. Thackeray's method is amusingly illustrated by his response to
an attack on a passage in *The Newcomes*. He quotes the
novel's "fatal words" in his reply:

" 'When pigtails grew on the backs of British gentry, and
their wives wore cushions on their heads, over which they
tied their own hair, and disguised it with powder and
pomatum; when Ministers went in their stars and orders to
the House of Commons, and the orators of the Opposition
attacked nightly the noble lord in the blue riband; when
Mr. Washington was heading the American rebels with a
courage, it must be confessed, worthy of a better cause,—
there came to London, out of a northern country, Mr.,' &c."

Defending his practice against the American reviewer
who had construed the phrase "with a courage, it must be
confessed, worthy of a better cause" as an insult to Washington and the Union, Thackeray explains the intention
of the paragraph: "I fancy the old society with its hoops
and powder—Barré or Fox thundering at Lord North
asleep on the Treasury-bench—the news-readers at the
coffee-room talking over the paper, and owning that this
Mr. Washington, who was leading the rebels, was a very
courageous soldier, and worthy of a better cause than
fighting against King George. The images are at least
natural and pretty consecutive. 1776—the people of London in '76—the Lords and House of Commons in '76—
Lord North—Washington—what the people thought about
Washington,—I am thinking about '76."[28]

"I am thinking about '76." This must be a constant guide
in reading Thackeray: whose mind or minds are perceiving

the event? The passage quoted from *The Newcomes* illustrates a related phenomenon—the swift movement of Thackeray's style into and out of dramatic presentation as the point of view intensifies and fades away. In the quoted lines, the first clause belongs to the narrative observer, factual but flavored with quizzical metaphor: "When pigtails grew on the backs of British gentry." In the next clause, the details become more intimate, the historian's tone begins to efface itself; by the time we have arrived at "the orators of the Opposition [who] attacked nightly the noble lord in the blue riband," a dramatic scene has been evoked, and the phrase "when Mr. Washington was heading the American rebels with a courage, it must be confessed, worthy of a better cause," although it is not enclosed in quotation marks, is evidently a piece of direct discourse, echoing, as Thackeray points out, the clichés appropriate to the period.

The subtly varying intensity of characteristic viewpoints, the fluent transitions and the points of sudden focus prefigure the later fiction of Henry James. James' celebrated "point of view" is not the simple-minded formula that has hypnotized later novelists and critics; his narrative is never pedantically constricted by the realistic limitations of a single observer. Throughout *The Ambassadors*, the specificity of the individual viewpoint alters continually, moving towards and away from the objectively dramatic. Somerset Maugham said that James' method was "only a slight variation from the autobiographical form";[29] but this is inaccurate. Strether's "he" in *The Ambassadors* is very different from the "I" of *Robinson Crusoe* which never transcends the hero's immediate experience and observation. In reality, *The Ambassadors'* third person is strikingly like the third person of *Henry Esmond*. The narrative viewpoint provides a similar flexibility in the two novels; it combines the intensity of a personal, emo-

199

tional focus with allusive textures that reflects a wider perspective and develops a versatile prose that modulates effortlessly from subjective response to dramatic event.

In *The Ambassadors* an excellent instance is the scene of Strether's first private interview with Mme. de Vionnet:

> "She occupied, his hostess, in the Rue de Bellechasse, the first floor of an old house to which our visitors had had access from an old clean court . . . he found himself making out, as a background of the occupant, some glory, some prosperity of the First Empire, some Napoleonic glamour, some dim lustre of the great legend; elements clinging still to all the consular chairs and mythological brasses and sphinxes' heads . . . the world of Chateaubriand, of Madame de Staël, even of the young Lamartine, had left its stamp of harps and urns and torches . . . across the room, he made out the great *Revue*; but even that familiar face, conspicuous in Mrs. Newsome's parlours, scarce counted here as a modern note . . .
>
> "She was seated, near the fire, on a small stuffed and fringed chair, one of the few modern articles in the room . . . one of the windows, at a distance, stood open to the mildness and stillness, out of which, in the short pauses, came the faint sound, pleasant and homely, almost rustic, of a plash and a clatter of *sabots* from some coach-house on the other side of the court. Madame de Vionnet, while Strether sat there, wasn't to shift her posture by an inch. 'I don't think you seriously believe in what you're doing,' she said; 'but all the same, you know, I'm going to treat you quite as if I did.' "[30]

The quoted passage begins with an objective setting of the scene. The narrator's voice emerges, suggesting at first an historian's factual description. As the voice proceeds, objective reality is partially effaced, while Strether's personal responses are increasingly emphasized. Allusive images not only reveal Strether's private associations, but function symbolically to juxtapose traditions of the past with events of the present—the heroic attitudes of Napoleonic legend with the present emotional heroism of Mme. de Vionnet, the "harps and urns and torches" of neoclassical love allegory with her spuriously aetherialized love for Chad. This associative exploration of history and tradition intensifies the dramatic effect of the return to a narrative present at the mention of Mrs. Newsome and the *Revue*; while it emphasizes the tension between old and new that is implicit throughout the scene, sustaining the novel's thematic American-European dichotomy. The thematic motif leads at once to the dramatic image of Mme. de Vionnet, sitting on her "modern" chair; and thus to the objective presentation of dramatic dialogue. Clearly, in this sequence, Strether's consciousness is a multiple, diffuse interpretive medium; and the scene derives a part of its suggestive range from the varying narrative perspectives.

Compare, from *Henry Esmond*, the scene of Esmond's return to Castlewood after a university session. The smallpox epidemic that disordered his adolescence has initiated a domestic readjustment that is now a permanent way of life:

"The old room had been ornamented and beautified not a little to receive him. The flowers were in the window in a china vase; and there was a fine new counterpane on the bed . . .

"The children, who are always house tell-tales, soon made him acquainted with the little history of the house and family. Papa had been to London twice. Papa often went away now. . . . Many gentlemen came to stop with papa, and papa had gotten a new game from London, a

French game, called a billiard . . . papa did not care about them learning, and laughed when they were at their books; but mamma liked them to learn, and taught them: and I don't think papa is fond of mamma, said Miss Beatrix, with her great eyes. She had come quite close up to Harry Esmond . . .

" 'You shouldn't say that papa is not fond of mamma,' said the boy, at this confession. 'Mamma never said so; and mamma forbade you to say it, Miss Beatrix.'

" 'Twas this, no doubt, that accounted for the sadness in Lady Castlewood's eyes, and the plaintive vibrations of her voice. Who does not know of eyes, lighted by love once, where the flame shines no more?—of lamps extinguished, once properly trimmed and tended? Every man has such in his house. Such mementos make our splendidest chambers look blank and sad; such faces seen in a day cast a gloom upon our sunshine. So oaths mutually sworn, and invocations of Heaven, and priestly ceremonies, and fond belief, and love, so fond and faithful, that it never doubted but that it should live for ever, are all of no avail towards making love eternal: it dies, in spite of the banns and the priest; and I have often thought there should be a visitation of the sick for it; and a funeral service, and an extreme unction, and an *abi in pace*. It has its course, like all mortal things—its beginning, progress, and decay. It buds, and it blooms out into sunshine, and it withers and ends. Strephon and Chloe languish apart: join in a rapture: and presently you hear that Chloe is crying, and Strephon has broken his crook across her back. Can you mend it so as to show no marks of rupture? Not all the priests of Hymen, not all the incantations to the gods can make it whole!

"Waking up from dreams, books, and visions of College honours . . . he found himself instantly, on his return home, in the midst of this actual tragedy of life."[31]

202

Here, as in *The Ambassadors,* the sequence progresses from a factual setting of the scene, executed with an impersonal objectivity, to an evocation of the narrator's emotional experience that is concurrently a realization of broader, traditional perspectives. The intensification of the observer's subjective response is indicated, as at other points in *Esmond,* by a momentary transition to the first person ("I have often thought") imitating the usage of eighteenth-century memoirs—a convention that emphasizes the presence of the old narrator, his unifying imagination re-creating the experiences of his youth. The allusive range of the prose is amplified in the long reflective paragraph which has the same commentating, interpretive, and assimilative quality as the development of Strether's reminiscent associations in James' novel. Beginning with pastoral motifs (love lamps, ritual oaths, invocations), the language gradually comes to echo the phrases of Christian tradition as a play on "priest" transforms the classical flamen to a parish clerk, pastoral ceremonies become marriage banns, and the visitation of the sick and the "extreme unction" lead to the climactic *abi in pace* that is medieval rather than classical. The initial images of ineffectual union, recalling the futile hymeneal rites of Orpheus and Euridice that recur thematically in the novel, are rephrased in the concluding pastoral burlesque of Strephon and Chloe, its sexual implications extending from neoclassical parody to biblical allusion, the symbolic fruition of Aaron's rod mocking the discredited sterility of the Augustan Arcadia.

What is especially striking is how James and Thackeray agree in varying the specificity of the narrative point of view, and in combining subjective response with objective drama. Like the sequence in *The Ambassadors,* the passage from *Esmond* moves in several dimensions, exploring simultaneously the narrator's subjective experience and the configurations of external event. Both James and Thackeray prepare for the objective dramatic sequence by minimizing the personal interior vision: James by calling attention to the alien "Revue," Thackeray by modulating to a passage of direct discourse, still nominally "narrated," but hardly distinguishable from dramatic dialogue—"Papa had been to London twice. Papa often went away now." Immediately Thackeray introduces, in a grammatical transition so skillfully prepared that its effect is felt but not at first defined, the direct quotation of little Beatrix's painful phrase, "I don't think papa is fond of mama"— and the situation is momentarily on stage, only to give way to a profounder exploration of the narrator's interior consciousness as Esmond's allusive reminiscences parallel Strether's historical associations.

In developing this narrative method, Thackeray was doubtless responding to requirements that would in some way have influenced later writers. If reality was no longer an absolute—if accepted "truths" now needed the observer's subjective confirmation—then the only approach to reality lay in the representation of individual responses. Thackeray could not offer a single, definitive version of the Castlewood sequence as Jane Austen could of *Emma's* Box Hill picnic. His vivid perception of the dependence of evaluation on perspective, of the relationship between his characters' emotions and their divergent "realities," made it impossible for him to subsume the ambiguities of event in an objective dramatization.

For Thackeray, artistic truth could be achieved only through the synthesis of individual response; his technical solution was the shifting kaleidoscope of the "point of view" with its imaginative approximation of simultaneity. *Henry Esmond* is the first sustained example of this technique in the English novel—the pressure of content has produced a mutation in style.

iii

The anticipations raised by Thackeray's chronology have done him great disservice. In the novels of his time, vigorous action and vivid characters are expected to compensate for static form and conventional texture. But Thackeray was also a gifted parodist. Successful parody depends upon critical distortions of form and style; its patterns must develop unexpected and meaningful shapes, its textures precise and revealing detail. In *Vanity Fair*, the satirical novel of manners is crossed with the fashionable novel: in *Esmond*, epic with historical romance; in *The Newcomes*, fairy tale and fable with Quixotic burlesque. The analytic requirements of parody trained Thackeray to recognize convention and to treat it with intense awareness; as a result; his synthesis of the literary heritage is purposeful and controlled, his expressive formulations experimental and creative rather than traditional.

A number of later novelists have developed Thackeray's intricate textures and expressive forms instead of the broad and vigorous or spectacular effects of the Brontës, Dickens, and Trollope. Thackeray is better compared with Meredith, George Eliot and Henry James than with writers of his own time; his special gifts are richness of language, subtlety of implication, psychological acuity. His novels cannot be approached, for instance, like those of Dickens, through the vivid memories of childhood; he is too sophisticated, too equivocal a writer for children. Nor does he develop the powerful, primitive symbolisms which have recently had sympathetic recognition in Dickens.

The new dimension of experience registered in Thackeray's novels was to find its most sensitive theoretical formulation in Pater. "To the modern spirit nothing is, or can be rightly known, except relatively and under conditions," Pater wrote in his essay on Coleridge (*Appreciations,*

1889). "The moral world is ever in contact with the physical, and the relative spirit has invaded moral philosophy," he goes on—and one is reminded of the critic in *The North British Review* (1855-56) who remarked, "We are all of us disciples of that school of the new science of moral anatomy of which Mr. Thackeray is emphatically the master." Pater continues—"Hard and abstract moralities are yielding to a more exact estimate of the subtlety and complexity of our life. . . . Man is the most complex of the products of nature. Character merges into temperament: the nervous system refines itself into intellect"—and, after Pateresque refinements, he relates his insights to the conditions of art: "It is the truth of these relations that experience gives us . . . a world of fine gradations and subtly linked conditions. . . . To the intellect, the critical spirit, just these subtleties of effect are more precious than anything else. What is lost in precision of form is gained in intricacy of expression." In the development of these "subtleties of effect," in the expression of this unfamiliar, relativistic reality, Thackeray —whose *Henry Esmond* was, for Pater, "a perfect fiction" —finds for his peculiar gifts their characteristic consummation.

Indeed, Thackeray is closer to Proust than to Dickens, and *Henry Esmond* has more in common with *Remembrance of Things Past* than with *Bleak House*. Like Proust, Thackeray insists that truth is a subjective value, defined by personal criteria, that reality is a variable in relation to the content of experience. If appearance is not identical with reality since it conceals discordant facts, these are, themselves, only further perceptions; beneath them may lie more ultimate realities that, in turn, resemble appearance. Human beings are also angels and monsters, ideas are contingent on emotion, time is relative to content. In both writers, behavior is a function of circumstance. So, for Proust's Narrator, "our virtues" are "closely linked

in our minds with the actions . . . if we are suddenly
called upon to perform some action of a different order, it
takes us by surprise"; Esmond comments "Who hath not
found himself surprised into revenge, or action, or passion,
for good or evil; whereof the seeds lay within him, latent
and unsuspected?"[32] For Proust, character is modified by
"the optics of our social perspective," and Esmond remarks
"We have but to change the point of view, and the greatest
action looks mean; as we turn the perspective-glass, and a
giant appears a pigmy."[33] In *Henry Esmond*, as in *Remembrance of Things Past*, point of view is constantly altering
value. In both, greatness is an ambiguous quality, and
famous men are victims of the incongruous effects of perspective. *Esmond's* Addison, Steele, and Marlborough,
like Norpois, Elstir, and the Guermantes Duke in Proust,
illustrate, beneath their types of public and artistic splendor, the pettiness of private individuals. The Narrator's
poetic and venerable image of the great writer, Bergotte,
is juxtaposed with an incongruous reality—"a young common little thick-set peering person, with a red nose curled
like a snail-shell and a black tuft on his chin"; Esmond
compares the art of Jonathan Swift to the agony of a
mythical hero—"Prometheus I saw," he remembers, "with
a tipsy Irish servant parading before him . . . whilst his
master below was as yet haggling with the chairman."[34]
As the two novels' narrators explore reality, appearances
disintegrate; beneath them are not only the hidden mean-
nesses of men, but also their types of mystery and power.
The intimacy between Swann and Odette has sordid and
tender aspects not perceived in their social image; Castlewood and Rachel inflict petty injuries and make mutual
sacrifices behind the decorum of their noble station.
Esmond perceives, beneath the apparent tranquillity of
the Castlewoods' marriage, the wife's "latent scorns and
rebellions" as well as the resentment of her husband who

"crushes the outbreak of all these, drives them back like slaves into the dungeon and darkness"; so the Narrator discovers that "we find as many surprises as on visiting a house of plain exterior which inside is full of hidden treasures, torture-chambers, skeletons, when we discover the true lives of other people, the real beneath the apparent universe."[35]

Like Thackeray, Proust developed elaborate, evocative textures to suggest the real beneath the apparent universe. In *Remembrance of Things Past*, he adumbrates "what Jung has called archetypes, that is to say the root fictions of the human mind. . . . Behind the Duchesse de Guermantes stands the figure of Geneviève de Brabant; behind the three trees . . . a lovely body of flesh and blood (Daphne) . . . behind the sleeping Albertine . . . the myth of Proteus."[36] Similarly, Thackeray combines classic myths in deft mutations. The huntress Diana is now the leopard Beatrix, now the witchlike Viscountess, her godmother; Rachel reveals herself as Venus to Aeneas, Venus becomes Eurydice, Aeneas leaves her to search for Venus in her daughter; Diana is transformed to Circe, while in France Ulysses meets an English Ajax and Achilles; the Stuart Atridae forfeit their English loyalties as Medea murdered her husband's children. In Thackeray, as in Proust, these metaphors produce an interaction between past and present that is at once an identification and an intensification. When *Esmond* evokes types from epic and fable, a fusion takes place between past and present, primitive and civilized. Aeneas personifies Esmond's passions, and Esmond's suffering recreates the image of Aeneas. Rachel is partly revealed, partly distorted in the hero's angel-fantasy, Lord Castlewood is both caricatured and amplified as a gothic tyrant. Ultimately, in Thackeray as in Proust, allusive metaphors suffuse dramatic event with a multiple and simultaneous reality.

The further relativity of time, structuring the expanse of
Remembrance of Things Past, enters *Henry Esmond* as an
aspect of the old man's memories of youth. Thackeray's
time-magic, unlike Sterne's temporal trickery, is a Proustian exploration of emotion. When the aged Esmond
describes his prison interview with Rachel—"Her words
as she spoke struck the chords of all his memory, and the
whole of his boyhood and youth passed within him"—
there is a triple synthesis; the old man's realization, the
young man's pain, the child's distress project a sudden
diverse fusion of perception and response. So Proust
writes: "Sorrows of this sort come to us . . . from without;
. . . The cruel memory . . . is one of the rare witnesses to a
monstrous past."[37] Emotional duration measures Esmond's
imprisonment, as he comes to terms with suffering, reflecting the relativity of time to content: "At certain periods
of life we live years of emotion in a few weeks—and look
back on those times, as on great gaps between the old life
and the new." So in Proust, "The time which we have at
our disposal every day is elastic; the passions that we feel
expand it, those that we inspire contract it; and habit fills
up what remains."[38] And recurrently Thackeray, like
Proust, reminds the reader of the novel's plural time-
context. In the midst of rapid action, thematic phrases
reveal the narrator's superintending mind: "Now, at the
close of his life, as he sits and recalls in tranquillity"; "To
return from it to the writer's private affairs, which here, in
his old age, and at a distance, he narrates"; and as *Esmond*
progresses, these phrases provide a cumulative continuity
for major temporal insights at the novel's emotional
climaxes:

"It seemed to Esmond as if he lived years in that prison:
and was changed and aged when he came out of it. . . . You
do not know how much you suffer in those critical mal-

adies of the heart, until the disease is over and you look back on it afterwards. . . . He is old now who recalls you. Long ago he has forgiven and blest the soft hand that wounded him: but the mark is there, and the wound is cicatrized only—no time, tears, caresses, or repentance, can obliterate the scar."

"I invoke that beautiful spirit from the shades and love her still; or rather I should say such a past is always present to a man; such a passion once felt forms a part of his whole being, and cannot be separated from it; it becomes a portion of the man of to-day, just as any great faith or conviction, the discovery of poetry, the awakening of religion, ever afterward influence him; just as the wound I had at Blenheim, and of which I wear the scar, hath become part of my frame."[39]

Memory is the motif upon which *Esmond's* epic, fantastic, historical continuities depend. It is the crux of the narrator's unifying vision, the point of perception in which the novel's expressive parabolas intersect. The inexplicable intensities and lapses of recall with their hints of intuitive meaning are repeatedly rephrased—"he scarce seemed to see until she was gone; and then her image was impressed upon him, and remained for ever fixed upon his memory"; "strange how that scene, and the sound of that fountain remain fixed on the memory of a man who has beheld a hundred sights . . . of which he has kept no account"— and these recurrent partial harmonies culminate in the deep resonance of the final book: "We forget nothing. The memory sleeps, but wakens again; I often think how it shall be, when, after the last sleep of death, the *reveillée* shall arouse us for ever, and the past in one flash of self-consciousness rush back, like the soul, revivified."[40]

If these resemblances suggest Proust in Thackeray, does it follow that there is Thackeray in Proust? A definitive

210

answer would provide comparatively little insight into the vast synthesis of *Remembrance of Things Past,* though, through writers like George Eliot and Ruskin, Proust shared a tradition that Thackeray helped create.[41] Comparison should end, in such a case, with isolating against the exotic Proustian context, those aspects of Thackeray's art which are especially relevant to the later tradition. Once identified, these qualities can be recognized in their native habitat.

Among English novelists, writers like George Eliot, George Meredith, Ronald Firbank, E. M. Forster, and Virginia Woolf represent a tradition that derives many of its qualities from Thackeray; but this is not commonly a question of imitation or even of explicit interaction. If there are instances of primary Thackerayan derivation—if George Eliot "learnt from him how to place commentary in the novel"[42]—nevertheless the most significant effects of Thackeray's expressive experimentation are to be found in the dissemination of a way of writing that continues to evolve after the fact of the original mutation. And, in Thackeray's time, it was not *Henry Esmond* but *The Newcomes* that most influenced other writers. *The Newcomes* adapted *Esmond's* expressive modes to a less rigorous concept; Henry James classed it among the "large loose baggy monsters" of fiction[43]—and it was the looseness of *The Newcomes* that enabled writers like James to isolate and develop those aspects of its fictional resources that were most congenial to their abilities. *Esmond's* subtlety and precision were almost prohibitive—George Eliot called it "the most uncomfortable book you can imagine"[44]; it was the later and lesser novel that had the most immediate effect. The question of conventional "influence" should seldom be pressed, however; it is interesting only when it defines and clarifies, rather than factitiously "explaining" an artistic achievement.

This may be the case, for example, with Henry James.[45] James has been too much detached from the English background, as Thackeray has been too much identified with it. To appreciate James' inspired extension of Thackeray's experiments in "point of view," evocative texture, subjective epic, makes it clear that he, like other great writers, was partly developing the implications of his literary heritage. If Thackeray's vision is more various and acute, Henry James' is richer in emotional subtleties and perceptual ambiguities. When James wrote about Thackeray he recognized some of the essential qualities of his own medium—"that combined disposition to satire and to literary form which gives such 'body,' as they say of wine, to the manner of Thackeray"[46]—but these qualities are cultivated, in the later writer, for the expression of a special kind of insight that transforms them into a characteristic mode of his own. Far more than the characters in *Esmond,* Jamesian actors move in an interior world that reflects a contemporary dissociation between subject and object. *The Ambassadors* is, in some respects, an international version of *Esmond's* epic voyage through the history of a culture; James' Newsome family are not unrelated to Thackeray's Newcomes, the Jamesian hero's image of Mme. de Vionnet resembles *The Newcomes'* portrait of Madame de Florac, and Strether's frustrated romance, his ambivalent relationships with Miss Gostray and Mme. de Vionnet, recall the patterns of Rachel and Beatrix in *Esmond.* But Thackeray's insights are effectively modified by James' American antitheses, his continental ironies, his perceptual paradoxes. As the American reality is less congruous than *Esmond's* world with the European imaginative tradition, so James' observers must fabricate more tenuous continuities between their fantasy-experience and the sequence of objective events. Unlike Esmond, Strether is not aware of the lag between his perceptions and the patterns of event until the end of the novel. In *Henry Esmond*, dramatic incident initiates subjective associations; in *The Ambassadors*, subjective response is the initial context, the medium through which reality is approached. James does not introduce an older Strether, like Thackeray's narrator, to correlate fact with fantasy. In *Esmond*, Beatrix is simultaneously idealized and satirized and her objective presence is established before her allusive personifications are developed; in *The Ambassadors*, Strether must adumbrate an imaginative persona for Mme. de Vionnet before he can approach her at all.

Such processes of transmission, evincing both the fertility of the original and the scope of the mutation, would make a study of influence extremely interesting. Throughout James' critical writing, his admiration for Thackeray is in evidence, as when he comments on an ephemeral anthology "It really strikes us as sad that this is the best that English literature should be able to do for a genius who did so much for it."[47] In the novels, there are explicit as well as implicit instances of discipleship. *Roderick Hudson*, James' first major work, summons Thackeray to define the atmosphere of a crucial scene (Baden has the quality of "Madame de Cruchecassée in Thackeray's novel, but of a Madame de Cruchecassée mature and quasi-maternal"[48]). And, so late as *The Wings of the Dove*, James twice cites Thackeray to describe the heroine's impressions ("What she already knew moreover was full, to her vision . . . of Thackerayan character"; "the adored author of 'The Newcomes,' in fine, had been on the whole the note"[49]). The fictional synthesis of action and response, so characteristic of James and so essential to his development of the "point of view," is one of the matters in which he invokes Thackeray's precedent; "doing" and "feeling," he insists, are inseparable in the novel: "What a man thinks and what he feels are the history and the character of what he does. . . . If I have called the most general state of one's most exposed and assaulted figures the state of bewilderment—the condition for instance on which Thackeray so much insists in the interest of *his* exhibited careers . . . so it is rather witless to talk of merely getting rid of that displayed mode of reaction."[50]

This fundamental insight, essential to James' method of presentation, finds in Thackeray its unmistakable provenance. The professional debt was not dishonored—James was generous in his critical acknowledgments; his special enthusiasms found expression in analyses of his art, and Thackeray owes to him perhaps the most judicious praise he ever received. It was James who said: "There is no writer of whom one bears better being reminded, none from whom any chance quotation, to whom any chance allusion or reference, is more unfailingly delectable. Pick out something at hazard from Thackeray, and ten to one it is a prize."[51]

REFERENCES

Two important sources for bibliographical information on Thackeray deserve mention here. The best single bibliography of Thackeray's own publications is *A Thackeray Library*, Henry Sayre van Duzer, privately printed, New York, 1919. This, although describing a single collection, is remarkably complete, and there is as yet no competitive publication.

A good coverage of critical and bibliographical work on Thackeray is included in *Victorian Fiction: A Guide to Research*, ed. Lionel Stevenson, Harvard University Press, Cambridge, Mass., 1964. Mr. Stevenson has prepared the article on Thackeray, which covers the important work in the field, emphasizing a particularly full survey of the more recent studies.

An authoritative biography, published in two volumes, with reference notes that offer an additional source for critical material, is *Thackeray: The Uses of Adversity, The Age of Wisdom* (two volumes), Gordon N. Ray, McGraw-Hill, New York, 1955, 1958.

In the reference notes that follow, *Letters* stands for *The Letters and Private Papers of William Makepeace Thackeray*, ed. Gordon N. Ray, Harvard University Press, Cambridge, Mass., 1964. *Works* stands for *The Works of William Makepeace Thackeray* (The Biographical Edition), Harper & Brothers, New York, 1899-1903.

Chapter One

1. Geoffrey Tillotson, *Thackeray the Novelist*, Cambridge University Press, 1954, Appendix II, pp. 288f.
2. *Works*, VII, 556 ("The English Humourists of the Eighteenth Century").

Chapter Two

1. Harry Levin, "What Is Realism?" *Contexts of Criticism*, Harvard University Press, Cambridge, Mass., 1957, p. 71.
2. *Contributions to the Morning Chronicle*, ed. Gordon N. Ray, University of Illinois Press, Urbana, 1955, p. 71.
3. *Works*, XIII, 495.
4. *Ibid.*, p. 500.
5. *Works*, IV, 533.
6. *Letters*, I, 198.
7. *Works*, IV, 519-20.
8. *Ibid.*, p. 555 (The Greek phrase is not transliterated in the text cited.)
9. *Ibid.*, p. 531.
10. *Ibid.*, p. 635.
11. *Ibid.*, p. 666.
12. *Ibid.*, pp. 667-68.
13. *Works*, I, 9, ch. 2.
14. *Ibid.*, p. 637, ch. 64.
15. *Ibid.*, p. 459, ch. 47.
16. *Ibid.*, p. 519, ch. 53.
17. *Ibid.*, p. 639, ch. 65.
18. *Ibid.*, p. 407, ch. 41.
19. *Ibid.*, p. 9, ch. 2.
20. *Ibid.*, p. 10, ch. 2.
21. *Ibid.*, p. 632, ch. 64.
22. *Letters*, II, 309.
23. *Works*, I, 45, ch. 6.
24. *Ibid.*, p. 30, ch. 4.
25. *Ibid.*, p. 112, ch. 13.
26. *Ibid.*, p. 42, ch. 5.
27. *Ibid.*, p. 658, ch. 66.
28. *Ibid.*, p. 672, ch. 67.
29. *Ibid.*, p. 676, ch. 67.
30. *Ibid.*, Before the Curtain (prologue).

Chapter Three

1. William Congreve, *Incognita*, in *Shorter Novels, Jacobean and Restoration* (Everyman Series), J. M. Dent & Sons, London, II, 241.
2. Tobias Smollett, *The Adventures of Count Fathom*, The Navarre Society, Ltd., London, I, 3.
3. Horace Walpole, *The Castle of Otranto*, Chatto and Windus, London, 1926, pp. lv-lvi.
4. Henry James, "Anthony Trollope," *The Future of the Novel*, ed. Leon Edel, Vintage Books (paperback), New York, 1956, p. 248.
5. *Letters*, II, 772-73.
6. *Letters*, I, 228.
7. *Letters*, I, 224-25.
8. *Works*, V, 53.
9. *Works*, VI, 417.

10. Alexandre Dumas, *Oeuvres Complètes,* Michel Lévy-Frères, Paris, 1867. ("Othon l'Archer" is included in a volume entitled "Les Frères Corses.")

11. George Saintsbury, *A Consideration of Thackeray,* Oxford University Press, London, 1931, p. 137.

12. *Works,* III, 435. A misprint in the text is not reproduced here.

13. *Letters,* II, 179 (quoted in editor's footnote).

14. *Works,* III, 451.   15. *Ibid.,* p. 461.
16. *Ibid.,* p. 474.   17. *Ibid.,* p. 478.
18. *Ibid.,* pp. 465-66.   19. *Ibid.,* p. 473.
20. *Works,* IX, 108.   21. *Ibid.,* p. 109.
22. *Ibid.,* p. 130.   23. *Works,* I, 41, ch. 5.
24. *Ibid.,* p. 43, ch. 5.   25. *Ibid.,* p. 92, ch. 11.
26. *Ibid.,* p. 85, ch. 10.   27. *Ibid.,* p. 123, ch. 14.
28. *Ibid.,* p. 519, ch. 53.   29. *Ibid.,* p. 285, ch. 30.
30. *Ibid.,* p. 43, ch. 5.   31. *Ibid.,* p. 285, ch. 30.

32. *Ibid.,* p. 9, ch. 2; p. 20, ch. 3; p. 145, ch. 16 and p. 502, ch. 51 and p. 633, ch. 64; p. 269, ch. 29; p. 519, ch. 53; p. 229, ch. 25; p. 621, ch. 63; p. 432, ch. 44; p. 491, ch. 51; pp. 407-8, ch. 41.

33. *Ibid.,* p. 118, ch. 13; p. 204, ch. 22; (two following) p. 106, ch. 12; p. 422, ch. 43; p. 660, ch. 66; p. 447, ch. 46.

34. *Ibid.,* pp. 38, 35, 36, ch. 5; p. 219, ch. 24; p. 38, ch. 5.

35. *Ibid.,* p. 284, ch. 30.   36. *Ibid.,* p. 131, ch. 14.
37. *Ibid.,* p. 658, ch. 66.   38. *Letters,* II, 309.

39. *Letters,* II, 309; *Works,* I, 643, ch. 65; p. 658, ch. 66.

40. *Works,* I, 108, ch. 13; p. 271, ch. 29; p. 193, ch. 21; p. 228, ch. 25.

41. *Ibid.,* p. 85, ch. 10; p. 84, ch. 10; p. 92, ch. 11; p. 204, ch. 22; p. 145, ch. 16.

42. *Ibid.,* p. 484, ch. 50; p. 345, ch. 35; p. 246, ch. 26; p. 176, ch. 19; p. 293, ch. 31; p. 442, ch. 45; (two following) p. 509, ch. 52.

43. *Ibid.,* p. 421, ch. 43; p. 365, ch. 37.

44. *Ibid.,* p. 293, ch. 31.

45. *Ibid.,* p. 4, ch. 1; p. 162, ch. 18; p. 246, ch. 26; p. 205, ch. 22; (two following) p. 273, ch. 29.

46. *Ibid.,* p. 132, ch. 14; p. 358, ch. 37; p. 366, ch. 37; p. 521, ch. 53.

47. *Ibid.,* p. 481, ch. 50; p. 482, ch. 50; (two following) p. 485, ch. 50.

Chapter Four

1. Charlotte Brontë, *Jane Eyre* (preface to the second edition).
2. John Henry Cardinal Newman, *An Essay in Aid of a Grammar of Assent,* Longmans, Green and Co., New York, 1947, p. 204, ch. 8.
3. Harry Levin, "The Example of Cervantes," *Contexts of Criticism,* Harvard University Press, Cambridge, Mass., 1957, p. 86.

4. C. S. Lewis, *English Literature in the Sixteenth Century*, Clarendon Press, Oxford, 1954, p. 334.

5. John Dryden, "Preface to Sylvae," *Essays of John Dryden*, ed. W. P. Ker, The Clarendon Press, Oxford, 1900, I, 265.

6. Alexander Pope, "A Discourse on Pastoral Poetry," *The Poems of Alexander Pope* (The Twickenham Edition), General Editor, John Butt, Methuen & Co., Ltd., London and Yale University Press, New Haven, 1939-61, I, 32.

7. Richard Steele, "On Pastoral Poetry," *The Guardian*, No. 30.

8. Alexander Pope, "Windsor Forest," ll. 7-8; this and subsequent citations of Pope's poetry refer to the text of The Twickenham Edition, cited above.

9. Pope, *Moral Essays*, "Epistle IV: Of the Use of Riches," ll. 119-20; "Epistle II: Of the Characters of Women," ll. 7-10.

10. Samuel Johnson, "Milton," in *Works*, Talboys and Wheeler, and W. Pickering, London, 1825, VII, 119.

11. Johann Wolfgang von Goethe, *Wilhelm Meister's Apprenticeship and Travels*, in the translation by Thomas Carlyle, S. E. Cassino & Co., Boston, 1882, I, 58.

12. *Works*, VII, 530-31. (*The English Humourists of the Eighteenth Century*, "Prior, Gay, and Pope.")

13. *Works*, I, 362-64, ch. 37.   14. *Works*, II, 217, ch. 22.

15. *Ibid.*, p. 238, ch. 25.   16. *Ibid.*, p. 246, ch. 25.

17. *Ibid.*, p. 365, ch. 37.   18. *Ibid.*, p. 366, ch. 37.

19. *Ibid.*, p. 634, ch. 63.   20. *Ibid.*, p. 634, ch. 63.

21. *Works*, I, 624-25, ch. 64.

22. Charlotte Brontë, *Jane Eyre* (preface to the second edition).

23. Samuel Johnson, "Butler," *Works*, VII, 155-56.

24. Boileau, "Au Lecteur," Preface (1st printed 1674) to "Le Lutrin," *Oeuvres Complètes*, Garnier Frères, Paris, 1872, II, 405.

25. Dryden, "A Discourse Concerning the Original and Progress of Satire," *Essays*, II, 107-8.

26. Johnson, "Pope," *Works*, VIII, 332-33.

27. *Ibid.*, p. 339.

28. Pope, "Dunciad," Book II, ll. 421-26.

29. Johnson, "Pope," p. 339.

30. *Works*, V, 625-27 ("A Journey from Cornhill to Cairo"); *Works*, VI, 80 ("Wanderings of Our Fat Contributor," in "Contributions to Punch").

31. *Works*, VII, 555 (*The English Humourists*, "Prior, Gay, and Pope").

32. Johnson, "Pope," p. 339.

33. *Works*, VII, 555-56 (*The English Humourists*, "Prior, Gay, and Pope").

34. *Works*, VIII, 286, ch. 28.   35. *Ibid.*, p. 216, ch. 22.

36. Lucretius, *De Rerum Natura*, Book I, ll. 1-2. Citations from the Latin text refer to the Loeb Classical Library edition; the present author's free translations are indebted to William Ellery Leonard's version in The Modern Library (New York, 1950).

37. *Works*, VIII, 289, ch. 28.

38. Lucretius, Book I, ll. 84-99.

39. *Works*, VIII, 288, (three following) pp. 291-92, ch. 28.

40. *Ibid.*, p. 245, ch. 24.

41. *Ibid.*, p. 486, ch. 46.

42. *Ibid.*, p. 559, ch. 53.

43. *Works*, VI, 64 ("Wanderings of Our Fat Contributor," in "Contributions to Punch").

44. *Works*, VIII, pp. 284-85, ch. 28.

Chapter Five

1. Horace, *Ars Poetica*, ll. 92, 119, 311. (Citations to classical texts refer to the Loeb Classical Library edition.)

2. Longinus, *Peri Hupsos*, l. 3.

3. Jane Austen, *Emma* (*The Novels of Jane Austen*, Volume IV), ed. R. W. Chapman, The Clarendon Press, Oxford, 1923, pp. 66, 64-65, ch. 8; p. 112, ch. 13; p. 129, ch. 15.

4. *Ibid.*, p. 64, ch. 8.

5. *Ibid.*, p. 137, ch. 16.

6. Emily Brontë, *Wuthering Heights*, The Shakespeare Head Press, Oxford, 1931, p. 192, ch. 16; p. 135, ch. 11.

7. Samuel Richardson, *Clarissa*, The Shakespeare Head Press, Oxford, 1930, VIII, 56, 57, 55, 66, 57, Letter cxxxviii.

8. *Works*, I, 284, ch. 30.

9. Brontë, *Wuthering Heights*, p. 93, ch. 9.

10. *Works*, I, 111-12, ch. 13.

11. Quoted by Gordon N. Ray, *Thackeray: The Age of Wisdom*, McGraw-Hill, New York, 1958, p. 420.

12. Laurence Sterne, *The Life & Opinions of Tristram Shandy, Gentleman*, The Shakespeare Head Press, Oxford, 1926, Vol. I, p. 77, ch. 22, Bk. I.

13. Thomas Carlyle, *Sartor Resartus*, ed. Charles Frederick Harrold, Odyssey Press, New York, p. 73, Bk. I, ch. 11; pp. 219-20, Bk. III, ch. 3.

14. *Works*, I, 487, ch. 51.

15. *Ibid.*, p. 520, ch. 53; p. 480, ch. 50; p. 666, ch. 67.

16. *Ibid.*, p. 481, ch. 50.   17. *Ibid.*, p. 482, ch. 50.

18. *Ibid.*, p. 543, ch. 55.   19. *Ibid.*, p. 311, ch. 32.

20. Austen, *Emma*, p. 431, ch. 13.

21. *Works*, I, 103, ch. 12; p. 111, ch. 13; p. 658, ch. 66; p. 672, ch. 67.

22. George Eliot, *Middlemarch*, Houghton Mifflin, Boston and New York, 1908, I, pp. 280, 284, ch. 20; George Meredith, *The Egoist*, Charles Scribner's Sons, New York, 1910, p. 150, ch. 13; Thomas Hardy, *Tess of the D'Urbervilles*, Harper & Brothers, New York and London, 1928, p. 173, ch. 21.

23. *Works*, I, 30, ch. 4; p. 18, ch. 3; p. 103, ch. 12; p. 124, ch. 14.

24. John Bunyan, *The Pilgrim's Progress*, ed. James Blanton Wharey, The Clarendon Press, Oxford, 1928, p. 94.

25. C. S. Lewis, *The Allegory of Love*, Oxford University Press, London, 1936, p. 68.

26. *Works*, I, 481, ch. 50.

27. *Letters*, II, 309.

28. *Works*, I, 112, ch. 13.

29. *Letters*, II, 309 (2 July 1847 to Mrs. Carmichael-Smyth).

30. *Works*, I, 111, ch. 13.

31. *Ibid.*, p. 642, ch. 65.

32. Charlotte Brontë, *Jane Eyre* (preface to the second edition).

33. *Works*, II, 143, ch. 15.

34. *Letters*, II, 424 (3 September 1848 to Robert Bell).

35. *Works*, I, 480-85, ch. 50.

36. George Henry Lewes, article on Thackeray in the *Morning Chronicle*, March 6, 1848 (quoted in the footnote for Thackeray's letter to Lewes, 6 March 1848, in *Letters*, II, 353).

37. *Works*, I, 285, ch. 30; p. 432, ch. 44.

38. *Letters*, II, 423-24.

39. *Works*, VIII, 491, ch. 47.

40. *Works*, I, 285, ch. 30; p. 311, ch. 32.

41. *Ibid.*, p. 273, ch. 29; p. 519, ch. 53.

42. *Ibid.*, p. 123, ch. 14; p. 246, ch. 26; p. 624, ch. 64.

Chapter Six

1. *Letters*, I, 396.

2. Thomas Carlyle, "Biography," *Critical and Miscellaneous Essays*, Boston, 1855, p. 313.

3. John Dryden, "Dedication of the Aeneis," *Essays of John Dryden*, ed. W. P. Ker, The Clarendon Press, Oxford, 1954. Vol. II, p. 154.

4. *Ibid.*, p. 160.

5. *Ibid.*, pp. 199-200.

6. *Ibid.*, p. 220.

7. *Letters*, III, 402 (to James Hain Friswell, 2 December).

8. *Letters*, III, 304.

9. *Letters*, II, 424 (3 December 1848, to Robert Bell).

10. *Letters*, II, 282 (24 February, to Mark Lemon).

11. *The Quarterly Review*, LXXXIV, John Murray, London, December 1848, pp. 156-57, 162.

12. Archimede Marni, *Allegory in the French Heroic Poem*, Princeton University Press, 1936, p. 5.

13. Fénelon, *Les Aventures de Télémaque, Fils d'Ulysse*, Firmin Didot Frères, Fils et Cie., Paris, 1862, p. 440.

14. *Works*, II, 162, ch. 17.

15. *Ibid.*, p. 431, ch. 44.

16. *Works*, X, 148-50, ch. 18.

17. Samuel Johnson, "Milton," *Works*, London, 1825, VII, 125.

18. Johnson, "Rasselas," ch. 10, *Works*, I, 221.

19. Johnson, *Idler* No. 84, *Works*, IV, 398.

20. *Ibid.*, p. 399.

21. Johnson, "Rasselas," p. 222, ch. 10.

22. Johnson, "Milton," p. 134.

23. Johnson, "Rasselas," pp. 221-22, ch. 10.

24. Johnson, *Idler* No. 84, pp. 398-400.

25. Carlyle, "Biography," *Essays*, p. 312.

26. *Works*, VIII, 238, ch. 24.

27. Carlyle, *Sartor Resartus*, ed. Charles Frederick Harrold, Odyssey Press, New York, 1937, p. 220, Bk. III, ch. 3.

28. Carlyle, "On History Again," *Essays*, pp. 422-23.

29. *Works*, XII, 178 ("The Roundabout Papers").

30. *Works*, V, 81 ("The Paris Sketch Book").

31. Johnson, *Idler* No. 79, *Works*, IV, 383.

32. *Works*, V, 154-55 ("The Paris Sketch Book").

33. Jane Austen, *Northanger Abbey* (*The Novels of Jane Austen*, Volume V), ed. R. W. Chapman, The Clarendon Press, Oxford, 1923, pp. 37-38, ch. 5.

34. James Boswell, *Life of Johnson*, Oxford University Press (Oxford Standard Authors), p. 389 (Spring 1768); *Works*, VII, 489 ("The English Humourists of the Eighteenth Century").

35. Johnson, *Idler* No. 84, p. 399.

36. *Works*, VII, 630 ("The Four Georges").

37. Henry James, "The Art of Fiction," *The Future of the Novel*, ed. Edel, Vintage Books (paperback), New York, 1956, pp. 5 and 6.

38. *Works*, VIII, 237-38, ch. 24.

39. Henry James, "Novels and Novelists," *The Future of the Novel*, p. 248.

40. Thomas Babington Macaulay, *The History of England*, ed. Firth, Macmillan and Co., Ltd., London, 1913, I, 2.

41. Samuel C. Chew, "The Nineteenth Century and After," in *A Literary History of England*, ed. Baugh, Appleton-Century-Crofts, Inc., 1948, p. 1,214.

42. *Works*, XII, 379 (*Roundabout Papers*, "On a Peal of Bells").
43. *Letters*, I, 396.
44. Carlyle, "Biography," pp. 312-13.
45. *Christian Remembrancer* (April 1848), p. 405. Quoted by Kathleen Tillotson, *Novels of the Eighteen-Forties*, Oxford, 1954, p. 13.
46. *The Quarterly Review*, XCVII, June and September 1855, pp. 352, 356.
47. *The Edinburgh Review*, No. 224, October 1859, p. 442.
48. *Works*, VII, 33, ch. 3.
49. *Letters*, III, 175 (editor's footnote).
50. *The Dublin Review*, XXXIV, March and June 1853, p. 176.
51. *The Dublin University Magazine*, CCXLI, January 1853, p. 71.
52. Gordon N. Ray, *Thackeray: The Age of Wisdom*, McGraw-Hill, New York, 1958, p. 191.
53. *The North British Review*, XXIV, November-February 1855-1856, p. 201.
54. James Boswell, *Journal of a Tour to the Hebrides* (September 18), ed. R. W. Chapman, Oxford University Press, London, 1961 (first published 1924), p. 310.
55. *Letters*, III, 24.
56. *The History of Henry Esmond, Esq.*: A Colonel in the Service of Her Majesty Q. Anne. Written by Himself. Smith, Elder, & Company, London, 1852. Book III, ch. vii, p. 166. (Here and subsequently, the page citations for *Esmond* refer to the first edition from which the text is quoted. Book and chapter citations are given as a means of reference to other editions.)
57. Horace, *Ars Poetica*, ll. 120-27. Translations of classical passages are the present author's, unless otherwise indicated, although they derive substantially from accepted readings, especially those given in the Loeb Classical Library editions.
58. Book II, ch. xi, p. 201.
59. John Dryden, "Examen Poeticum," *Essays*, II, 13.
60. Book III, ch. viii, p. 189.
61. *Ars Poetica*, l. 240.
62. Horace, *Satires*, I, i, ll. 69-70 (*mutato nomine de te fabula narratur*—change the name and the story applies to you). Thackeray's running-heads for *Esmond* appear in the first edition; in later editions, they are commonly altered by an editor to suit the pagination or discarded altogether. Many of them add a suggestive emphasis to the allusive materials, but, since they are not essential to the reading of the text and are not available to most readers, they are not quoted in the rest of this discussion.
63. Book II, ch. xi, p. 196.
64. *Letters*, II, 815.

Chapter Seven

As in the preceding pages, references to *Henry Esmond* in this and the following chapters cite the first edition (see chapter six, note 62). Book and chapter citations are included to facilitate reference to other editions.

1. See, for instance, the opening pages of *The Newcomes*.
2. *Letters*, II, 263.
3. *Ibid.*, IV, 152.
4. Book I, ch. i, p. 33.
5. *Aeneid*, I, 329.
6. Book I, ch. i, p. 33.
7. *Aeneid*, I, 384.
8. Book I, ch. i, p. 33.
9. *Aeneid*, I, 378.
10. *Ibid.*, I, 402-4.
11. *Ibid.*, I, 327-28.
12. Book I, ch. i, pp. 33 and 35.
13. Book I, ch. i, p. 33.
14. *Aeneid*, I, 630.
15. Book I, ch. vii, p. 132.
16. Book I, ch. i, p. 38.
17. Book I, ch. iii, p. 61.
18. Book I, ch. iii, p. 63.
19. Book I, ch. iii, p. 70.
20. Book I, ch. ii, pp. 51-52.
21. Book I, ch. ii, p. 50.
22. Book I, ch. iii, p. 75.
23. Book I, ch. v, p. 116.
24. *Odyssey* I, 242-43 and 215-16; xv, 8; I, 444.
25. Book I, ch. vi, pp. 145-46.
26. Book I, ch. vi, p. 147.
27. Book I, ch. vii, p. 148.
28. *Satires*, XIV, 47-48.
29. Book I, ch. vii, p. 151.
30. Book I, ch. ix, p. 222.
31. Book I, ch. vii, p. 156.
32. Book I, ch. vii, p. 157; *Histories*, v, 9.
33. Book I, ch. vii, p. 176.
34. Book I, ch. vii, p. 177.
35. *Aeneid*, IV, 300.
36. *Ibid.*, ii, 590-93.
37. Book I, ch. viii, p. 182.
38. Book I, ch. ix, p. 197.
39. *Metamorphoses*, x, 6-7.
40. Book I, ch. xi, pp. 243, 246, and 247.
41. Book I, ch. xi, p. 243.
42. Book I, ch. xi, p. 247.
43. Book I, ch. xi, p. 250.
44. Book I, ch. ix, p. 201; *Metamorphoses*, I, 758.
45. Book I, ch. ix, p. 220; ch. x, p. 228.
46. Book I, ch. ix, p. 211.
47. Book I, ch. ix, p. 221.
48. Book I, ch. ix, pp. 221-22.
49. Book I, ch. x, p. 224.
50. Book I, ch. xii, pp. 280-81.
51. Book I, ch. xii, p. 265.
52. Book I, ch. xiv, p. 343; *Aeneid*, x, 907-8.
53. Book I, ch. xiv, p. 342.
54. Book I, ch. xi, p. 243; ch. xiii, p. 293; ch. xiv, pp. 314 and 343.
55. Book II, ch. i, pp. 3 and 10.
56. Book II, ch. i, p. 7; *Heroides*, VII, 127-28.
57. Book II, ch. i, pp. 7-8; *Aeneid*, IV, 552.
58. Book II, ch. i, p. 8; *Aeneid*, IV, 596.

59. *Paradise Lost*, VI, 312-13. (This and subsequent citations of *Paradise Lost* refer to the text of *The Poetical Works of John Milton*, ed. Helen Darbishire, Oxford, 1952.) Book II, ch. i, p. 9.
60. Book II, ch. i, p. 18; *Odes*, I, xxxiv, 14-16.
61. Book I, ch. ix, p. 199; *Odes*, I, i, 17-18.
62. Book II, ch. i, pp. 20-21.
63. Book II, ch. iii, p. 43.
64. Book II, ch. ii, p. 31.
65. *Iliad*, I, 231 and 158-60.
66. Book II, ch. iii, pp. 57-58; *Odyssey*, I, 32-34. (The Greek text is given as it appears in the first edition of *Esmond*.)
67. Book II, ch. i, p. 14.
68. Book II, ch. v, p. 84.
69. Book II, ch. vi, p. 98; *Iliad*, XI, 385.
70. Book II, ch. vi, p. 102.
71. Book II, ch. vi, p. 107; *Psalms* 126.
72. Book II, ch. i, p. 14; *Psalms* 126.
73. Book II, ch. vi, pp. 107-8.
74. Book II, ch. vi, pp. 108-9; *Odes*, III, xxx, 6.
75. *Odes*, I, xxviii, 3; Book III, ch. vi, p. 163.
76. *Eclogues*, x, 69.
77. Book I, ch. iii, p. 75; *Aeneid*, III, 163-64.
78. Book II, ch. vi, p. 109.
79. Book II, ch. vii, p. 117; *Paradise Lost*, VIII, 472-77.
80. *De Rerum Natura*, IV, 1173; *Paradise Lost*, IX, 1,029-32.
81. Book II, ch. vii, p. 124; *De Rerum*, IV, 1,089-90.
82. Book II, ch. vii, p. 133.
83. Book II, ch. ix, p. 155.
84. *Aeneid*, IX, 525-26.
85. Book II, ch. ix, p. 156; *Iliad*, XX, 98.
86. Book II, ch. ix, pp. 156-57.
87. Book II, ch. x, p. 170; "The battel of Audenard," anonymous poem, London, 1708.
88. *Paradise Lost*, IX, 1,036; Book II, ch. ix, pp. 166-67.
89. Book II, ch. ix, p. 167.
90. Book II, ch. x, p. 181.
91. Book II, ch. x, p. 179; *Epodes*, XIV, 13-14.
92. Book III, ch. ii, p. 33.
93. Book II, ch. xi, p. 192.
94. *Aeneid*, I, 294-95; Book II, ch. xi, p. 197.
95. Book II, ch. xi, pp. 195 and 197.
96. Book II, ch. xi, p. 198; *Georgics*, IV, 520-23; III, 163; IV, 176 ff.
97. Book II, ch. xi, pp. 198-99; *Ars Poetica*, l. 73; *De Laudibus Stilichonis*, III, xiii, 48-50.

98. Book II, ch. xi, p. 201.
99. Book II, ch. xi, p. 202; *Heroides*, I, 31-34.
100. *Odyssey*, XI, 154 and 87.
101. *Aeneid*, VI, 190 ff.
102. *Georgics*, IV, 221-22.
103. *Odyssey*, XI, 157-58; I, 161-62.
104. Book II, ch. xiii, pp. 245-47.
105. *Iliad*, III, 18-19.
106. Book II, ch. xiv, p. 250.
107. Book II, ch. xv, pp. 274-75.
108. Book II, ch. xv, p. 276.
109. *Aeneid*, VIII, 537; IX, 525-26; *Satires*, VIII, 108-112.
110. Book II, ch. xiv, p. 261.
111. Book II, ch. xv, p. 315.
112. *De Rerum Natura*, IV, 1135-40.
113. Book II, ch. xv, pp. 316-17.
114. Book III, ch. ii, p. 56.
115. Book III, ch. xiii, p. 321.
116. Book III, ch. i, p. 16; *Iliad*, IV, 44-47; XVIII, 288-90.
117. Book III, ch. i, p. 15.
118. Book III, ch. i, pp. 17-18.
119. Book III, ch. ii, pp. 58-59.
120. Book III, ch. ii, p. 60.
121. Book III, ch. iii, pp. 81-82.
122. Book III, ch. iii, p. 95.
123. Book III, ch. v, p. 132.
124. Book III, ch. v, p. 133.
125. Book III, ch. v, p. 136.
126. Book III, ch. iii, p. 87.
127. Book III, ch. iv, p. 109; Book I, ch. vii, p. 156.
128. Book III, ch. iv, pp. 105-6.
129. Book I, ch. xiv, p. 331.
130. Book II, ch. xv, p. 282.
131. Book III, ch. vi, p. 161.
132. Book III, ch. vi, pp. 154-55; *De Rerum Natura*, I, 32-37.
133. *Odes*, I, xxviii, 2-3; *Georgics*, IV, 86-87; Book III, ch. vi, pp. 162-63.
134. Book III, ch. vii, p. 166.
135. *Georgics*, II, 325-36.
136. Book III, ch. vii, pp. 176-77.
137. *Paradise Lost*, XII, 648-49.
138. Book III, ch. vii, p. 185 and ch. viii, p. 204.
139. Book III, ch. viii, p. 189.
140. Book III, ch. viii, p. 191.
141. *Odyssey*, IV, 247-49; Book III, ch. viii, p. 191.
142. Book III, ch. ix, p. 208.
143. Book III, ch. ix, p. 218.
144. Book III, ch. ix, p. 220.
145. Book III, ch. x, pp. 255-57 and ch. vi, p. 164.
146. Book III, ch. xi, p. 269.
147. *Paradise Lost*, IX, 901; Book III, ch. xiii, p. 305.

148. Book III, ch. xiii, p. 310.
149. *Paradise Lost*, IX, 892-93; Book III, ch. xiii, p. 316.
150. *Paradise Lost*, X, 517-18; Book III, ch. xiii, p. 316.
151. Book III, ch. vi, p. 152.
152. Book III, ch. vii, p. 172 and ch. ix, pp. 233-34 and ch. xiii, p. 320.
153. Book III, ch. viii, p. 203.
154. Book III, ch. vii, p. 177.
155. Book III, ch. xiii, p. 321.
156. *Eclogues*, X, 64-69; *Paradise Lost*, XII, 575-85.
157. Book III, ch. xiii, p. 323; *Paradise Lost*, IV, 492-501.
158. Book III, ch. xiii, p. 324.
159. Book III, ch. xiii, p. 324; *Georgics*, I, 508.
160. Book III, ch. xiii, p. 324; E. M. Forster, *Aspects of the Novel* (first published 1927), Harcourt, Brace & Co., p. 166.
161. [Edward Bulwer Lytton] Lord Lytton, *Devereux*, The Walter Scott Publishing Co., Ltd., London and New York, 1852, "Dedication," p. vii.
162. Book II, ch. iii, p. 48; *Satires*, VIII, 20.
163. Book I [prologue], p. 31.
164. Book III, ch. i, p. 23.
165. Book III, ch. ix, p. 234.
166. Book III, ch. ix, p. 228; *Satires*, VIII, 173-76.
167. Book III, ch. ix, p. 224.
168. Book III, ch. v, p. 131.
169. Virginia Woolf, *To the Lighthouse* (first published 1927), The Hogarth Press, London, 1955, pp. 61-62, I, 7.
170. E. M. Forster, *A Passage to India* (first published 1924), Harcourt, Brace and Company, New York, 1952, p. 162, ch. 17.
171. James Thomas Fields, *Yesterdays With Authors*, Houghton Mifflin and Company, Boston and New York, 1900, p. 17.

Chapter Eight

1. Book I, ch. ix, pp. 204 and 212-13.
2. Book II, ch. ii, p. 37 and ch. i, p. 9.
3. Book I, ch. xii, pp. 280-81; Book II, ch. vi, pp. 101, 108, and ch. vii, p. 133.
4. Book II, ch. x, p. 186.
5. Book III, ch. vi, p. 155.
6. Book II, ch. xiv, p. 259.
7. Book III, ch. i, p. 4; Book II, ch. xv, p. 290; Book III, ch. i, p. 10.
8. Book III, ch. vii, p. 164.
9. Book III, ch. v, p. 133.
10. Book III, ch. xiii, p. 320.

11. Book I, ch. xiv, p. 314.

12. Book I, ch. vi, p. 146; Book II, ch. ii, pp. 20-21 and ch. xiii, p. 247.

13. Book I, ch. xiii, p. 67.

14. Book III, ch. vii, p. 174.

15. Book III, ch. xiii, p. 304.

16. E. M. Forster, *Aspects of the Novel* (first published 1927), Harcourt, Brace & Co., New York, p. 239.

17. Book I, prologue, p. 28 and ch. v, p. 109; Book II, ch. vii, p. 131.

18. Book III, ch. vi, p. 152.   19. Book II, ch. vii, p. 128.

20. Book II, ch. viii, pp. 140-41.   21. Book III, ch. iv, p. 111.

22. Book II, ch. vi, p. 109.

23. Book I, ch. xii, p. 280; Book II, ch. ii, p. 27 and ch. ix, p. 167.

24. Book I, ch. xii, p. 276.

25. Book II, ch. i, p. 8 and ch. vi, p. 111.

26. Virginia Woolf, *To the Lighthouse* (first published 1927), The Hogarth Press, London, 1955, pp. 206-7, 11, 6.

27. *Ibid.*, pp. 9-10.   28. *Ibid.*, pp. 99-100.

29. *Ibid.*, p. 59.   30. Book II, ch. i, p. 18.

31. Book III, ch. iv, pp. 106-7.

32. Leonard Woolf, ed., *A Writer's Diary*, The Hogarth Press, London, 1953, pp. 52 and 69.

33. Forster, *Aspects of the Novel*, p. 18.

34. *Ibid.*, p. 239.   35. Book I, ch. xiv, p. 344.

36. Book II, ch. xv, pp. 318-19.   37. Book II, ch. x, p. 184.

38. Book III, ch. i, pp. 25-26.

39. Book I, ch. iii, p. 61 and ch. xii, p. 271; Book II, ch. v, p. 89; Book III, ch. x, p. 263 and ch. ii, p. 57.

40. Book III, ch. xiii, p. 321; Book I, ch. ix, p. 190.

41. Book II, ch. vii, p. 125 and ch. vi, pp. 108-9; Book III, ch. vi, p. 162.

42. Book III, ch. vi, pp. 152-53.

Chapter Nine

1. *Works*, v, 619 ("A Journey from Cornhill to the Grand Cairo").

2. *Letters*, III, 12-13.

3. *Works*, II, 230, ch. 24.

4. *Works*, IV, 533 (*Catherine*, ch. 1).

5. *Works*, VI, 83.

6. For Victorian reactions, see John E. Tilford, Jr., "The 'Unsavoury Plot' of 'Henry Esmond,'" in *Nineteenth-Century Fiction*, VI, 121-30.

7. Book I, ch. ix, pp. 193-94.
9. Book I, ch. xiv, p. 323.
11. Book II, ch. x, p. 186.
13. Book III, ch. iii, pp. 93-94.
15. Book III, ch. vii, p. 183.
17. Book III, ch. iii, p. 94.

8. Book I, ch. ix, p. 194.
10. Book II, ch. vi, pp. 107-8.
12. Book III, ch. vii, p. 182.
14. Book III, ch. iv, p. 113.
16. Book III, ch. x, p. 264.

18. Book I, ch. ii, pp. 50, 52, 53, and 53-54; ch. viii, p. 167; and ch. ix, p. 188.

19. Book I, ch. ix, pp. 192, (two following) 193, and 194.

20. For a discussion of classical red-symbolism, see N. G. McCrea, "Ovid's Use of Colour and of Colour Terms," in *Classical Studies in Honour of Henry Drisler*, Macmillan and Co., New York, 1894, pp. 180-94; *Paradise Lost*, VIII, 619; Book I, ch. xii, p. 269.

21. Book II, ch. iv, p. 72.

22. Book II, ch. vii, (two following) pp. 115, 129, and 121.

23. Book II, ch. xiv, p. 259; Book III, ch. i, p. 4.

24. Book II, ch. iii, p. 44 and ch. xv, pp. 301-2; Book III, ch. xiii, p. 316.

25. See Basil Willey, *More Nineteenth Century Studies*, Columbia University Press, New York, 1956, p. 101; Matthew Arnold, "Empedocles on Etna," Act II, 352.

26. *Letters*, III, 217.

27. Book II, ch. x, p. 173.

28. *Letters*, III, 320-21.

29. W. Somerset Maugham, *The Summing Up*, Doubleday, Doran & Company, Inc., New York, 1938, p. 217.

30. Henry James, *The Ambassadors*, Charles Scribner's Sons, New York, 1909, I, 243-47.

31. Book I, ch. xi, pp. 240-44.

32. Marcel Proust, *Remembrance of Things Past*, tr. Moncrieff, Random House, New York, 1934, I, 332; Book II, ch. i, p. 14.

33. Proust, I, 582; Book II, ch. x, pp. 173-74.

34. Proust, I, 417; Book III, ch. v, pp. 133-34.

35. Book I, ch. xi, p. 247; Proust, I, 562.

36. André Maurois, *Proust*, tr. Hopkins, Harper & Brothers, New York, 1950, p. 176.

37. Book II, ch. i, p. 9; Proust, I, 477.

38. Book II, ch. i, p. 20; Proust, I, 465.

39. Book I, ch. vii, pp. 154-55; Book II, ch. xiii, p. 230 and ch. i, pp. 19-20; Book III, ch. vi, p. 152.

40. Book I, ch. viii, p. 182 and ch. xiv, p. 315; Book III, ch. vii, p. 177.

41. For Proust's interest in Eliot and Ruskin see, for example, André Maurois, *Proust, passim*.

42. Geoffrey Tillotson, *Thackeray the Novelist*, Cambridge University Press, 1954, p. 192.

43. Henry James, *The Art of the Novel*, ed. Blackmuir, Charles Scribner's Sons, New York, 1947, p. 84 (preface to *The Tragic Muse*).

44. *The George Eliot Letters*, ed. Haight, Yale University Press, New Haven, 1954-1955, II, 67.

45. For a discussion of Thackeray's effect on James, see Geoffrey Tillotson, *Thackeray the Novelist*, Appendix II.

46. Henry James, "Anthony Trollope," *The Future of the Novel*, ed. Edel, Vintage Books (paperback), New York, 1956, p. 237.

47. *The Nation*, New York, 9 Feb. 1875, p. 376; quoted in Tillotson, p. 296.

48. Henry James, *Roderick Hudson*, Charles Scribner's Sons, New York, 1909, I, 139.

49. James, *The Wings of the Dove*, Charles Scribner's Sons, New York, 1909, I, Pt. IV, p. 167, ch. ii; p. 192, ch. iii.

50. James, *The Art of the Novel*, p. 66 (preface to *The Princess Casamassima*).

51. *The Nation*, New York, 9 Dec. 1875, p. 376; quoted by Tillotson, p. 24.

INDEX

Aaron's Rod (Lawrence), 164
Addison, Joseph, 104, 114, 116, 125, 137, 140, 151, 172, 173, 181
Adventures of Count Fathom, The (Smollett), 34
Aeneid (Virgil), 94, 116, 121-122, 124, 127, 132, 134, 139, 140, 143, 145, 147, 152
Agassiz, Louis, 89
Allegory in the French Heroic Poem (Marni), 96
Allegory of Love, The (Lewis), 85
Ambassadors, The (James), 199, 200, 203, 211, 213
Amelia (Fielding), 7
Andersen, Hans Christian, 120
"Anthony Trollope" (James), 36, 212
Appreciations (Pater), v, 205-206
Arcadia (Sannazaro), 53
Arnold, Matthew, 93; *Empedocles on Etna*, 197
Ars Poetica (Horace), 73, 74, 111-112, 114, 115, 143
"Art of Fiction, The" (James), 104
Art of the Novel, The (James, ed. Blackmuir), 211, 213-214
Aspects of the Novel (Forster), 161, 172, 181, 182
Austen, Jane, 3, 10, 12, 14, 36, 76, 77, 180; *Emma*, 74, 75, 81, 82, 180, 204; *Northanger Abbey*, 103

Barry Lyndon, The Luck of (Thackeray), 11, 22
"Battel of Audenard, The" (anon.), 141
"Biography" (Carlyle), 93, 101, 106
Bleak House (Dickens), 10, 80, 206
Boileau-Despreaux, Nicolas, *Le Lutrin*, 63, 64
Book of Snobs, The (Thackeray), 37, 39
Bossu, René Le, 94, 96
Boswell, James, 102, 109; *Journal of*

a Tour to the Hebrides, 109; *Life of Samuel Johnson*, 99, 101, 104
Brimley, George, 108
Brontë, Charlotte, 51, 61, 87, 89; *Jane Eyre*, 51, 61, 87
Brontë, Emily, *Wuthering Heights*, 76, 77, 83
Brontës, 4, 76, 205
Bulwer-Lytton. *See* Lytton
Bunyan, John, 96, 99, 108; *The Pilgrim's Progress*, 85, 86-87, 95, 96
Burney, Frances, 10
"Butler" (Johnson), 63
Butler, Samuel, *Hudibras*, 66
Byron, George Gordon (Noel) Byron, 6th baron, 14, 18, 65, 146

Carlyle, Thomas, 14, 54, 77-78, 93, 102, 109, 112, 125, 141, 146, 161; "Biography," 93, 101, 106; *Critical and Miscellaneous Essays*, 106; "On History," 102; "On History Again," 102; *Sartor Resartus*, 78, 79, 95, 99, 101
Castle of Otranto, The (Walpole), 9, 34, 35
Catherine (Thackeray), 10, 11, 19-22, 25, 26, 27, 31, 54, 57, 83, 189
Cervantes Saavedra, Miguel de, 9, 63, 94; *Don Quixote*, 94, 109, 116
Chaucer, Geoffrey, 33, 63
Chew, Samuel C., quoted, 105-106
Christian Remembrancer, 106-107
Clarissa (Richardson), 76-77
Classical Dictionary (Lemprière), 61
Claudian, 151; *De Laudibus Stilichonis*, 143
Coleridge, Samuel Taylor, 146, 205-206
Congreve, William, 35; *Incognita*, 34
Conrad, Joseph, 90
Consideration of Thackeray, A (Saintsbury), 37
Contexts of Criticism (Levin), 14, 52

Contributions to the Morning Chronicle (Thackeray, ed. Ray), 15

Cooper, James Fenimore, 10, 164

Critical and Miscellaneous Essays (Carlyle), 106

David, Jacques Louis, 36

Decline and Fall of the Roman Empire, History of the (Gibbon), 99, 102

"Dedication of the Aeneis" (Dryden), 93

Defoe, Daniel, 74, 103; *Robinson Crusoe*, 95, 199

De Laudibus Stilichonis (Claudian), 143

De Quincey, Thomas, 78

De Rerum Natura (Lucretius), 68, 139-140, 147, 153

Devereux (Lytton), 161

Dickens, Charles, 18, 102, 105, 189, 205, 206; *Bleak House*, 10, 80, 206; *Great Expectations*, 10, 101; *Oliver Twist*, 19, 101; *Pickwick Papers*, 10

"Discourse Concerning the Original and Progress of Satire, A" (Dryden), 64

"Discourse on Pastoral Poetry, A" (Pope), 53

Donne, John, 78, 79

Don Quixote (Cervantes), 94, 109, 116

Dryden, John, 33, 53, 93, 94, 107, 114; "Preface to Sylvae," 53; "Dedication of the Aeneis," 93; "Discourse Concerning the Original and Progress of Satire," 64; "Examen Poeticum," 114, 115; *MacFlecknoe*, 94

Dublin Review, 108

Dublin University Magazine, 108

Dumas, Alexandre (père), 37, 120; "Othon l'Archer," 35, 37

Dunciad, The (Pope), 65, 66, 94, 116

Eclogues (Virgil), 139, 160

Edgeworth, Maria, 10

Edinburgh Review, 107

Egoist, The (Meredith), 10, 33, 83, 165

Eliot, George, 3, 5, 88, 164, 205, 211; *Middlemarch*, 83, 104, 165

Emma (Austen), 74, 75, 81, 82, 149, 180, 205

Empedocles on Etna (Arnold), 197

"English Humourists of the Eighteenth Century, The" (Thackeray), 11, 54, 66, 70, 104

Epodes (Horace), 142

Ernest Maltravers (Lytton), 19

Essay in Aid of a Grammar of Assent, An (Newman), 51

Eugene Aram (Lytton), 18, 19

"Examen Poeticum" (Dryden), 114, 115

Faerie Queene, The (Spenser), 45, 49

Fénelon, François de Salignac de la Mothe, *Télémaque*, 96, 97, 98, 108

Fielding, Henry, 4, 5, 10, 12, 22, 24, 51, 73, 74, 76, 103, 164; *Amelia*, 7; *Jonathan Wild*, 11, 103; *Tom Jones*, 7, 94, 105, 116

Fields, James T., *Yesterdays with Authors*, 166

Firbank, Ronald, 86, 211

Flore et Zephyre (Thackeray), 58

Forster, E. M., 3, 4, 9, 181, 183, 211; *Aspects of the Novel*, 161, 172, 181, 182; *A Passage to India*, 165, 180, 181

"Four Georges, The" (Thackeray), 104

Fraser's Magazine, 87, 120

Gay, John, 54

Georgics (Virgil), 143, 145, 151, 153, 154

Gibbon, Edward, 102; *Decline and Fall of the Roman Empire*, 99, 102

Goethe, Johann Wolfgang von, *Wilhelm Meister's Apprenticeship*, 54

INDEX

Gore, Catherine, 10, 16, 18, 19, 20, 23, 28
Grammar of Assent, An Essay in Aid of a (Newman), 51
Great Expectations (Dickens), 10, 101
Guardian, 53-54

Hardy, Thomas, 76; *Tess of the D'Urbervilles*, 83
Heartbreak House (Shaw), 95
Henry Esmond, The History of (Thackeray), v, 6, 7, 8, 9, 12, 35, 62, 63, 66, 72, 88, 91, 92, 93, 94, 95, 98, 99, 105, 106, 107, 108, 109, 110-117, 118ff.
Heroides (Ovid), 134, 144
Histories (Tacitus), 128
"History, On" (Carlyle), 102
"History Again, On" (Carlyle), 102
History of England from the Accession of James II (Macaulay), 105
Homer, 96, 105, 116, 131, 141, 146, 149, 150, 151, 156, 165; *Iliad*, 115, 136, 137, 141, 144, 146, 149, 150; *Odyssey*, 61, 62, 69, 94, 95, 98, 124-125, 136, 141, 144, 145, 156
Horace, 116, 131, 134, 137, 139, 153, 172; *Ars Poetica*, 73, 74, 111-112, 114, 115, 143; *Epodes*, 142; *Odes*, 139, 153, 154
Hudibras (Butler), 66
Hugo, Victor, *Notre Dame de Paris*, 36
Hume, David, 102
Hurd, Richard, 34, 35

Idea of a University, The (Newman), v
Idler (Johnson), 100, 103, 104
Idylls of the King (Tennyson), 120
Iliad (Homer), 115, 136, 137, 141, 144, 146, 149, 150
Incognita (Congreve), 34
In Memoriam (Tennyson), 118
Ivanhoe (Scott), 10, 37, 39, 43, 45, 46, 50, 105

James, Henry, v, 3, 4, 9, 12, 36, 103, 105, 108, 196, 203-204, 205, 211, 213, 214; *The Ambassadors*, 199, 200, 203, 211, 213; "Anthony Trollope," 36, 212; "Art of Fiction," 104; *Art of the Novel* (ed. Blackmur), 211; "Novels and Novelists," 105; *Roderick Hudson*, 213; *The Wings of the Dove*, 213
Jane Eyre (Brontë), 51, 61, 87
Johnson, Samuel, 54, 64, 65, 66, 93, 104, 109; "Butler," 63; *Idler*, 100, 103, 104; "Milton," 99, 100; "Pope," 64, 65, 66; "Savage," 100; *Rasselas*, 95, 99-100
Jonathan Wild, The Life of Mr. (Fielding), 11, 103
Journal of a Tour to the Hebrides, The (Boswell), 109
"Journey from Cornhill to Cairo, A" (Thackeray), 65-66, 189
Joyce, James, 5, 7, 24, 76, 108; *Ulysses*, 7, 33, 94, 116
Juvenal, 115, 116, 125, 162, 163; *Satires*, 126, 147, 162, 163

Kafka, Franz, 90
Kingsley, Charles, 105

Lamb, Charles, 78
Lawrence, D. H., *Aaron's Rod*, 164
Legend of the Rhine, A (Thackeray), 10, 37-39, 41, 42, 43, 50, 58
Lemprière, John, *Classical Dictionary*, 61
Letters and Private Papers of William Makepeace Thackeray (ed. Ray), 19, 28, 36, 38, 46, 47, 85, 86, 87, 89, 93, 94, 96, 106, 110, 117, 120, 189, 197, 198, 215
Lewes, George Henry, on Thackeray, 88, 108
Lewis, C. S., 85; *The Allegory of Love*, 85; *English Literature in the Sixteenth Century*, 53
Lewis, Matthew Gregory, 10
Levin, Harry, *Contexts of Criticism*, 14, 52
Life of Samuel Johnson, The (Boswell), 99, 101, 104

233

Locke, John, 78
Longinus, *Peri Hupsos*, 74
Lucretius, 68-69, 116, 139, 140, 147, 153; *De Rerum Natura*, 68, 139-140, 153
Lutrin, Le (Boileau), 63, 64
Lycidas (Milton), v
Lytton, Edward Bulwer-Lytton, 1st baron, 10, 18, 19, 20, 21, 22, 23, 26, 50, 105, 163, 164, 166; *Devereux*, 161; *Eugene Aram*, 18, 19; *Ernest Maltravers*, 19

Macaulay, Thomas Babington Macaulay, 1st baron, 102, 103, 161; *History of England*, 105
MacFlecknoe (Dryden), 94
Marni, Archimede, *Allegory in the French Heroic Poem*, 96
Maugham, W. Somerset, *The Summing Up*, 199
Maurois, André, Proust, 208
Meredith, George, 3, 9, 86, 205, 211; *The Egoist*, 10, 33, 83, 165
Metamorphoses (Ovid), 128, 129
Middlemarch (Eliot), 83, 104, 165
Milton, John, 78, 79, 93, 95, 111, 116, 136, 141, 149, 151, 160, 165, 194; *Lycidas*, v; *Paradise Lost*, 26, 66, 100, 134, 139, 140, 141, 149, 155, 158, 159, 160, 194
"Milton" (Johnson), 99, 100
Moral Essays (Pope), 54
Morning Chronicle, 88; Thackeray in, 15
Mrs. Dalloway (Woolf), 179

Nabokov, Vladimir, 5, 22, 105
Newcomes, The (Thackeray), 12, 52, 63, 67-72, 89, 94, 101, 105, 198, 199, 205, 211, 212
Newman, John Henry, v; *Grammar of Assent*, 51
Notre Dame de Paris (Hugo), 36
"Novels and Novelists" (James), 105
Northanger Abbey (Austen), 103
North British Review, 109, 206

Odes (Horace), 139, 153-154

Odyssey (Homer), 61, 62, 69, 94, 95, 98, 124, 134, 136, 144, 145, 156
Oliver Twist (Dickens), 19, 101
Orlando (Woolf), 164
"Othon l'Archer" (Dumas), 35, 37
Ovid, 128, 129, 134, 144, 194; *Heroides*, 134, 144; *Metamorphoses*, 128, 129

Paradise Lost (Milton), 26, 66, 100, 134, 139, 140, 141, 149, 155, 158, 159, 160, 194
Paris Sketch Book, The (Thackeray), 36, 103
Passage to India, A (Forster), 165, 180, 181
"Pastoral Poetry, On" (Steele), 53-54
Pater, Walter, v; *Appreciations*, v, 205-206; "Style," v
Pendennis, The History of (Thackeray), 12, 51, 52, 55, 57-60, 98, 189
Peri Hupsos (Longinus), 74
Perrault, Charles, 120
Pickwick Papers (Dickens), 10
Pilgrim's Progress, The (Bunyan), 85, 86-87, 95, 96
Pope, Alexander, 11, 53, 54; "Discourse on Pastoral Poetry," 53; *Dunciad*, 65, 66, 94, 116; *Moral Essays*, 54; *Rape of the Lock*, 64, 66; "Windsor Forest," 54
"Pope" (Johnson), 64, 65, 66
"Preface to Sylvae," (Dryden), 53
"Princess, The" (Tennyson), 120
Professor, The (Thackeray), 10, 16, 17, 20, 28
Prudentius, *Psychomachia*, 85, 96
Proust, Marcel, 5, 7, 73, 164, 165, 206, 208, 210; *Remembrance of Things Past*, 181, 206, 207, 208, 209, 211
Proust (Maurois), 208
Psalms, 138
Psychomachia (Prudentius), 85, 96

Quarterly Review, 96, 107

Rabelais, François, 14

Radcliffe, Ann, 10
Rape of the Lock, The (Pope), 64, 66
Rasselas (Johnson), 95, 99-100
Ray, Gordon N., *Thackeray*, 77-78, 108, 215
Rebecca and Rowena (Thackeray), 10, 37, 39-41, 43, 46, 50
Remembrance of Things Past (Proust), 8, 181, 206, 207, 208
Richardson, Samuel, 5, 9, 14, 16, 74, 104; *Clarissa*, 76-77
Robinson Crusoe (Defoe), 95, 199
Roderick Hudson (James), 213
Roderick Random (Smollett), 10
Romola (Eliot), 164
"Roundabout Papers, The" (Thackeray), 102-103, 106

Saintsbury, George, *A Consideration of Thackeray*, 37
Sannazaro, Jacopo, *Arcadia*, 53
Sartor Resartus (Carlyle), 78, 79, 95, 99, 101
Satires (Juvenal), 126, 147, 162, 163
"Savage," (Johnson), 100
Scott, Sir Walter, 3, 9, 10, 12, 35, 36, 102, 105, 106, 120, 164; *Ivanhoe*, 10, 37, 39, 43, 45, 46, 50, 105; *Waverley Novels*, 105
Second Funeral of Napoleon, The (Thackeray), 10
Shakespeare, William, 63
Shaw, George Bernard, *Heartbreak House*, 95
Sidney, Sir Philip, 86
Smollett, Tobias, 3-5, 74, 76, 102; *Adventures of Count Fathom*, 34; *Roderick Random*, 10
Spectator, The, 108
Spenser, Edmund, 15, 46, 86, 89, 94, 96; *The Faerie Queene*, 45, 49
Steele, Sir Richard, 53-54, 125, 173; "On Pastoral Poetry," 53-54
Sterne, Laurence, 10, 14, 16, 78, 79, 125; *Tristram Shandy*, 79
Stevenson, Lionel (ed.), *Victorian Fiction: A Guide to Research*, 215
"Style" (Pater), v

Summing Up, The (Maugham), 199
Swift, Jonathan, 125, 151; *Tale of a Tub*, 22, 78
Synge, John Millington, 108

Tacitus, 125; *Histories*, 128
Tale of a Tub, A (Swift), 22, 78
Tale of Two Cities, A (Dickens), 164
Télémaque (Fénelon), 96, 97, 98, 108
Tennyson, Alfred, 1st baron, 125, 189; *Idylls of the King*, 120; *In Memoriam*, 118, reviewed, 197; "The Princess," 120; "Ulysses," 111
Tess of the D'Urbervilles (Hardy), 83
Thackeray, William Makepeace, v, vi, 3, 4-13, 14-19, 22, 33, 35-37, 51-53, 65-67, 73, 74, 92-109, 188-190, 196-199, 205-214; *Barry Lyndon*, 11, 22; *Book of Snobs*, 37, 39; *Catherine*, 10, 11, 19-22, 25, 26, 27, 31, 54, 57, 83, 189; *Contributions to the Morning Chronicle* (ed. Ray), 15; "English Humourists of the Eighteenth Century," 11, 54, 66, 70, 104; "Four Georges," 104; *Henry Esmond*, v, 6, 7, 8, 9, 12, 35, 62, 63, 66, 72, 88, 91, 92, 93, 94, 95, 98, 99, 105, 106, 107, 108, 109, 110-117, 118 ff.; "Journey from Cornhill to Cairo," 65-66, 189; *Legend of the Rhine*, 10, 37-39, 41, 42, 43, 50, 83; *Letters*—see *Letters and Private Papers of William Makepeace Thackeray*; *Newcomes*, 12, 52, 63, 67-72, 89, 94, 101, 105, 198, 199, 205, 211, 212; *Paris Sketch Book*, 36, 103; *Pendennis*, 12, 51, 52, 55, 57-60, 98, 189; *Professor*, 10, 16, 17, 20, 28; *Rebecca and Rowena*, 10, 37, 39-41, 43, 46, 50; "Roundabout Papers," 102-103, 106; *Second Funeral of Napoleon*, 10; *Vanity Fair*, 5, 6, 7, 8, 9, 10, 11, 12, 13, 14, 15, 16, 22, 23-32, 33,

36, 37, 40, 41, 42-50, 51, 52, 53,
54, 55-57, 58, 59, 60-62, 66, 70,
72, 73, 77-91, 95, 96, 108, 109,
115, 167, 172, 175, 176, 178, 189,
197, 205; *Virginians*, 98, 107;
"Wanderings of Our Fat Contributor," 66
Thackeray (Ray), 77-78, 108, 215
Thackeray Library, A (van Duzer),
215
Thackeray the Novelist (Tillotson),
5, 211
Theocritus, 53
Tillotson, Geoffrey, *Thackeray the
Novelist*, 5, 211
Times, The (London), 88, 108
To the Lighthouse (Woolf), 86,
164-165, 177-179
Tolstoy, Leo, 164
Tom Jones, The History of (Fielding), 7, 94, 105, 116
*Tristram Shandy, The Life and
Opinions of* (Sterne), 79
Trollope, Anthony, 3, 205

Ulysses (Joyce), 8, 33, 94, 116, 164,
165
"Ulysses" (Tennyson), 111

van Duzer, Henry Sayre, *A Thackeray Library*, 215
Vanity Fair (Thackeray), 5, 6, 7, 8,
9, 10, 11, 12, 13, 14, 15, 16, 22,
23-32, 33, 36, 37, 40, 41, 42-50,
51, 52, 53, 54, 55-57, 58, 59, 60-62,
66, 70, 72, 73, 77-91, 95, 96, 108,

109, 115, 167, 172, 175, 176, 178,
189, 197, 205
Victorian Fiction: A Guide to Research (ed. Stevenson), 215
Virgil, 96, 116, 132, 140, 149, 153,
154, 160; *Aeneid*, 94, 116, 121-122,
124, 127, 128, 132, 134, 139, 140,
143, 145, 147, 152; *Eclogues*, 139,
160; *Georgics*, 143, 145, 151, 153,
154, 160
Virginians, The (Thackeray), 98,
107
Voltaire, 164

Walpole, Horace, *The Castle of
Otranto*, 9, 34, 35
"Wanderings of Our Fat Contributor" (Thackeray), 106
Waverley Novels (Scott), 105
Wilhelm Meister's Apprenticeship
(Goethe), 54
"Windsor Forest" (Pope), 54
Wings of the Dove, The (James),
213
Woolf, Virginia, 3, 76, 86, 164, 211;
Mrs. Dalloway, 179; *To the Lighthouse*, 86, 164-165, 177-179; *A
Writer's Diary* (ed. Leonard
Woolf), 180
Wordsworth, William, 18
Writer's Diary, A (Woolf, ed.
Leonard Woolf), 180
Wuthering Heights (Brontë), 76, 77,
83, 166

Yesterdays with Authors (Fields),
166